Casanova Was a Book Lover

Other books by John Maxwell Hamilton

Main Street America and the Third World

Edgar Snow: A Biography

*Entangling Alliances: How the Third World
Shapes Our Lives*

Hold the Press: The Inside Story on Newspapers
(coauthor George Krimsky)

Casanova
Was a
Book Lover

And Other Naked Truths
and Provocative Curiosities
about the Writing, Selling,
and Reading of Books

John Maxwell Hamilton

LOUISIANA STATE UNIVERSITY PRESS

BATON ROUGE

MM

1661 5534

Designer: Laura Roubique Gleason
Typeface: Adobe Caslon
Typesetter: Crane Composition, Inc.
Printer and binder: Thomson-Shore, Inc.

Library of Congress Cataloging-in-Publication Data:
Hamilton, John Maxwell.
    Casanova was a book lover : and other naked truths and curiosities about the writing, selling, and reading of books / John Maxwell Hamilton.
      p. cm.
    Includes bibliographical references and index.
    ISBN 0-8071-2554-7 (alk. paper)
    1. Books and reading. 2. Books and reading—United States. 3. Authorship. 4. Authorship—United States. 5. Publishers and publishing—United States.   I. Title.

Z1003.H194 2000
028'.9—dc21

99-059582

The paper in this book meets the guidelines for permanence and durability of the Committee on Production Guidelines for Book Longevity of the Council on Library Resources. ∞

———∽∾∿∾∽———

To Paula and Jack
. . . because they are such good friends and because
I'm running out of family suitable for dedicating purposes.

To all reviewers
. . . because only ungrateful asses would pan a book after having
it dedicated to them.

———∽∾∿∾∽———

Contents

Illustrations

—⟨∾∾⟩—

Acknowledgments

Whom can we blame?

Let's start with the students who helped with research: Kenneth Damann, Anita Chang, Christie David Duet, Jane Perrone, and Nicholas Kahn-Fogel. Bonnie Bauman, my graduate assistant during the most important period of writing this book, made significant editorial suggestions, unearthed obscure information, and tracked down pictures. I believe that Bonnie did a better job at the research than she does balancing her checkbook.

Les Phillabaum, Maureen Hewitt, John Easterly, Laura Gleason, Jean C. Lee, and Sylvia Frank at LSU Press got into the spirit of this venture and cheerfully offered valuable ideas. As the chief editor of this book, Sylvia Frank bears the most responsibility for it. Come what may, I enjoy working with LSU Press.

George Garrett at the University of Virginia vetted this book for the LSU Press. I appreciate his generous comments—and the fact that he surrendered his anonymity, thus ensuring he is implicated along with everyone else.

Many other knowledgeable professionals of one kind or another helped with odd facts and perceptive interpretations. I mention these people in the Notes on Sources to tie them as closely as possible to any gaffes for which they should be accountable.

With one exception, friends and colleagues happily made suggestions. Among the generous helpers are Lou Day, Meg Ross, Len Sanderson, and Jack Sullivan. Sullivan offered chapter-by-chapter criticism that typically began in this vein: "Since my tuba lesson is off because I got my lip caught in the breadmaker, I am able to render my judgments immediately and get the draft back to you." Along with Ron Garay, he helped me make up the advance quotes for the book, which have been printed accurately on the back cover. The one exception was Mary Ann Sternberg, who refused to read the book or make any suggestions at all. She is a smart friend as well as a good one.

My wife Gina read several of the chapters, but wisely confined herself to saying mostly nice things about them. Drawing on his wide reading, our son Maxwell directed my attention to a number of useful anecdotes and quotations. He allowed that this is a book someone might want to read, not that he was risking *his* reputation on it.

Author's Warning

I have spotted a trend: authors inserting a warning in the front of their books. The leaden hand of the lawyer is apparent in many of these opening salvos. The "**Important**" notice beginning Donald S. Passman's *All You Need to Know About the Music Business* is full of language such as "The materials in this book represent the opinions of the author. . . . In addition, laws and customs change over time, and by necessity of the lapse in time between the writing and printing of this book, some aspects may be out of date even upon first publication. . . ."

At first I dismissed these disclaimers as examples of our highly litigious society combined with really bad marketing judgment. On reflection, I changed my mind about the bad marketing judgment. These warnings can do the opposite of what they purport to do. Instead of putting people on notice that the book has weaknesses, they advertise its strongest selling points.

Here is Roger Shattuck in *Forbidden Knowledge: From Prometheus to Pornography*: "Parents and teachers should be aware that Chapter VII does not make appropriate reading for children and minors." Shattuck can't really think the little ones would plead for a copy of this scholarly tome full of sentences such as "Sade discovers a moral order based on the self-preservation of the bourgeois individual." Let's face it, very few parents would have an interest in this book. If they saw their kid reading it they would think they were blessed with a child prodigy. There can only be one reason for Shattuck's warning. He draws attention to the dirty parts in hopes of tricking someone—parent or child—into buying the book. Not that I blame him. Scholars need to do a better job of marketing.

Hit Man: A Technical Manual for Independent Contractors gives instructions on how to bump off someone the way a professional would. A typical chapter is titled "The Direct Hit Is Not Your Only Alternative." The book has been the object of a lawsuit. After allegedly reading the alleged book, someone allegedly killed three people. Palladin Press, the publisher, allegedly protects its interests by "**Warning**" readers that *Hit Man* is "**For**

informational purposes only!" The legal and promotional departments are sometimes at odds over the best course of action. But here is wording that should have induced everyone at Palladin to break out the champagne, at least until the court case was settled in 1999. Palladin's insurance company finally agreed to a multimillion dollar settlement with the victims' families. Palladin itself is making annual contributions to two charities picked by the plaintiff. The publisher also agreed to take the book from the market. All of this goes to show that the only value of a warning is as an advertisement, not as legal protection.

Anyway, the warning craze leaves the rest of us authors desperate to appear dangerous, even if we are shooting blanks. Hence, I provide these safety instructions to readers who dare to venture farther into this book:

Warning
Wear gloves! Paper cuts are possible.

An Introduction to the
Proper Study of Mankind

—◦◦◦—

In which it is shown that the best way to
study books, reading, and people is not to
take them too seriously.

—⁓—

The proper study of mankind is books.
—ALDOUS HUXLEY

Dear Friend, I believe, contrary to the fashion among our
contemporaries, that one can have a very lofty idea of literature,
and at the same time have a good-natured laugh at it.
—MARCEL PROUST

—⁓—

Early in 1990, I wrote a piece for the *New York Times Book Review* on the fatuousness of book acknowledgments and dedications. Only once before had an article of mine drawn so much attention. That was a profile for a Catholic magazine of an American missionary whom I met on a reporting trip to Venezuela. In an accompanying photograph, Father Mel Krumdick was shown at a beach near Caracas with a few young parishioners, among them a voluptuous, bikini-clad teenager. In the flesh, Father Mel was entirely priestly. The camera angle in the photo, however, did him no favors. He was wearing swim trunks, and an errant shadow made it appear as though he had squeezed something the size of a football inside them.

The unhappy mail that followed would have filled the Sistine Chapel. A writer from Manchester, New Hampshire, expressed shock over "a girl in a 'swimsuit'?? talking to a priest. . . . Such style is surely the work of the devil. (Our Lady of Fatima warned certain fashions will offend Our Lord.)"

The difference in the response to the *New York Times* essay was that the mail was positive. People sent me examples of their favorite front-of-the-book dreck and wit. One reader, who was also a writer, mailed her own book, which was dedicated to her psychotherapist and contained long, sexually explicit disclosures involving a ménage-à-trois that would have made Father Mel lock himself in his confessional.

The episode revealed something I had not known. People who read books cherish them and are fascinated by the processes that produce them, no matter how humble or mean. We don't care much about our plumber's foibles and tribulations. We want him to fix the leak in the sink and move on. John Milton is another matter altogether. We love to know that Milton composed while lying in bed, that Vladimir Nabokov wrote on three-by-five-inch index cards, that John Keats dressed in his best clothes to write poetry, and that Thackeray reached the point where he could not write at home. "There is an excitement in public places which sets my brain working," he said of his need to write in hotels and clubs. Somewhere, years ago, I read that Alexander Pope—I think it was Pope— could only write if he had a crate of old apples nearby; the rotting smell inspired him. This is not important. Nonetheless, the story has lodged in my memory. One of the successes of Brian Lamb's C-SPAN program

"Booknotes" is that authors reveal themselves, as when Forrest McDonald reported that he wrote naked on his porch in Alabama. We hunger to know about authors' tribulations and foibles, expecting that they are every bit as interesting as their books.

This is not to say that all is well in the world of books. On the contrary. We have every reason to worry that the quality of writing has gone to hell. After renovation, the Algonquin Hotel reopened in 1991 and, to whip up a little nostalgia, published a service directory with an essay celebrating the hotel's history as a literary hangout. The directory was full of misplaced modifiers, missing articles, and the like. The essay is symbolic of our times.

Corporate executives decry illiteracy. They spend large amounts of money on programs to train their employees. Yet, at the same time, they pay marketing experts big bucks to help their corporations violate all the rules of good writing. First National City Bank of New York turned itself into Citicorp, a word that has more things wrong with it than would seem possible with any combination of eight letters. Control Data is now Ceridian Corporation. Don't bother to look it up; "Ceridian" isn't in the dictionary. Before Levi Strauss & Company came out with its new brand of slacks, the marketing staff spent four months looking for a name *without* meaning, "an empty vessel." Their name-that-did-not name was *Slates*.

A new store opens every day with signs over the door like one I saw in a small southern town: Ammo and Stuff. In a commentary on public radio, I once mused that a shop called Things 'N' Stuff surely must exist. Sure enough, someone called in to say there was one in Garden City, New York.

Stephen Vincent Benét's poem "American Names" should be required reading in corporate boardrooms:

> I have fallen in love with American names,
> The sharp, gaunt names that never get fat,
> The snakeskin-titles of mining-claims,
> The plumed war-bonnet of Medicine Hat,
> Tucson and Deadwood and Lost Mule Flat.

We live in a Hallmark culture where we buy our loftiest personal feelings on manufactured cards sold in drug stores. Or if we have the money, we pay Love Letters, Ink (sic), a Beverly Hills, California, company, to write synthetic sentiments for us at the price of fifty-five dollars each. No surprise then that the polls tell us, as an Associated Press poll did in 1992, that 30 percent of families earning more than forty thousand dollars annually have no books at home. Other studies report that 21 percent of the adult population "had only rudimentary reading and writing skills" and that nearly half of all American adults "are not proficient enough in English to write a letter about a billing error."

Nor is the United States alone. A 1995 survey by the Organization for Economic Cooperation and Development found that Americans are about average among industrialized countries. The percent of illiteracy in France, which is intent on keeping language pristine, was twice as high. The French spend twice as much on their pets as on books.

This illiteracy makes what I learned from that *Times* article all the more poignant. People who care about books care profoundly. What they lack in numbers they make up for in passion. A typical mid-1980s study illustrates the fidelity of readers to reading. Only half of the American public, the study found, had read at least one book in the past six months. Of those "readers," however, almost one-third devoured at least one book a week. A 1997 Pew Center survey found that slightly more than one-third of respondents had read a book the day before outside of school or work; 77 percent of those people who had read a book the day before did so for at least thirty minutes and many for much longer. This reading intensity explains the rise of book discussion clubs, which according to some estimates now total 250,000. "Book festivals," *The Economist* reported in 1999, "are multiplying almost as fast as espresso franchises. At the moment there are 148 in Britain alone."

Books are like Swiss Army knives. They offer endless creative and revealing possibilities for those who like to interact with them.

Not only can we get even by writing a book, we can get even by reading a book. "There are few things I enjoy so much as talking to people about books which I have read and they haven't," crusty Edmund Wilson said, "and making them wish they had—preferably a book that is hard to get or in a language that they do not know."

The story is told that Brian Courthorpe Hunt shot himself to death while in the venerable London Library. The proximate cause seems to have been the news that the second volume of some book he was reading was unavailable. This tells us something about Hunt. The story also tells us much about Thomas Carlyle, the Scottish historian, who was elsewhere in the library at the time. Unfazed by news of the suicide, he asked the librarian to bring him Motley's *Rise of the Dutch Republic* and remarked, "There's another of Thornton Hunt's bastards gone." Carlyle took the measure of people by counting the number of books in their libraries.

We can take the measure of Evelyn Waugh by his actions during World War II. During the London blitz, the literature-loving author ordered that his books be taken to a safe haven in the country. He told his son, Auberon, to stay in London.

Some years ago, while writing a biography of foreign correspondent Edgar Snow, who was viewed by many as an un-American pro-Communist, I came across copies of some of the actual books he had read. Leafing through a volume by Harold Laski, an English scholar and left-wing activist, I found a comment Snow had scribbled in the margin: "See Mark Twain on this." Here in Laski's book was a piece of evidence for my thesis: Snow's leftist views sprang from an intensely American point of view, not in spite of it.

To love books is to write in them the way the Chinese, having acquired a painting, sometimes write their names right next to the artist's. At least that is my view. In truth, there are many views on how to treat books. Charles Darwin went further. When someone sent him a book, he would cut off the spine with a knife, throw away the cover, and put the loose pages in a box. The sheets were easier to turn that way. On the other end of the spectrum is Salman Rushdie. As a boy he learned to kiss any book he dropped "by way of apology for the act of clumsy disrespect."

One does not have to read books to interact with them. In the hands of an interior decorator, a book is like a throw pillow. It adds a spot of color here or there. It can dress up an entire wall. "The rich colors of bookbindings are made only the lovelier, when their setting is a paneled room," *Good Housekeeping* advised in 1925. A southern woman I know doesn't shelve books; she "hangs" them. As noted later in this book, Dallas Cowboys owner Jerry Jones and his wife, Gene, made a large donation in 1999 to help the Library of Congress reassemble Thomas Jefferson's original book collection. They don't go in much for reading, though. "We have a beautiful library. It's one of the most important rooms in our house," Gene Jones noted in earshot of a *Washington Post* reporter. At a Library of Congress event to celebrate the donation, Jerry Jones observed that Thomas Jefferson was author of those hallowed lines about Americans being entitled to life, liberty, and—oops—the "pursuit of property."

In the pursuit of property, happiness, or whatever, people like the Joneses do considerable business with Levenger, a mail order company that sells "tools for serious readers." There are statues of Shakespeare, special light bulbs, footrests, and wristwatches. Everything, except books. Other mail order companies offer those—with expensive leather bindings. A promotional flyer advertises "The 100 Greatest Books Ever Written: A Rich Addition to Your Home." The brochure reveals all the merits of the books, except the titles. "Genuine-premium-quality leather," it says; ". . . how surprised your guests will be to discover that the impressive foil edging serves an important purpose!" (*i.e.*, to keep out moisture). Books, as poet Robert Southey said, are furniture for the rich.

The most passionate book readers share these acquisitive sentiments, although much more than crude materialism is at work. Well-displayed books, a sixteenth-century Italian scholar commented, "will form a complete library, which will ornament first your study, and then, to a much greater degree, your soul." Dr. A. S. W. Rosenbach, a well-known bookseller, often could not bear to lose a special book, no matter how much profit it would fetch. The widowed wife of a famous British journalist decided to part with some of her old furniture but refused to sell anything to an interested young woman I know unless the would-be customer promised to read her late husband's memoirs.

I was in Sarajevo shortly after the Serbian siege was lifted. Not far from my office stood the remains of the National and University Library. Serb bombing in 1993 had turned much of the Moorish-style building to charred rubble; more than 90 percent of the 1.5 million books burned. That had been big news around the world; the ordeal of a veteran Bosnian journalist I met was commonplace, unreported, and even more depressing. For years he had collected books, he told me in his husky cigarette-smoker's voice. When he had run out of firewood in the winter, he burned more than five hundred books, about one-fifth of his library. First he chose "the big ones. They burn best." Now, he said, he didn't care about property anymore. "After you burn books, why would you care about a chair?"

After restoring long-packed-away books to shelves, German author Walter Benjamin reflected on the way readers become one with their personal book-sorting schemes. "For what else is this collection," he wrote in a short essay, "but a disorder to which habit has accommodated itself to such an extent that it can appear as order?" Thomas Jefferson, who said he "could not live without books," kept his Monticello library under lock and key. To keep track of his books, he created a classification system, divided into forty-four subject areas based on the Baconian structure of knowledge. Carlyle carefully shelved his books level with each other. One man I knew removed the dust jackets from each volume he had read. At a glance he knew how many books he had conquered. Another acquaintance challenged me to divine *his* private bookshelf formula. The answer: No two books of the same color were allowed next to each other. Carter Burden, a businessman and art lover, assembled one of the finest personal libraries in the country before he died in 1996. He fastidiously arranged his books alphabetically by author. When someone looked as if he or she might be moving a book from its proper spot, Burden would shout across the room, "What are you doing?"

Elitists often sniff at readers who enjoy simple romantic novels, Luke Short Westerns, and other easy reading. This is misguided on two counts. First, reading should be fun. Not everyone wants to run three miles on a hot Sunday afternoon. Sometimes a stroll through the park is in order. If some people never want to break a sweat, so what? We should rejoice that they are, after all, reading, not lying in front of the television all the time. Second, people's diverse reading habits make books and people more interesting and more worthy of serious study. In Aldous Huxley's words, "The proper study of mankind is books."

The elitists, sad to say, have had such a strong grip on our thinking that, until recently, only a few scholars stood back to survey the vast panorama presented by books. One of these exceptions was Isaac D'Israeli, father of the colorful British prime minister and author, who wrote essays in the mid–nineteenth century about the evolution of literature. This has begun to change, thanks to creative historians such as Robert Darnton. He looks at the naughty books that people have read, at the sub rosa systems publishers and booksellers used to distribute books, and at the dirty tricks authors used to survive. He has found that booksellers during the Enlightenment wanted copies of *Margot the Campfollower* every bit as much as they wanted copies of *The System of Nature.*

Inspired by the response to my first article on acknowledgments and dedications, and intrigued by such histories, I have occasionally detoured from my work as a journalist, government bureaucrat, and now academic to explore the underworld of books. The fruits of these explorations have figured prominently in my teaching, for it has become clear to me that one cannot understand modern journalism and letters, or for that matter modern economics and politics, without appreciating the rich, quirky history of writing.

One of the more entertaining characters in this history is Giacomo Girolamo Casanova. We know Casanova best as the eighteenth-century lover of women, although we may not realize that he belongs to our polit-

Giacomo Girolamo Casanova, a lovable symbol of the raucous world of books, had a Renaissance résumé: minor orders in the Catholic Church, violinist, soldier, occultist, diplomat, theatrical producer, dancer, prisoner many times over, actor, silk manufacturer, con man, spy, publicist, and, yes, book writer. A Venetian police report noted that he traveled "under the title of man of letters."

Casanova, engraving by Johann Berka, 1788, copyright the British Museum

ically correct age. He respected women, rather than took advantage of them, and they loved him in return. Less well known, but equally true, Casanova was an ardent book lover, an emblem of the raucous reality of books and literature. Like many of our best writers, Casanova had a Renaissance résumé: minor orders in the Catholic Church, violinist, soldier, occultist, diplomat, theatrical producer, dancer, prisoner many times over, actor, silk manufacturer, con man, spy, and publicist. He helped start the first Parisian lottery with Abbé de Bernis. Writing was as ever-present in this exuberant life as were women. A Venetian police report noted that Casanova traveled "under the title of man of letters."

Casanova's most famous incarceration was beneath the Leads, as the upper chambers of the Doge's Palace in Venice were called because of their lead roof. The state inquisitors never held a proper trial, thus leaving Casanova uncertain which of his transgressions offended the authorities. Historians have concluded that he was imprisoned for atheism. If so, books figured prominently in the evidence. A spy had induced him to recite a sexually charged heretical poem, and the constables who came to arrest him found books on the occult in his quarters. His spectacular escape was by the book, too. He made plans with a fellow prisoner by writing notes in the books they exchanged, and he passed an iron bar to a conspirator inside a Bible. When he was a free man, Casanova wrote *Flight from the Leads*.

Casanova translated Homer's *Iliad* into Italian. He created *Opuscoli miscellanei,* a monthly review devoted to his own writing, and another journal of dramatic criticism to stimulate interest in his theatrical productions. He scripted plays and may have helped revise Lorenzo da Ponte's libretto for Mozart's *Don Giovanni*. A partial list of Casanova's books includes *History of Unrest in Poland; The Philosopher and the Theologian; Critical Essay on Morals, The Science, and the Arts; Musing on the Mean Measurement of Time According to the Georgian Reform;* and a utopian novel called *Icosaméron, or The History of Edouard and Elisabeth Who Spent Eighty-one Years among the Megamicres, Aboriginal Inhabitants of the Protocosm Inside our Globe.* At the end of his life, while a librarian in the Dux castle in Bohemia, he wrote the twelve-volume *Historie de Jacques Casanova de Seingalt, Venetian, écrite par lui-même à Dux, en Bohême.* "His every word is a revelation," the Prince de Ligne said of Casanova, "and every thought a book."

The book you are holding in your hands does not seek to glorify writing or writers the way that so many books on the subject do. I assume the reader does not need to be persuaded that books are important. Instead of pounding on that familiar theme, I take a cue from Casanova. Some "fine ladies," as he called them, criticized his earthy description of his loose bowels during his imprisonment in the Leads. "I would perhaps have omitted it in talking to a lady," he said; "but the public is not a lady, and I like to be instructive."

In that spirit, this book answers this question: Can writers make a living writing? (Rarely.) And this one: Do I have to buy my friend's new book? (No, but you should.) And this one: Should I consider dropping dead in order to sell my book? (Absolutely.) This book explains why one of the greatest threats to good literature is the proliferation of writers, why books are an ideal way to market yourself, why librarians need to throw out more books, and why presidents should not write. It reports which books are most often stolen, a theme that in much shorter form was a second essay for the *New York Times Book Review* and also generated substantial mail (including the offer from one reader to give his edition of Abbie Hoffman's *Steal This Book* to the Library of Congress, which I had reported was missing its copy).

Although I employed serious research techniques in this book, I confess to having made liberal use of the wonderfully weird information that lies everywhere waiting to be picked up. Like the day I was leafing through the Manila phone book and came across a local establishment called Jargon Publishers. Or the day I learned that someone designed a bulletproof *New Testament,* an invention that gives new meaning to the concept of a *hardback* book. The best place to glean insights on the real world of books is the daily newspaper. Carlin Romano, a literary critic for the *Philadelphia Inquirer,* disputes this. "Perhaps the most remarkable aspect of American newspapers in the 1990s," he writes, "is their hostility to reading in all forms." Romano is correct in the sense that book reviewing is half-hearted and feeble, which is the subject of another chapter in this book. But tidbits about books and authors appear in news pages all the time.

As a test of this proposition, I asked Anita Chang, a bright journalism student at our school, to look at one issue each of *USA Today* and the *Wall Street Journal.* The former is not commonly thought of as highbrow. She found mention of eight books in it. The *Journal* mentioned twenty-eight books. This is an unusually high number. Twenty-two of the books were connected to an article about the Booker Awards. Nevertheless, that left six books, one of which is mentioned on the front page. The article described the cutthroat competition among onion farmers in Vidalia, Georgia. One of the most entrepreneurial of these men of the soil sold 100,000 copies of the *Vidalia Onion Lover's Cookbook*.

Perhaps the news is all about crime, terrorism, and mayhem. But those stories often involve books. One day, the *New York Times* reports that a Memphis judge punishes first offenders by making them write a ten-page essay on *The Autobiography of Malcolm X*. Another morning, we learn that the head of the National Endowment for the Arts has canceled a grant for a bilingual children's book, *The Story of Colors*, published by a small press in El Paso, Texas. The author is Subcomandante Marcos, the renegade Zapatista guerrilla leader in southern Mexico. The subcomandante appears on the inside flap of the book jacket wearing ammo belts across his chest and a ski mask to hide his face. Yet another day, an online news service tells us that Chicano students at Michigan State University "took 4,500 university library books hostage for a day and presented the administration with a list of demands." The demands included asking the university to inaugurate a Hispanic studies major.

So, as we set sail for the out-of-the-way literary islands, let's agree that Casanova's rationale for writing his memoirs should be a creed for all who truly love books: "I know that I am being unwise. But I need something to occupy me, something to make me laugh; so why should I deny myself?"

ONE

T. Roger Claypool's Fish Store

———✳———

In which it is argued that the economics
of authorship have evolved without really
changing and that we should be glad
money is the ultimate writer's block.

—ᴄᴠᴄ—

But just understand the difference between a man like
Reardon and a man like me. He is the old type of unpractical
artist. . . . Literature nowadays is a trade. Putting aside men of
genius, who may succeed by mere cosmic force, your successful man
of letters is your skillful tradesman. He thinks first and foremost of
the markets; when one kind of goods begins to go off slackly, he is
ready with something new and appetizing. . . . Reardon can't do that
kind of thing, he's behind his age; he sells a manuscript as if he lived
in Sam Johnson's Grub Street. But our Grub Street of to-day is
quite a different place: it is supplied with telegraphic communication, it knows what literary fare is in demand in every part of the
world, its inhabitants are men of business, however seedy.
—Jasper Milvain speaking in George
Gissing's 1891 novel, *New Grub Street*

—ᴄᴠᴄ—

A *New Yorker* cartoon that has hung on my wall for years depicts two types of "Writer's Block." In the first frame, the writer has risen from his typewriter and stares out the window. He is experiencing "temporary" writer's block. In the second frame, he stares at the sign over the front window of his business, "T. Roger Claypool's Fish Store." Mr. Claypool suffers from "permanent" writer's block. I've hung this cartoon within eyeshot of my desk to remind me that a person can't be a writer if he or she doesn't write. Yet I've come to realize that the cartoon overlooks a much more fundamental truth.

Writing dwells in the popular imagination as a romantic occupation. Authors do not punch in to the nine-to-five job that most people know. They pad around the house in baggy pants and roomy old sweaters. Their daily routine is one long coffee break, an endless sipping while thinking big thoughts. Even if they scribble away in cramped quarters, writers are free. This is a myth.

Anyone who thinks full-time authors are liberated because they wear comfortable clothes while staying at home might as well conclude that birds sit in trees and chirp because they are happy. "There is no difference between the writer in his garret, and the slave in the mines," James Ralph wrote in *The Case of Authors by Profession or Trade, Stated, 1758.* As George Gissing showed in his minor classic about Grub Street, writing is a tough business. Very few make it as full-time authors. If they do, they generally possess Jasper Milvain's entrepreneurial savvy. Meanwhile, the majority of authors pack a lunch pail off to work like everyone else, writing on the side, when their neighbors are asleep.

This category of part-time writers includes the pitifully small number of authors who rise above what Samuel Johnson famously called the "mean production" of Grub Street. Indeed, a discursive tour through the history of authorship arrives at that fundamental truth that a day job in T. Roger Claypool's Fish Store is often the best place to produce good literature.

A Short Economic History of Writing: Part I

Historians have suggested that the capitalist economic system began in the mid-fifteenth century when Johannes Gensfleisch zur Laden gennant Gutenberg printed for the first time with movable type. The mechanized production system foreshadowed by Gutenberg's press made a mass market economy possible. Not only did Gutenberg use movable type, but he also developed a method for casting type in large quantities and invented a new press and oil-based printing ink.

Gutenberg seems to have been one of those habitual experimenters who, if he lived today, would have been the first on his block to have an electric juicer—even if he didn't really want any juice. When he wasn't working on printing, he tinkered with polishing precious stones and making mirrors. Whatever aspirations Gutenberg had for his improvement to the printing process, he could not have foreseen it as a predecessor to a free-market economy any more than Henry Ford could foresee that his Model T would lead to suburban sprawl. If anything, Gutenberg was probably disappointed in his invention. As historian John P. Feather has noted, he "was not only the first printer, he was also the first printer to go bankrupt." Much of what we know about Gutenberg comes from the financial litigation in which he was embroiled.

Nor could Gutenberg have foreseen that movable type would transform writing into a booming business with thousands of new book titles each year. He invented his press in order to crank out the religious manuscripts that monks formerly copied by hand. He and other early printers strove for a monkish look in their books. It was common for some time afterward to print books with wide margins that could be illuminated by hand. Readers considered printed books vulgar.

Original writing for publication at the time was a small province. Not yet invented—in Isaac D'Israeli's words—was "that race of writers who have been designated in the modern phrase as 'authors by profession.'" Rarely did authors strive to make money from their writing, for little money could be made. As uncertain about how to make the book system pay as we are today about making the Internet pay, authors and publishers experimented with a wide variety of financial arrangements. Sometimes an author helped with the printing chores and paid the printer to sell the books on commission; sometimes an author dedicated a book with the expectation of payback from the dedicatee; sometimes the printer paid the author. A sixteenth-century Dutchman, who had profited handsomely from writing, advised his nephew that "some authors, having seen that their work was beautifully printed, have presented [the printer] with a silver bowl."

Chaucer, Shakespeare, and Milton are perhaps the three most important figures in early English literary history. Not one of these preeminent authors wrote books to put bread on the table.

Geoffrey Chaucer, who preceded Gutenberg, made his living as a career public servant. He began as a page in the household of Prince Lionel of Clarence. After the French imprisoned him in 1359, Chaucer served kings Edward III and Richard II as justice of the peace in the county of Kent, diplomat, controller of the King's Custom and Subsidy of Wool and Hides, and clerk of the King's Works, a demanding post in which he oversaw various building schemes. He also was a member of Parliament and ended his career as subforester in North Petherton.

Sir Geoffrey wrote on the side. He may have been thinking of himself when in "The House of Fame" the eagle chides the poet: "For when your work is all done and you have finished all your accounts, instead of resting or doing different things, you go home to your house at once and sit as dumb as any stone with another book until your eyes are completely dazed."

Although his work was collected in books, Chaucer wrote for his amusement and the amusement of the elites he served or worked with. Storytelling was a common form of after-dinner entertainment. A famous

Geoffrey Chaucer, one of early English history's holy trinity of authors, was not a book writer by profession. Among his many government jobs, Chaucer was controller of the King's Custom and Subsidy of Wool and Hides, and clerk of the King's Works. He ended up as subforester in North Petherton.

The Harvard portrait of Geoffrey Chaucer, Houghton Library, Harvard University. Bequest of Charles Eliot Norton to Widener Library in memory of Francis James Child and James Russell Lowell

illumination from a manuscript of *Troilus and Criseyde* shows Chaucer reading to a royal circle in a castle garden. No existing manuscripts of Chaucer's poems date from his own day. Chapters from *The Canterbury Tales* circulated piecemeal well before he was done with what would become a whole book of stories. Because of its rarity, an early copy of *The Canterbury Tales* fetched a record $7.5 million at Christie's in 1998.

And what of William Shakespeare? Suppose he actually wrote the material attributed to him; Shakespeare wasn't thinking about selling books when he did so. A principal shareholder and actor in the Lord Chamberlain's (later King's) Men, he was expected to create new material to attract patrons. His colleagues wanted him to think like a television script writer. "Hey, Bill, you better come up with a revenge play, because that is what is showing down the street." So, Shakespeare writes *Hamlet*. Just how much of his theater income came from writing is not clear, but a common method of payment for scripts was to give a playwright the box office proceeds, minus the company's expenses, from the second performance. Shakespeare acted year round, but wrote only from November to February.

At the beginning of his career, Shakespeare arranged publication of his poems *Venus and Adonis* and *The Rape of Lucrece* with a friend from Stratford who had set up shop in London and remained in business when the plague had forced theaters to close. Money, though, probably was less a motive for Shakespeare to seek publication than the opportunity to en-

In the end what counted for Will Shakespeare was real estate, not book royalties. At the time of his death, he had the second largest house in Stratford, owned 107 acres of surrounding farmland, and was invested heavily in local agricultural leases. He also owned property in London.

The Chandos portrait of William Shakespeare, attributed to John Taylor. By courtesy of the National Portrait Gallery, London

hance his name recognition in London. "Throughout his life, he had little to gain from seeing his name in a London bookshop," concludes one of Shakespeare's leading biographers, Park Honan.

Printers published a grand total of only five or six new plays a year in Shakespeare's time. Because no copyright laws existed, they could avoid paying the playwrights a single shilling. Shakespeare's first published play was a pirated version. When Shakespeare and his company sold play-books for *Richard III* and a few other dramas in the late 1590s, they essentially were doing the same thing as farmers who sell their seed corn for cash. The printed plays also advertised that the company was desperate, and who wants to see a desperate acting company? As for his sonnets, Shakespeare wrote those for his own pleasure, not publication.

In the end, what counted for Shakespeare was real estate, not book royalties. At the time of his death, he owned the second largest house in Stratford and 107 acres of surrounding farmland and was invested heavily in local agricultural leases. He also had property in London.

About half of his plays appeared in book form for the first time when two colleagues who outlived him published them "without ambition, either of self-profit, or fame: only to keep the memory of so worthy a friend and fellow alive."

John Milton, the third member of our holy trinity of early English

At various times John Milton lived off his prosperous father, tutored youngsters, and, because he was a good propagandist, landed a political job in Cromwell's regime. When it came time to seek a publisher for *Paradise Lost* toward the end of this life, Milton settled for a five-pound up-front payment.

Engraving of the Faithorne portrait of John Milton. Princeton University Library

writers, was born to a rising middle-class family in 1608, eight years before Shakespeare's death. After earning his bachelor's and master's degrees from Christ College, he lived off his prosperous father while writing and traveling more or less at leisure. Later, he tutored youngsters and became entangled in politics as a propaganda writer and activist on behalf of the Parliamentary government.

Following the execution of Charles I in 1649, Milton was appointed Latin secretary during Cromwell's regime. The post drew on his writing skills. One day he translated a letter of state from Parliament to Hamburg. Another day he examined the papers of John Lee, who was arrested on suspicion of dealing with the enemy. On yet another day the Council of State directed him "to make some observations" on affairs with Ireland. For this he received an annual salary of £288.13s.6½d and lodgings in Whitehall. The position harbored other writers. George Rudolph Wecklein and Richard Fanshawe—his predecessor and successor respectively—were poets. (Milton asked to have Andrew Marvell as his assistant, but the young poet ended up tutoring one of Cromwell's protégés.) Milton stayed in Whitehall until the Restoration in 1660, although he lost his sight soon after taking the job.

Milton viewed himself as a spokesman for the Truth, whether writing polemics on the Reformation or penning poetry. He wrote his famous pamphlet on free speech, *Areopagitica,* to make trouble, not money. If he expected any reward, it may have been jail. He had not bothered to get the required license or registration for his tract against the evils of prior restraint against writing.

After Milton was ousted from Whitehall, his financial situation went to hell. He lost all the savings he had accumulated as Latin secretary. The house his father had left him burned down in the Fire of London. He sold off his substantial library to raise a little cash. His books were of less use to him as he grew older, and he realized that his three ungrateful daughters, on whom he had wasted much money for education, would not make good use of them. As he grew still older, booksellers saw a profit in reprinting familiar letters and academic exercises from his school days. He probably cooperated less out of interest in profit, small as it was, than out of pride. He wanted to preserve his literary legacy.

When it came time to seek a publisher for *Paradise Lost* toward the end of his life, Milton settled for a five-pound up-front payment and another five pounds for each of three printings, to be paid in installments when each printing of 1,300 copies was sold out. In exchange for the prospect of a whopping sum of twenty pounds, he had relinquished all future rights on the poem. The sale could hardly have changed his quality of life. As one Milton scholar has noted, five pounds was about the price of repainting a gentleman's coach.

Well beyond Milton's time, writing remained a by-product of leisure, which meant it was largely a pursuit of the nobility. Wellborn gentlemen, who had time and taste for the arts, became patrons of writers. This was the case on the continent as well as in England. Louis XVIII and Charles X gave Victor Hugo two thousand francs a year. If a gentleman chose to write, itself the mark of a gentleman, he sometimes would not sign his name to his work, take payment for it, or even consent to have it published formally. He distributed his scribblings discreetly among intimates. Some argue that Shakespeare did not author the work under his name; his learning and background were too humble for such great results. Most of those credited as the real authors belonged to the aristocracy: the earls of Oxford, Derby, Rutland, Essex, and Southampton. (Shakespeare dedicated poems to the earl of Southampton, and an active society celebrates the seventeenth earl of Oxford, Edward de Vere, as the real "Shakespeare.") Money, according to the prevailing aristocratic sentiment, tainted art by forcing the writer to produce what others wanted instead of what should be written. Ultimately, however, the forces put in place by Gutenberg would not be denied.

The Industrial Revolution advanced the technology for mass producing books: presses powered first by horses, later by steam; typesetting machines; machine-made paper that came in rolls, not sheets; mechanical folders. Gas lighting, a by-product of industrialization, ended centuries of dark, gloomy nights. The growing middle class, with better educations and disposable income to spend on books and periodicals, could read at home after it had flipped the switch at work.

As industrialization steamed ahead, the aristocracy lost its hegemony over book writing. Reading and writing became important marketable skills for the armies of clerks that appeared. One such clerk, Benjamin Hayne, advertised himself as doing "the buisnesse of writeing for any person who will employ him." As his "writeing" suggests, it would be some time before spelling and punctuation became as standardized as factory products. Producing literature became a job, too. Responding to the idea that books were a product, countries agreed to copyright regimes ensuring royalties for authors. Increasingly the bookseller took over the aristocracy's role of feeding writers. "Money has emancipated the writer," pronounced Emile Zola, "money has created modern letters."

The early professional writers sometimes felt ill at ease with their role. Oliver Goldsmith looked "to the bookseller for support, they are my best friends." Yet, he also condemned the Grub Street "author who draws his quill merely to take a purse." When reports circulated that Lord Byron was profiting handsomely from his poetry, he considered issuing a public statement that he never took money for his work. Although he did accept "brain money" as time went on, Byron nobly waved off a publisher's advance later in life when he dearly needed it. A British magazine noted in 1847 the "unwillingness of literary men to own themselves professional authors; they almost all pretend to be barristers or gentlemen at large."

But no amount of subterfuge could change the economic reality. The often acerbic Dr. Johnson, a friend of Goldsmith and a skilled writer for hire, pronounced his enduring credo for the profession of writing. "No man but a blockhead," he declared, "ever wrote, except for money."

But the economic history of writing does not end there.

A Short Economic History of Writing: Part II

United States book sales hit $23 billion in 1998, a 6.4 percent increase over the previous year, according to the Association of American Publishers. To say that the market for books is now greater than at any other time in history, however, is to leave much unsaid about the contemporary writer's predicament.

Modern economic forces swooped down and freed writers from one set of circumstances only to chain them to new circumstances that have more or less the same result. One of the outcomes of industrialization is that virtually everyone in the modern economic system it created can read *and* write. Sometimes it seems as if the number of readers and writers is equal. This proliferation of writers divides the market into tiny shares that make it nearly impossible for all but a few highly popular authors to prosper by their books. In the words of Gertrude Stein, "In the eighteenth century not enough read to make any one earn their living and in the twentieth century too many read for anyone to make their living."

Some 140,000 new books were published in the United States in 1998, according to *Books in Print*'s managing editor, Andrew Grabois. Using 1990 census data, that is one new book for every 1,264 American citizens over the age of twenty-four. And new authors poke up their heads each year. A wild (and probably conservative) guess is that 35,000 of those 140,000 books are by first-time authors. By this calculation, 455,000 different people—or one out of every 388 Americans—write at least one published book each decade.

Admittedly these are crude calculations. Each decade some authors die. Some authors listed in *Books in Print* are not Americans. These factors lower the totals. Many books have joint authors, which raises the numbers. And *Books in Print* does not list the many books published by small presses for non-bookstore markets.

Even as gross generalizations, these estimates should unnerve authors—especially when low literacy rates are also taken into account. A Department of Education study of adults found that 18 to 21 percent of those tested "demonstrated proficiencies associated with the most challenging tasks in this assessment, many of which involved long and complex documents and text passages." Assuming that books are written by such people—a risky assumption perhaps—one out of every sixty-six to eighty-one highly literate Americans writes a book each decade.

The trend toward more competition shows no sign of abating. The *Statistical Abstract of the United States* reported only 125,000 "authors" in 1992, a ridiculously low estimate but a telling one insofar as it is a more than 100 percent increase over the previous decade. *Writer's Digest,* a self-help magazine for writers, had an 81 percent increase in paid subscribers in the twenty-year period up to 1998. Its total circulation that year was 250,000. In the early 1980s, a *New Yorker* editor suggested the following odds against publication in his magazine: "novels, approximately 29,998 to 2; stories, 249,511 to 489." He noted that his magazine received at least 25,000 poetry submissions a year. It is difficult to imagine the odds being more favorable today, and it is easy to imagine that they are far worse.

Statistics such as these, which show the number of writers growing faster than the overall population, cast a long shadow over what should be the good news of increased life expectancies. The longer people are around, the greater the possibility that they will start to write books. Consider the most common answer to the question "What will you do when you retire?" "Write a book" comes second only to "play more golf." Many never get around to writing, but as more people live longer, more likely will. One of the popular enrichment programs for seniors is the writing workshop, in which they learn to put their thoughts on paper. Retired folk living off pensions do not need to worry if what they write sells.

Most others must worry that stiff book writing competition makes it difficult to earn a living. A depressing point of departure in assessing this dog-eat-dog climate is a 1994 Gallup study of readers' habits. The study, done for the American Booksellers Association, found 106 million American adults purchasing an average of about 457 million books in any given quarter.

To take the brightest scenario possible, let's make several assumptions dramatically in favor of an author who has just published a book. First, assume the book-buying Americans in the Gallup study bought only books published that year. That is to say, they did not buy classics or even books that were published the year before. Second, assume that only established, reputable houses published all the books bought in the Gallup study. Under these circumstances, our average author is competing with about 50,000 books, instead of the 140,000 books mentioned above or the more than 1.6 million books listed in the 1998–1999 edition of *Books in Print.*

The result? Each title averages 915 sales per quarter. Because respondents in the Gallup survey said they spent an average of $15 for each book, a book selling the average of 915 copies each quarter would earn $13,725. That comes out to $54,900 a year, a tidy sum until one delves a little further into the numbers.

Book publishing involves paper, printing and binding, editing, promotion, and warehousing, all of which must be paid for. Also, book distributors and bookstore owners want their share. From the point of view of authors, the magic of the marketplace is how much money disappears into other people's pockets. Authors are workers whose wages are paid in royalties, a handful of free copies of their own book, and the privilege of buying more at a discount. Royalty scales differ depending on the book and the author's prestige. A romance novel, often written under a pseudonym and sold by the truckload, may pay out only 4 percent on the first 150,000 copies and sometimes 2 percent, 3 percent, or possibly a bit more on sales after that. A serious nonfiction hardcover book generally pays 5 to 10 percent for the first 5,000 copies, and in the 10 to 15 percent range on increments thereafter. So, to continue our Gallup study example, let's remain on the generous side. Suppose our average author receives 15 percent royalties for all sales. This brings the author $8,235 in royalties in a year.

In a world where a few authors do stunningly well, distorting the statistics wildly, most authors consider themselves lucky to reach the averages. Even if they do, they must buy their own paper and pencils, pay for Social Security and medical benefits, and cover the cost of research and travel to libraries. A literary agent, almost a necessity to securing a decent publishing contract, will take at least 10 percent of the author's share and, more frequently, as much as 15 percent.

Ireland has made its writers tax exempt. Authors everywhere else I know about not only pay taxes but also find it difficult to take tax deductions. James Wilcox, a Reardon-type character if ever one existed, made $11,800 in 1985 and tried to deduct a third of the rent for his small apartment. "The auditor," a *New Yorker* writer reported, "examined the table where Wilcox worked—which, given the size of the apartment, was close to the refrigerator—and accused Wilcox of eating there. Wilcox said he didn't ('It's much too depressing to eat next to the typewriter'), but the auditor argued that he *could* eat there, so the area wouldn't count as an office. It also lacked a solid wall, which would have cut off his view of both windows."

Money can disappear quickly even from a lucrative book. Rudy Maxa and Marion Clark wrote *Public Trust, Private Lust,* an account of congressional wrongdoing published in 1977. As Maxa recalls, "We got an advance of $30,000 to split . . . and after my agent's 10 percent and my expenses, I had about $7,000. But I had taken off time from work, which cost me over $6,000 in salary. That left me almost $1,000 to the good. Then Marion talked me into having the book party, which *we* paid for (the publisher sent down twenty free copies of the book) at F. Scott's in Georgetown, with an open bar featuring ice-cream drinks and Chivas Regal! The bill for the party came to more than $2,000."

Although professional writers can supplement book income by writing articles, this is really a from-the-frying-pan-into-the-fire scenario. "Since these are confessions," author Paul Gallico observed many years ago in *Further Confessions of a Story Writer*, "I will confess to you that from the time I resigned from the [*New York Daily*] *News* a quarter of a century ago up to and including this very moment I have never had a single moment of security." A journalism school dean in the 1970s calculated that twenty-five thousand citizens call themselves freelancers but fewer than three hundred make a living at it. It is worse now, as the nearby table shows.

Many writers have seen article writing as a warm-up to book writing. John Updike questioned this practice when the commercial market for

Writing for Free(lance)

The Decline in Freelance Magazine Rates in 1982 Dollars per Article

Publication	1960	1994
Cosmopolitan	$3,378	$2,362
Family Circle	4,223	2,699
McCall's	8,446	2,699
New York Times Magazine	1,014	2,024
Popular Science	1,351	1,687
Reader's Digest	6,757	2,699
Redbook	4,730	2,699
Woman's Day	2,250	2,699

NOTE: These numbers estimate typical payments per article at the high end of prevalent freelance rates. They are based on data from the *Columbia Journalism Review* (September/October 1981), the *National Writers Union Guide to Freelance Rates & Standard Practice* (1995), and interviews with editorial assistants at the magazines noted in the chart. As the interviews confirmed, what an author receives for an article is flexible, depending on a variety of factors, such as fame. These variables aside, it is clear that the rates overall are far less than they were thirty-five years ago.

Compiled by Kenneth Damann

fiction shrank. "When I began, I could support myself and my growing family on the six stories a year I sold to the *New Yorker*. Now there's hardly anywhere to sell stories, and without that it's harder to establish a track record" that will impress book publishers. In the 1920s, the *Saturday Evening Post* published 250 stories a year and twenty to twenty-five serialized novels. It paid $5,000 for the former and $50,000 or more for the latter. The old weekly *Saturday Evening Post* is now out of business.

Norman Mailer, who gets married the way everyone else dates, makes enough money to support a wife and five former wives, five daughters and three sons of his own, and one adopted son. But he is the exception. Battalions of struggling full-time writers cannot afford to get married unless their spouses have good jobs. Frank Sulloway toiled for years on *Born to Rebel*, which explored the relationship between birth order and intellectual creativity. Nearly fifty years old when the book came out in 1996, he had never owned a car or paid a mortgage. He wasn't married. He had to use $3,000 of his own money to pay for the cover art he wanted.

The most definitive study of writers' incomes, based on a 1980 survey of those who had at least one book published, showed that median writing income was $4,775 a year. Given that estimate, increased competition, the failure of publishers to keep up with inflation, and the fact that the money American households spent on reading in 1994 ($165 per household) was less than one-half annual household purchases of personal care products and services ($397), it is reasonable to assume that writers today are not doing any better in real terms and probably far worse.

Dr. Johnson stressed the importance of writing for pay, perhaps because he was always in debt. Most contemporary authors must have other jobs as Chaucer, Shakespeare, and Milton did. Or, if they write full time, they approach their work the way a factory executive does. To understand this aspect of the economics of authorship more clearly, let's look first at the men and women who write on the bosses' time.

Writing on the Bosses' Time

Although we may be in the age of "authors by profession," strictly speaking, authors aren't professionals. Professionals must have special educations and review boards to establish minimum levels of competence.

These do not exist for authors; neither do binding codes of ethics nor the seeming imperative that they speak mumbo jumbo as lawyers and doctors do. Their supposed goal is to be understood. While some authors show remarkable entrepreneurial instincts, they don't like to be called business people. They can't be called blue-collar workers either, although many like to wear denim. Skilled workers know how to organize themselves. Authors occasionally make common cause, but without much real enthusiasm. But the biggest reason authors defy categorization is that they are in every category.

Walk down the street, enter any shop, and an author may very well greet you. Writers do—and have done—everything to earn their living. They have been clergy (Horatio Alger), governesses (Anne, Charlotte, and Emily Brontë), school inspectors (Matthew Arnold), exterminators (William Burroughs), firemen (Larry Brown), tinkers (John Bunyan), oil company executives (Raymond Chandler), bank clerks (T. S. Eliot and Stephen Leacock), stockbrokers (Jules Verne), architects (Thomas Hardy), apothecaries (John Keats), longshoremen and truck drivers (Jack London and Arthur Miller), spies (Christopher Marlowe), advertising men (F. Scott Fitzgerald, Sherwood Anderson, James Dickey), tailors (Henry Miller), insurance men (Franz Kafka and Tom Clancy), physicians (Arthur Conan Doyle, William Carlos Williams, Anton Chekhov, Louis Ferdinand Céline), dentists (Zane Grey), pencil sharpener salesmen (Edgar Rice Burroughs), merchant seamen (Joseph Conrad), miners (Brett Harte), and farmers (J. Hector St. John de Crèvecoeur).

Even the guy who holds you up may be a writer. The sixteenth-century Englishman Robert Greene deserted his wife and entered a bohemian life "among cutpurses, rogues, and prostitutes, and died of a surfeit of pickely herrings and Rhenish wine." When we die, a writer may be there with a shovel. Michigan poet Thomas Lynch is an undertaker. Is murder suspected? Before she became a popular mystery writer, Patricia Cornwell worked in the Richmond, Virginia, medical examiner's office.

Working for the Barron Collier Advertising Agency, F. Scott Fitzgerald coined an ad slogan for a steam laundry in Iowa: "We keep you clean in Muscatine." Next he fixed train roofs for the Northern Pacific Railroad. That job lasted two weeks. When *This Side of Paradise* was accepted for publication, he became a full-time writer.

Many other notable writers did not give up their day jobs to write books. Sir Walter Scott practiced law throughout his productive literary career. Charles Lamb clerked in the South Sea House for several years and after that at the East India Company for thirty-three years. William Carlos Williams was a doctor until the end of his life. His fellow physician, Chekhov, called medicine "my lawful wife and literature . . . my mistress."

Wallace Stevens, trained as a lawyer, went into the insurance business in 1908 and sat at his Hartford office desk well past mandatory retirement and almost to the day he died in 1955. When asked about poets in similar circumstances to his own, Stevens favorably noted the nineteenth-century poet Clarence Stedman. Stedman entered banking after his first book appeared and later opened a brokerage firm, where he worked most of his life. He devised a poetic telegraphic code: Keats meant "cancel order to buy" and Shelley meant "select and sell at discretion." This is not to say that Stevens sought inspiration from his regular job. He wanted money.

"A writer faces the point of honor that concerns him as a writer," Stevens wrote a friend. "He must apparently choose between starvation and that form of publishing (or being published) in which it is possible to make money. His problem is how to support himself while engaged in the most honorable capacity. There is only one answer. He must support himself in some other way." In other words, he must get a steady, well-paying job. "I cannot accept one bedroom as being liberty in comparison with my present life," said T. S. Eliot, who disliked his job at Lloyds Bank but relished poverty less.

"Most authors would find themselves in a state of virtual poverty if they had to depend solely on their writing income," according to the 1980 wage survey mentioned earlier. While the median annual income reported in the study was just under $5,000, the total median income from all sources was $27,000 a year. Other surveys confirm that few writers live adequately by writing. A 1979 poll of the membership of the Authors Guild found that only about one-third held no job other than writing. The median annual income from writing for these full-time writers was a mere $11,000.

The *New York Times*'s book review is as good a standard as any for identifying the important books that come out each year. As such, it also offers an opportunity to categorize the employment patterns of our more important authors. With this in mind, one of my graduate assistants researched each American author whose book was reviewed during August 1996.

The result is the pie chart (page 31). The chart tells us some things we could guess. Predictably journalism nurtures a large number of book writers. Margaret Mitchell, Walt Whitman, and Ernest Hemingway left journalism. But H. L. Mencken continued to write a column for the *Baltimore Sun* until 1941, when he was older than sixty. The reason for staying is obvious. Real dramas play out daily for newsroom workers. The old French saying that journalism is a great profession as long as you get out of it doesn't really apply if you want to be a book writer.

At the same time, the chart may be misleading about the number of full-time writers. That is to say that some of those full-time writers may not make enough money from their writing to support themselves, but rely instead on some form of coupon clipping. As she wrote in *A Room of One's Own*, Virginia Woolf thought it far more important to inherit five hundred pounds a year from an aunt who died in a fall from her horse than to get the right to vote from suffrage-minded legislators. No more reading to old ladies or making artificial flowers for Woolf. William Burroughs, that writer of erotic and bizarre prose, was a grandson of the inventor of the adding machine, something the family needed to total up all its profits. Or one can fall in love with the right person. While Lord Byron was reluctant to take money for his work, marrying for money was quite all right. Actually, it was expected. The equivalent in our more class-free society is a hardworking spouse. No doubt spousal support explains the statistics in the Authors Guild study, which showed that full-time authors with a median income of eleven thousand dollars from their writing had enjoyed a *family* income three times as high.

Still, the majority of writers get by writing on the bosses' time. That's the ticket to high literary output and financial comfort. To understand how this process works, let's look at five categories of work that have been especially attractive historically to the wordsmith who wants to tinker at someone else's expense.

How Writers Really Put Pie on Their Tables

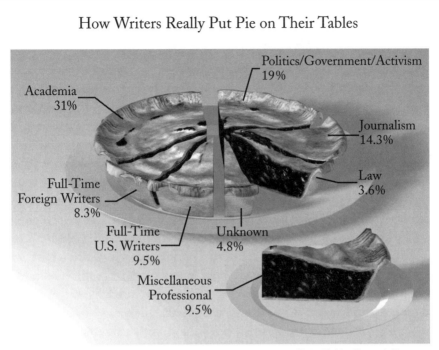

Politics/Government/Activism 19%

Academia 31%

Journalism 14.3%

Full-Time Foreign Writers 8.3%

Law 3.6%

Full-Time U.S. Writers 9.5%

Unknown 4.8%

Miscellaneous Professional 9.5%

Compiled by Kenneth Damann

Few book writers live chiefly by writing books. As this pie chart shows, they typically do something else to keep food on the table.

The chart is based on the books reviewed in the Sunday *New York Times* during August 1996. All authors whose books received substantial reviews were included, except for two long-deceased foreign writers whose works had come out in new translations. Authors of children's books and authors of books reviewed in brief were not included.

Contemporary Authors and other such sources consulted often describe authors as having double-barreled occupations (e.g., diplomat-writer). For the purposes of this chart, the job that appeared to account for the greatest share of the author's income was considered the chief occupation. In some cases it was difficult to establish the primacy of one job over another. How, for instance, does one categorize a science fiction book writer who is a columnist for a monthly magazine (unless one actually looks at the book writer-columnist's tax return)? Kenneth Damann, who did the research for this chart, gave the benefit of the doubt to full-time writing in such cases. It is possible, of course, that some of the "full-time" writers were not actually making a living from writing, but were supported by a working spouse, such as is the case of book writer James Trilling. His wife is a tenured professor at Brown University. The miscellaneous professional category included occupations that ranged from neuroanatomist at a medical institute to architect.

Vows of Poverty, Silence, and Writing

This trend started in Europe's monasteries and continues to the present day. Monks who previously would have copied illuminated manuscripts now write books of their own. Instead of dank scriptoria, they have cozy quarters and computers—as well as that other essential convenience of the modern writer, an agent. Hotshot New York agent Mort Janklow, the same guy who handles Judith Krantz and Danielle Steel, sold Pope John Paul II's *Crossing the Threshold of Hope* to Knopf for a reported $6 million.

But in thinking about the special enticements the Catholic Church offers writers, don't concentrate on *Crossing the Threshold of Hope*, which in its various translations earned between $100 million and $200 million, and don't focus on the fact that the pope-approved *Catechism of the Catholic Church*, which came out in the United States in 1994, had limited bookstore discounts because of the royalties required by the Vatican. Think, instead, about the vow of poverty. Better than any publisher's contract, this self-denial ensures that priests and nuns always get what they need to live no matter how ungainful their daily work.

Praying does not interfere with writing. Sister Wendy Beckett, the buck-toothed English nun who has become an art critic, prays seven hours a day and writes for only two hours. She has more than a dozen books to her credit. Between rosaries, she has also squeezed in a delightful television series on the history of art. Both praying and writing require reflection that overlaps. A writer can get a lot of work done on God's time.

The Church has always managed to generate intense hostility and angst. This wonderfully energizes writers, whose emotions roiled not long after Gutenberg's invention. With mechanized printing, the church mass-produced forms that sinners could buy to lessen their sufferings after death. The corruption of indulgences, as these preprinted passes out of Purgatory were called, ignited heretical thoughts among people like Martin Luther. Luther has gone down in history as the renegade who nailed his ninety-five theses to the door of the Augustinian Chapel at Wittenberg on All Saints' Day, October 15, 1517. In truth, he probably didn't do any nailing at all. Even if he had, translation of the theses from Latin into German, and their printing and wide dissemination within a month of Luther's writing them, stirred up far more trouble than a little hammering on a church door ever could. And Luther had only just begun his troublemaking in print. "I am publishing a book in the German tongue about Christian reform, directed against the pope, in language as violent as if I were addressing Antichrist," Luther wrote to a pal later. Writing in vernacular irritated the church leadership, which preferred Latin, a language on which it had a corner.

Accustomed to having their way, church fathers in Rome foolishly thought that they could foil the upstart German cleric and other writers who challenged them. They burned books that questioned papal authority, which was a waste of time considering the large numbers of volumes that now floated around as a result of mechanized printing. They forbade the publication of new books without Vatican imprimatur, equally silly since the Vatican did not control printing presses the way it controlled monasteries. And in 1559, they issued a list of forbidden books, perhaps the world's first consumer's guide to literature. As the church found itself besieged by more and more doubters, it tried more creative approaches. In the nineteenth century, it unveiled the divinely revealed dogma that it was infallible in matters of religion and morals.

As the centuries have rolled by, this holier-than-thou attitude has remained both irritating and inspirational to authors. Father Tissa Balasuriya, a Sri Lankan priest, has challenged church beliefs on original sin and the Virgin Mary, whom he believes is portrayed as too submissive and pious. His book *Mary and Human Liberation* describes her as a robust peasant woman. It also includes a special appendix of letters from the Vatican explaining why it excommunicated him.

Father Andrew Greeley writes catechisms and devotional books, articles for *TV Guide* and the *Chicago Sun-Times,* and novels with titles such as *Thy Brother's Wife, The Cardinal Sins,* and *Ascent into Hell.* Crimson and flesh tones dominate the covers of his novels. A social scientist by training, Greeley conducted surveys that have found that Catholics have more sex than non-Catholics. He also polled his readers and came up with a happy conclusion that the sex in his books "is not overdone and that the mixture of religion and story in the books responds to both market and human needs." Better yet, the Chicago Archdiocese in which Greeley works will not accept the prodigious royalties from his books. According to Greeley, church officials fear the Vatican's disapproval for taking money from a priest who writes steamy novels (Greeley prefers the adjective "erotic") and holds liberal views on homosexuality and the ordination of women. Father Greeley has the best of the secular and religious worlds.*

Going Postal and Other Public Service

In 1865, poet Walt Whitman lost his job clerking for the Bureau of Indian Affairs, part of the Department of the Interior. The Interior secretary, a staunch Methodist, wasn't concerned that Whitman used government time to revise *Leaves of Grass,* but that the book and its author, in his consideration, were immoral. In any event, being fired made little difference to Whitman. He went to the attorney general's office and got a new job. Besides, the news of his firing gave *Leaves of Grass* publicity.

William Charvat estimated in his valuable history of American authorship that from 1800 to 1870, 60 to 75 percent of all male American writers "who even approached professionalism either held public office or tried to get it." Nor have cushy government appointments for writers been a strictly American phenomenon. Thanks to Napoleon, Henri Beyle (Stendhal) served in the war commissary and as inspector of Imperial Crown Furniture. The English dramatist William Congreve was at various times the commissioner responsible for licensing hackney coaches, commissioner of wines, and secretary to the island of Jamaica. Richard Steele was commissioner of forfeited estates; Joseph Addison, commissioner of trade and secretary of state; Edward Gibbons, a member of Parliament and lord of trade; Richard Brinsley Sheridan, also an MP, treasurer of the navy. The Duke Carl August appointed Johann von Goethe to his council in Weimar as a privy legation councilor, where he was responsible for the committees on war and roads. At length he became the chamberlain, the equivalent of finance minister.

Of all the public troughs, none has offered more to authors than the post office. The large and far-flung postal bureaucracy had many places to

---

*Lest any think that Catholics are the only ones to deserve credit for supporting writers, let it be said that other religions have created a good writing environment too. Martin Luther's followers became rigid. "The dogmatists held that God spoke directly to simple men in simple language, that they instinctively understood him, and that the true Christian spurned literature, even reading and writing," William Manchester notes. This promoted alienated Lutheran humanists to write furiously against these conservative views.

hide. (In the United States alone, it offered 78,500 patronage slots in 1896.) Mail sorting and other routine work required little concentration. Clerks could read the unclaimed periodicals, as William Faulkner did when he was postmaster at the University of Mississippi postal station. He called his part of the post office "the reading room." *

In Anthony Trollope's mid–nineteenth century, one plucked these plums by standing on the backs of patrons (he landed his job thanks to a close friend of his mother, who in turn lobbied her father-in-law, who was secretary in the post office where the nineteen-year-old Anthony went to work). One kept these jobs depending on whom one knew and not what one did. This nurtured a fine tradition of bureaucratic unresponsiveness. Says one historian of the postal system, "Many seem to have regarded their inability to support themselves at some other line of work as their primary qualification for a government job." The inability to support oneself could be the textbook definition of a struggling but worthwhile belletrist.

Trollope, who worked in the post office for twenty of his thirty-five-year writing career, may have had the most successful literary experience. At his death in 1882, he had written sixty novels (many two or three volumes in length), five volumes of collected short stories, four travel books, four collections of sketches, four or five volumes of miscellaneous articles, two studies of classical authors, an autobiography, and plenty of polemic.

After Nathaniel Hawthorne unsuccessfully lobbied for an appointment as postmaster of Salem, Massachusetts, he settled for a job in a customs house, which, having a similarly bureaucratic routine, was almost as inviting. In an essay on the experience, he noted that in this line of work he was preceded by Chaucer, who was in customs work for twelve years in the Port of London, and Robert Burns, who became an excise officer after failing as a farmer and succeeding as a poet. Among the many others in

---

*Perhaps this also helps explain why many aspiring writers have worked in the private equivalent of post offices. D. H. Lawrence worked in the mail room at a local surgical goods firm after leaving Nottingham High School and for a time received inspiration from Blanche Jennings, a progressive suffragette who worked in the Liverpool post office. William Saroyan delivered telegrams for the Postal Telegraph Company. In addition to working as a tailor, Henry Miller worked for the Western Union telegraph service, where he did his first writing. His boss had suggested he write a Horatio Alger–type story about messengers.

the odious business of tax collection were: the Roman poet Horace (who previously turned down the job as private secretary to Augustus, possibly because it would have been too demanding); Jean de La Bruyère, who bought an absentee post in the Caen revenue department; poets Matthew Prior and William Wordsworth; novelist Daniel Defoe; and firebrand Thomas Paine.

The New York Customs House, the largest single federal office in the country in the 1870s and 1880s, was particularly rich in talent, as well as notorious for corruption. After years of episodic jobs, including setting pins in a Hawaiian bowling alley, Herman Melville finally cornered a customs position. He kept his job as deputy inspector of customs for nineteen years. Teddy Roosevelt, our most literary president, placed the poet Edwin Arlington Robinson in the New York Customs House.

Here is the New York Customs House. Notice how the customers wait while the clerks work at their desks, head down, the way writers do. The largest single federal office in the country in the late nineteenth century, this customs house was a sinecure for such literary greats as Herman Melville and Edwin Arlington Robinson.

New York City Customs House. Franklin D. Roosevelt Library

In the old patronage system, what one politician gave, another could take back in a wink. Hawthorne owed his $1,200-a-year, three-and-a-half-hours-a-day job in the Salem Customs House to his allies in the Democratic Party. A "besom of reform," as Hawthorne quaintly referred to the spoils system, swept him out when Zachary Taylor became president and put a Whig in the job.* Hawthorne wrote a campaign biography for Franklin Pierce, his close friend and classmate at Bowdoin College. When Pierce became president, he appointed Hawthorne the U.S. consul to Liverpool. During a housecleaning under the Hayes administration, two hundred employees were fired at the New York Customs House. Herman Melville survived, possibly because a Shakespearean scholar was a member of the review team, but he had to endure the indignity of increased working hours. Previously from ten-to-three, they were upped to nine-to-four.

As countries go through various stages of industrialization, good government types surface and eventually get around to civil service reform. When that happens, rules and regulations, not personal favors, decide who will have their noses in the government oat bag. Faulkner came to his postmaster job when patronage was waning. After about three years, he got the boot. A postal inspector's report noted that "you mistreat mail of all classes, including registered mail; that you have thrown mail with return postage guaranteed and all classes into the garbage can by the side entrance." Patrons had to go through the garbage to get their magazines.

Richard Wright had it worse. As a young man contemplating a writing career during the 1920s, the aspiring novelist desperately wanted a Chicago post office job. He scored a respectable 94 percent on the required written test, but did not meet another requirement that had nothing to do with literature or postal clerking. He was supposed to weigh a minimum of 125 pounds. He finally passed after gorging himself on buttermilk and bananas, but even then the post office showed no respect for his literary talent. It laid him off. Back on the street, he sold insurance and for a brief moment contemplated participating in a postal fraud scheme proposed by a friend who had also worked in the post office.

Today, as the earlier pie chart revealed, many "government-supported"

*Melville's short story "Bartleby" tells of the sad end of a disoriented "subordinate clerk in the Dead Letter Office at Washington [who] . . . had been suddenly removed by a change in the administration."

writers work for activist organizations that exist to change government policy. These agitators write books as part of their jobs. All that is left from that golden time when Faulkner read in the back room of his little post office are postal facilities full of slow-motion clerks who languidly eye the long lines that snake their way to counters.

Throwing the Book at Them

Walter Scott and Wallace Stevens, mentioned above, are not the only authors to have practiced law. James Boswell was a lawyer. Henry Fielding, the father of the English novel, was a barrister, magistrate, and justice of the peace for Westminster and eventually all of Middlesex. Washington Irving was admitted to the bar after dawdling around as a law clerk for eight years. Edgar Lee Masters practiced law in Chicago. Anthony Hope Hawkins, a British novelist and a lawyer, came up with the plot for *The Prisoner of Zenda* when walking back to his office after winning a case and noticing two men in the street who looked alike.

In recent years, the law has produced bumper crops of professional scribblers. Louis Auchincloss began producing novels and collections of short stories, many of which had legal themes, soon after he began his law practice in New York City in the 1940s. When he was at the prestigious firm of Sullivan and Cromwell, his colleague John Foster Dulles complained Auchincloss was writing when he should have been doing the firm's work. For a brief time, the young attorney tried writing full time. Ultimately, though, he preferred writing on the job. Critic John Leonard has decreed Auchincloss "the only serious writer seriously writing about the American business world—our ruling class, after all."

More recently, Scott Turow, John Grisham, George V. Higgins, Steve Martini, John Martel, Grif Stockley, and William Lashner have turned law into literature. Ken Ludwig, who specializes in theater law, has written *Lend Me a Tenor* and other plays. Some attorney-authors don't wait to become full-fledged lawyers before they write. Brad Meltzer wrote a legal thriller while studying law at Columbia, *Dead Even*.

The law is of increasing interest in our litigious society. If you haven't been sued yet, you figure it is only a matter of time. But this is not the only explanation for the proliferation of attorney-authors. With the number of lawyers increasing faster than the number of writers, attorneys need outside work. Besides that, many young lawyers find themselves in the same predicament as Robert Louis Stevenson, hating their trade. (As an advocate at the Scottish Bar, he earned a grand total of four guineas, about .2 percent of what it cost him to go to law school.) Writing legal fiction and nonfiction is a lot more interesting than writing legal documents. John Grisham, who disliked brief writing as a lawyer, now hires assistants to do the legal research for his books.

Then, too, there is what we might call Grisham's law: making a fast buck by chasing a book contract instead of an ambulance. First came Turow, a Harvard Law School graduate who reaped high financial rewards for his best seller *Presumed Innocent* in 1987. When Grisham's *The Firm* appeared four years later, Grisham has said, many lawyers figured it was time to cash in on the books they were quietly writing on the side. "An epidemic of sabbaticals and leaves of absence hit law firms across the land," Grisham said, "as budding writers left their offices to finish their books."

The argot of the legal profession provides an endless list of catchy title possibilities. Already we have had *Burden of Proof, The Runaway Jury, Compelling Evidence, Expert Testimony, Presumed Innocent, Hostile Witness, Conflict of Interest.* William Bernhardt alone has had *Primary Justice, Blind Justice, Deadly Justice, Perfect Justice, Cruel Justice,* and *Naked Justice,* not to mention *Double Jeopardy.*

Lawyers who may not have thought much about writing a book get the itch to sit at the computer as soon as they land a legal case that receives attention from the public and publishers. When appealing his conviction for the Oklahoma City bombings, Timothy McVeigh asked to dismiss his attorney. McVeigh complained that his counsel had signed a $600,000 book contract before the sentence was rendered. The attorney countered that he had not kept his book aspirations secret from McVeigh and that McVeigh "asked me to find an agent for Jennifer, his sister, because he wanted her to write a book. I declined."

As McVeigh's attorney may have understood, criminals already have such vast opportunities to build writing careers, they don't deserve any additional help from lawyers.

Serving a Sentence

Jail has a fine tradition of nourishing literature. Unlike the postal service, these advantages have not fallen victim to reform. Prison reforms have promoted writing. "By the late 1970s," H. Bruce Franklin observed, "the river of prison literature was overflowing its banks, pouring out to the American public in mass-market paperbacks, newspapers, magazines, and major motion pictures." PEN, a worldwide organization dedicated to promoting writing and writers, does its part by sponsoring an annual literary competition for prisoners.

The common view is that prison is unpleasant. And it can be. Sir Thomas More had to give up writing in the Tower of London when his jailers took away his writing tools. Oscar Wilde's two years at hard labor broke his health. But better accommodations are possible. The best, as Robert Graves has noted, are like those Cervantes found himself in, that is, "an old-fashioned jail where the prisoner is not required to break rocks, pick oakum or sew mailbags, but where the turnkey will provide pen, ink, paper and a writing table—not to mention food—for a small fee." Sir Walter Raleigh wrote his *History of the World* in the Tower of London without interruption.

The Bastille could be especially kind to French literature. One playwright described the food: "an excellent soup, a succulent side of beef, a thigh of boiled chicken oozing with grease; a little dish of fried, marinated artichokes or of spinach; really fine Cressane pears; fresh grapes, a bottle of old Burgundy and the best Moka coffee." The marquis de Sade sodomized women and men, deflowered young girls, knifed whores when he wasn't whipping them, and masturbated on a crucifix. While in the Bastille, where he secretly wrote *The 120 Days of Sodom* and other works, Sade had with him his finest clothes and elegant household furnishings. His wife supplied erotic novels to keep him amused when he wasn't writing them.

The big advantage of writing in jail is that a writer need not worry about making money or fret about having to take time out for cooking or doing the laundry. A grant from the National Endowment for the Humanities covers *some* expenses. A life sentence covers everything, plus offers peace and quiet. "So much lovely time stretches out before you," notes a modern prison writer, James Blake, "time to read, to write, to play, to practice, to speculate, contemplate."

Rogues Gallery of Writers

NELSON Algren: Lifted a typewriter from Sul Ross Teachers College in Alpine, Texas; spent month in the jug. Sometimes called "the poet of the jail and the whorehouse."

JIM BAKKER: Discredited televangelist; wrote *I Was Wrong* while serving time in federal pen. (The Reverend Richard Dortch, Bakker's accomplice, served less time more productively. After sixteen months in slammer, he wrote three I-am-sorry books.)

MIGUEL DE CERVANTES SAAVEDRA: Incarcerated first during war with the Turks. When imprisoned in Spain for fraud, a crime he committed while a tax collector, began his classic *Don Quixote*. Wrote another book, *Persiles and Sigismunda*, upon release. It is forgotten.

JOHN CLELAND: Thrown into Fleet Prison for debt. Completed *Memoirs of a Woman of Pleasure*, better known as *Fanny Hill*. Publisher paid Cleland's debts in exchange for rights to book.

ADOLF HITLER: Incarcerated for stirring up the 1923 Beer Hall Putsch. Dictated the first volume of *Mein Kampf* to two jailmates, one of whom was Rudolf Hess.

RICHARD LOVELACE: Jailed when he sided with the king during England's seventeenth-century civil wars. During first stint behind bars, he supposedly wrote "To Althea, From Prison."

THOMAS MALORY: The fifteenth-century author of *Le Morte d'Arthur*, went to prison at different times for church plundering, rape, extortion, etc. Buried close to Newgate, where he may have died a prisoner.

NORIO NAGAYAMA: While in jail for killing four people, became award-winning author. His last words before being hanged at the Tokyo Detention House in 1997 were to donate the royalties from his last novel to poor children.

CÉSAR VALLEJO: Peruvian poet who wrote part of one of his finest works, "Trilce," while in jail on a false charge.

FRANÇOIS VILLON: French contemporary of Malory and, like him, often in jail. Wrote beautiful poem while awaiting his hanging. Reprieved at last minute and disappeared for good shortly afterward.

"I saw literary glory illuminate the walls of my prison," one French writer mused. "Once persecuted I would be better known." In addition to giving authors notoriety, prison gives them book material. Simon Linguet wrote *The Bastille Revealed*. Despite the difficult conditions, Oscar Wilde wrote *De Profundis* while in jail and afterward wrote *The Ballad of Reading Gaol*, which he dedicated to C. T. Wooldridge, a fellow inmate who murdered his wife and was executed. Wilde initially used C3.3, his prison number, as his author's credit. This was his only major work based on personal experience. Poet Robert Lowell went to jail in 1943 because he refused to go into the wartime military. His Pulitzer Prize–winning book, *Lord Weary's Castle*, included a poem on his jail experience.

Sade's "passionately fixated hatred" of those who put him behind bars "helped to transform the early society dramatist and casual pornographer into something quite different," notes one scholar. It made him into a great writer. Says Robert Darnton, Sade "has to some degree inspired nearly every movement of the French avant-garde." After many ruinous financial ventures, including his stint with the taxation bureaucracy, Daniel Defoe went to Newgate. Defoe "was a busy, slip-shod journalist and a keen politician," E. M. Forster wrote. "But something happened to him in prison and out of its vague, powerful emotion, Moll Flanders and Roxana are born." Moll is literally born in Newgate to a mother condemned to hang for petty theft. Alexander Solzhenitsyn penned his first poetry while in a Soviet labor camp, which he described as "a spiritual birthplace." Before going to jail himself, Wilde had observed that a merely "clever rhymer" named Wilfrid Scawen Blunt became "an earnest and deep-thinking poet" after going to the pokey.

Criminals whose only past writing involved bad checks often discover their vocation for the written word in jail. Jean Genet, the French writer whose works included *Thief's Journal*, picked pockets, stole cattle, deserted from the military, lifted manuscripts, distributed counterfeit money, and trafficked in drugs. He said he "began writing in jail to clarify my ideas and amuse myself." (Other times he said he began to write as a teenager in reform school.) With time on his hands, Malcolm X taught himself to read and write in prison, as did Eldridge Cleaver, who "started to write. To save myself." The *New York Times* called Cleaver's *Soul on Ice* one of the ten best books of 1968. "One of the things you need to get started [as a writer] is a lot of time," said G. Gordon Liddy, a Richard

Nixon henchman who felt that he had books inside of him that wanted to get out, "and in prison I had all the time in the world."

A highly productive writer who goes to jail may find the change of scenery distracting. English author P. G. Wodehouse, who blithely stayed in France after the outbreak of World War II, was put in a Polish prison, which had previously been a lunatic asylum.* His output declined to three hundred words a day, compared with two thousand when he was free. After he was released, he foolishly agreed to broadcast over German networks to his American readers. This was a technically treasonable offense, which landed him in Allied custody after the war, this time in a Paris maternity ward. Nevertheless, by the time his prison days were over, he had written five novels, as well as a book about his internments.

In many more cases, getting out of jail is disconcerting. William Sydney Porter embezzled money from a bank where he worked as a teller and fled to Honduras. When he returned, he was sentenced to five years. A licensed pharmacist, he worked in the prison infirmary at night, a good, quiet place to write. An inmate's sister helped spirit his work to the outside world, where it was published under the alias of O. Henry. He died less than ten drunken years later, broke. Pramoedya Ananta Toer, considered by many to be Indonesia's greatest contemporary writer, composed the *Buru Quartet* while a political prisoner. He spent most of his fourteen years of incarceration on Indonesia's remote prison island of Buru, where he did hard labor and foraged for food. After his release in 1979, he was under house arrest for a dozen years or so, during which time he reported suffering from acute writer's block. His output since 1979 includes a recently published prison memoir, *The Mute's Soliloquy,* a novella, and a few articles. Pramoedya, who reportedly spends five hours a day cutting stories from newspapers, says he is "overwhelmed by information." In prison, he said, "there were not so many problems."

The one drawback is that our judicial system frowns on miscreants profiting from their transgressions. In 1977, New York passed the Son of

---

*After knifing his wife, Norman Mailer was adamant about going to jail rather than a mental institution. According to his friend at the time, Norman Podhoretz, Mailer said he would not be taken seriously if he were considered insane. This is wrong. Murderer and lunatic asylum resident Dr. William C. Minor contributed ten thousand entries to the *Oxford English Dictionary.* Ezra Pound spent more than a decade in St. Elizabeth's, where he remained productive.

Sam law. Named after the alias used by murderer David Berkowitz, it barred criminals from earning money writing about their crimes. The Supreme Court overturned the law on First Amendment grounds, saying that it targeted expression. New York rewrote the law to include "all profits from a crime." Other states have passed similar laws to ensure that prison writers stay poor.

If a criminal wants to make writing pay, the example to follow is Ronnie Biggs. One of the team of bandits in the famous 1963 Great Train Robbery, he escaped from jail, went to Australia, and ended up in Brazil. Having none of the dough from the heist left, he says, he's made his living selling "Ronnie Biggs" T-shirts to tourists and writing his life story. He has also made a little money from autobiographical films and, as he reports in his book, *Odd Man Out: My Life on the Loose and the Truth About the Great Train Robbery*, several gentlemen of the press offered to pay him if he would wear a Princess Di T-shirt and comment on her visit to Rio.

The Writing Academy

In 1995, for the first time in its history, the United States spent more money building prisons than building universities. Conceivably, this marks a turning point in literature, but that is unlikely. Prisoners can chose between writing and making license plates. Writing on someone else's time is part of the job description of a professor. As the pie chart on page 31 shows, professors dominate part-time writing.

The university culture is a more bookish culture than any other. Young men and women with an inordinate interest in books do best in school. They become the ones most likely to hang around and get a doctorate. I am unaware of any doctoral programs that require budding professors to pass a teaching competence examination. All require that doctoral candidates write a dissertation. This is quite a lot of dissertating. Some forty-seven thousand are done each year. It's also quite a lot of publishing, since newly minted Ph.D.s are expected to turn that dissertation into their first book.* This interest in books has been so intense over the centuries that professors have convinced themselves that book publishing is the single most important measure of whether a professor should be given tenure in

---

*The output of dissertations has grown over time just as the number of books has. The *Comprehensive Dissertation Index* lists total 417,000 dissertations from 1861 (the year of

the humanities. They also try to convince outsiders that authorship is the most sublime expression of humankind. Alumni magazines often have a special section showing off recent books by graduates. None has a special showcase for "Life Insurance Policies Sold" or "Successful Employee Downsizing Programs."

A general perversity characterizes academic life. Remember that this is the one endeavor in which the employee, the professor, is supposed to torment the employer, the student. More to the point, as far as this essay goes, writing without making any money is considered a virtue on campus. Prisoners are disappointed when elected officials try to take away their royalties. The university credo is that faculty members are expected to write books that no one wants to buy in order to keep their low-paying jobs. I have actually heard senior professors say that in considering tenure for a junior professor, they don't count articles for which payment is made.

It should be no surprise therefore that a National Writers Union survey found that more than 60 percent of scholarly journals never pay a cent to authors. The writers union also found that nearly 20 percent of academic journals at least occasionally charge a "reading fee" to authors who submit a manuscript on speculation. Some scholarly presses require authors to help subsidize publication.

This is not difficult to understand in view of the writer-to-market ratio for academics. As an extreme example, consider an almost purely scholarly activity, philosophy. The Philosophy Documentation Center in Ohio reported in the mid-1990s that there were 184 journals in the United States devoted to philosophy and only 8,500 American philosophers. That is one journal for every forty-six philosophers. These publishers have no incentive to pay anything to the writers.

In this economically surreal academic world, book ideas often sound like parodies of themselves. Editors at Louisiana State University Press, publisher of this book, tell of authors who suggested books on Hitler's retirement plan or gay generals who served with Stonewall Jackson. Nevertheless, many marginal titles get published. A single issue of the *Chronicle of Higher Education* announced these new books: *Void Where Prohibited: Rest Breaks and the Right to Urinate on Company Time*, which

---

the first doctoral degree awarded in the United States) to 1972; and 351,000 from 1973 to 1982. It lists 39,345 new U.S. dissertations for 1998 alone.

discusses "the legal struggles over . . . rest and bathroom breaks"; and *Matters of Face: Reading Nonfiction Over the Edge,* which "argues that the experience of reading and writing nonfiction fundamentally differs from even the most realistic fiction."

Greenwood Press, which specializes in academic books, doesn't bother to dress them up with a dust jacket or generally to promote them much. The editors know their books will appeal to a handful of academics and university libraries, who buy them based on scholarly reviews. University presses occasionally seek a wider market, although the American Booksellers Association estimates that only 1 percent of consumer book sales comes from university presses.

Not long ago, the *New York Times* reported that university presses, originally created to publish scholarly books, are becoming more market sensitive in order to remain viable. But while this is happening with the university press on one side of campus, professors on the other haven't changed at all. The *Times* quoted a young scholar who was unable to find a university press publisher for his doctoral dissertation: "I was astonished that they explicitly cited sales [as] a criterion for considering a manuscript's worth."

A few academics, however, are like jujitsu masters, using perversity to beat perversity. Realizing that students are a captive market, they write textbooks. Robert Samuelson's economics textbook made him rich, and one of his successors, Gregory Mankiw, received a seven-figure advance for *Principles of Economics,* published in 1997. Or they follow the example of John Kenneth Galbraith, the Harvard professor who has written popular books about economics as well as nonfiction books in other areas and novels. He once confessed that "faced with the choice of spending time on the unpublished scholarship of a graduate student or the unpublished work of Galbraith, I have rarely hesitated."

One last virtue of writing on someone else's time should be noted. When bricklayers are laid off, they are out of work. When write-on-the-job authors are laid off, they become full-time writers.

Niccolò Machiavelli did serious memo writing while working for the Medici in Florence. After being tossed out of office and into the torture chambers for a while, and not knowing what else to do, he wrote *The Prince, Discourses on Titus Livy, The Art of War,* poems, and a play, *La*

Mandragola, which has been called the greatest Italian comedy ever. Restored to Medici graces, Machiavelli received a commission to write a history of Florence. At the end of his life he signed a letter "Niccolò Machiavelli, historian, comic author, and tragic author."

Large gaps of joblessness in a bricklayer's resume raise worrisome questions in employers' minds. But a writer's résumé is always full. This makes it much easier to get a new job in which they hope not to break a sweat.

But enough of this. Let's now talk about authors who write full time. They have to show up for work every day too. And unlike those postal workers, they can't goof off for long or they will starve.

The Author-Industrialist

The discriminating reader may say, "Ha! Yes! But there is another kind of writer, like Milvain or, say, Stephen King. They write for a living and have no other jobs." But they, too, are hyphenated writers. The Industrial Revolution created professional writers, and most who would succeed by that craft alone must be industrialists in their outlook and manner of production. They write on schedule, day after day. The late literary critic Maxwell Geismar told me that he made himself sit in his office every morning. If he didn't have anything to write, he would clean his typewriter. He understood that writing is a job, and one cannot afford to get into slovenly habits.

James Fenimore Cooper was the first Jasper Milvain of American fiction. Cooper lived exclusively by his pen and described his work as "mere articles of trade." In his thirty-one-year career, he averaged a novel a year and wrote twenty other books and several magazine articles. He did not wait leisurely for the muses to drop by for a visit. He wrote at a set time each day. In the interests of efficiency he revised little, leaving clean-up work to printers and proofreaders. He did not make improvements in published novels out of an intense desire to make them better. He improved them to make a little extra money with a new edition. Sounding like a car salesman drawing the customer's attention to white sidewalls and leather interior, he told a publisher that a certain nautical tale he had written was worth more because it had "Indians intermingled." He averaged $6,500 income a year in the 1820s, a hefty sum in those days.

With payment based on the final product, the quest began for increased efficiency in its production. In his autobiography, Charles Chaplin reported that he dictated about 1,000 words a day in rough dialogue, which later resulted in about 300 words of finished script. Always wanting to speed up production, he was interested in how the competition worked. He was impressed with Alexander Woollcott, who wrote a 750-word review in fifteen minutes, then joined a poker game, and especially impressed with Georges Simenon. Simenon completed an "excellent" short novel in a month writing in very tiny script. When Chaplin asked why he wrote so small, Simenon replied, "It requires less effort of the wrist."

Simenon had other labor-saving techniques. When writing, he put up a "Do Not Disturb" sign, pulled down the shades in his office, and filled five or six pipes so he would not have to interrupt his work in order to keep puffing. Like a prize fighter, he weighed himself before and after writing each book. Between 1924 and 1931, he wrote nearly two hundred pulp novels. He slowed down as he matured, but in his case slowing down was relative. By the end of his life in 1989, he had more than four hundred books to his credit.

Other literary machines stand out. After giving up his job as a broker, Jules Verne pounded away at his writing day after day. He produced about one hundred books. Isaac Asimov, another writeaholic, typed ninety words a minute, wrote twelve hours a day, rarely went on vacation, and said he never experienced writer's block. He wrote more than four hundred books and, counting his articles and stories, produced more than twenty million printed words. For him everything could be a story. He once wrote a novel about the annual meeting of the American Booksellers Association. Television interviewer Barbara Walters asked Asimov what he'd do if he had only six months to live. His answer, "I'd type faster."

More productive still is Ryoki Inoue, a Brazilian pulp fiction novelist. In 1986, he left his medical career to write mostly Westerns. Ten years later, he had more than one thousand Portuguese-language books using thirty-nine pseudonyms. He is supposed to have written an entire book while waiting in a garage for mechanics to fix his truck. "Truthfully," he has said, "I haven't even read all the books I've written."

Modern capitalism is the breeding ground of writer-industrialists. Wang Shuo, one of a new breed of Chinese, disdains Marxist dictates about serving the state. "I want to earn lots of money," he says. His books have sold more than two million copies. Highly motivated by the market, he is becoming the Ryoki Inoue of China. He already has written two dozen novels about the seamy side of Chinese life.

"A very considerable part of the output of the literature industry in this country is not what somebody wanted to write," Elmer Davis said in a 1940 New York Public Library lecture, "but what somebody wanted to get written." This dictates that authors understand public taste and write to satisfy it. It also dictates that they remember that time is money and that they should always try to beat the clock with efficient routines. Inoue uses a formula that permits him to write as many as three books a day. A book must have a minimum of five killings and at least two romantic scenes; no more than twenty characters are allowed. What happens when the story gets complicated? "Dynamite resolves a lot of narrative complications," Inoue told a *Wall Street Journal* reporter. Agatha Christie with her mysteries and Grace Livingston Hill with her romance novels recycled the same plots over and over again.

Taken to its logical extension, the owners of a formula should put others to work on a literary assembly line with them. This is called mass production. James Michener used as many as three secretaries and employed teams of researchers to help him write his mammoth books. Helpers commented on his draft manuscripts and made changes. He told an interviewer how he sent aides out to get books for him. "I don't read them all, but I read indexes with a skill that's frightening." A reviewer of his book *Centennial* warned prospective readers not to deceive themselves about the book's "proper genre. It wasn't 'written,' it was compiled."

The most recent edition of *The Joy of Cooking* carries the triple-barreled credit of its creator, the late Irma S. Rombauer, her late daughter Marion Rombauer Becker, and their living heir, Ethan Becker. "The revision . . ." noted a *New York Times* reporter, "was actually the work of 150 chefs, nutritionists and writers (many of them accomplished cookbook authors) and others."

"As oil had its Rockefeller, literature had its Stratemeyer," *Fortune* observed of the "author" of more than thirteen hundred books. Starting in 1900, Edward Stratemeyer, a New Jersey author who looked like Dudley Do-Right, produced the Hardy Boys, Nancy Drew, the Bobbsey Twins, Tom Swift, and many other literary products under the made-up names of Franklin W. Dixon, Carolyn Keene, Laura Lee Hope, and Victor Appleton. At first he wrote the books himself. Then he wrote three-page outlines and gave them to hungry young writers who filled in the narrative. A quality control inspector, Stratemeyer reviewed the final product to ensure consistency.

Understanding that it was better to sell many copies for a modest price than a few copies for a high price, Stratemeyer convinced a publisher in 1906 to charge fifty cents instead of $1.25 for each book. He also sought low production costs by paying writers $50 to $250 for a book. He made $50,000 a year in an era when one dollar could buy a fine three-course meal.

Like a good capitalist, Stratemeyer was anonymous and wanted his writers to be as well. The authors signed an agreement with the Stratemeyer Syndicate promising not to divulge that they were the men behind the pen names assigned them. They never met each other. Stratemeyer had other writing rules: three books were written before a series was introduced; the first chapter of each new book previewed the previous books so young readers knew what good stuff they had missed; the last chapter temptingly foreshadowed the next book.

This formula worked so well that anyone could do it. When Stratmeyer died in 1930, his daughter inherited the factory and kept it going by producing still more books, using hired writers and rewriting old books that needed modernization. Long after she died in 1982, the Stratemeyer Syndicate was selling more than two million books a year.

Another tactic is what corporate moguls call horizontal integration. This means the writer compartmentalizes his skills to sell as separate, but related, services. A professional writer can work as a professional reader. Some go around reciting poems to highbrow groups, some seek smaller audiences. The French poet Paul Valéry wrote largely for himself at the break of dawn and went to work during the regular day as a reader to the director of the Havas News Agency, a task he did for twenty-two years. The director liked to hear and discuss seventeenth-century prose. William C. Davis, who writes on southern history and the Civil War, edits Civil War books and takes people on Civil War riverboat cruises, earning more money and building expertise in his subject. Also, he serves as a correspondent to media types and is one of the main talking heads on "Civil War Journal," a television series.

From the time of its invention, the silver screen has been a haven for book authors, albeit a haven with frustrations. Writers had to check pride of authorship at the studio gate, because inside the producers treated screen writers no different from stunt men. Frustration, nevertheless, has had its rewards. Ben Hecht, one of more than a thousand writers in Hollywood in the mid-1930s, observed that "My own discontent with what I was asked to do in Hollywood was so loud that I finally received $125,000 for four weeks of script writing." The average earnings for film and television writers in 1995 was $72,500, according to the Writers Guild of America, West. The Guild had 7,500 members on the West Coast; 40 of them earned more than $1 million in 1995. In addition, 200 earned more than $515,300 and 1,000 at least $176,560. Between screen writing gigs that gave him a financial cushion, William Faulkner wrote some of his best books. And a screen writer can receive a measure of fame. Anita Loos, the first writer to receive a movie credit, was listed as coauthor with William Shakespeare in the 1916 film adaptation of *Macbeth.* "If I had asked," she later said, they "would have given me top billing."

The only real problem with following the dictates of modern economic management is that inefficient writers are more likely to produce great literature than efficient ones. The production of *Ulysses* would drive the boys and girls at the Harvard Business School nuts. James Joyce spent seven years writing the book, investing twenty thousand working hours in some 2,500 eight-hour days. He rewrote some episodes nine times. Appropriately, the book prompted Ezra Pound to suggest a new system of time. The first year after its publication was 1 p.s.U. (post scriptum Ulysses).

Conclusion

Writers, like farmers, are their own worst enemies. Farmers earn more money per bushel of grain if they grow less and create scarcity. Instead, they are inclined to work harder and grow more. Farmers, a powerful political force, can lessen the ill effects of their hard work by lobbying the government to subsidize prices. Besides, the finite amount of tillable land limits the number of farmers. No such palliatives apply to writers. Anyone can aspire to write a book, and authors have no political clout.

Avid readers typically miss this point. They think that if the First Amendment is good for the nation because people *can* write as they please, the nation will be even better off if as many people as possible do write all that they please. "More speech, not less speech, is always what we should prefer in this society," Cameron DeVore, a First Amendment attorney, told a television audience.

Authors perversely share this feeling. The owners of Coca-Cola would never sell the secret formula for their drink to Pepsi. Authors give it away for pennies. Novelist John Irving has argued that teaching creative writing courses is "an economic necessity for writers in this country. For the writers who teach them, they are essential to their lives *as writers*. And for those few students who truly benefit from them, they are a gift of encouragement and time; writers—young writers, particularly—need more of both."

Marion Yule, the real hero of *New Grub Street*, is a woman capable of deep love and full of good sense. Milvain has a temporary romance with her, but his logic can never be hers. "I love books," Yule says, "but I could wish people were content for a while with those we already have."

It is not practical to suppose that publishers will take Yule's advice to stop producing books for a few years. They need new titles the way Dracula needs blood. That said, we can at least recognize three laws that demonstrate that more is not better and that greater writing production hurts authors and the quality of the literature they produce.

Law Number 1: The more books that are produced,
the harder it is for any one to survive.

The habits of the modern bookstore are a metaphor for this truism. With more and more new books coming out, stores can handle fewer copies of each new title and must cram the volumes on their shelves so that few books appear front cover out. As a result, customers sweep a hurried eye over rows of thin spines and gravitate toward the handful of books featured in displays. Books that don't sell quickly must be returned to the publisher to make way for the next wave of books to roll in. Bookstores have a great advantage in that they take books on what amounts to consignment. The author and publisher make no money on the returned books.

"The life of a book is one of the most terrifying phenomena of publishing . . . ," said O. H. Cheney's report to the National Association of Book Publishers. "The most frequent length of active life is between four and five months." Cheney's report appeared in 1931, a tame time by today's intensely competitive standards. Now, as one wag has put it, books have the shelf life of yogurt.

Law Number 2: A decrease in book production will not reduce the number of good books that are written.

Quite the opposite is probably true. A decrease in book production would increase the total number of good books that come out each year. A new field of economics, sportometrics, found that running times in races are faster when fewer people compete. Runners in a smaller field recognize that they have a better chance to win, hence they try harder. If runners competed in the circumstances suggested by law number 1, they would walk around the track. As Cicero said, "Times are bad. Children no longer obey their parents, and everyone is writing a book."

Law Number 3: Writers with second jobs have less time to write, but may have more to say.

Franz Kafka abhorred working in the Statistical and Claims Department of the Workmen's Accident Insurance Institute for the Kingdom of Bohemia. He hated running the family's asbestos factory as much. He led, he said, a "horrible double life, from which madness probably offers the only way out." But for Kafka everything was Kafkaesque. He only worked the 8 A.M. to 2 P.M. shift in the insurance business. Besides, as Leonardo da Vinci said, experience "has been the mistress of all those who wrote well."

We are better off because Chaucer went on diplomatic missions as far away as Italy, all the while collecting experiences for use in the pilgrims' stories in his *Canterbury Tales*. (In Florence, he also became acquainted with the writings of Dante, Petrarch, and Boccaccio, which directly influenced his work.) Because Melville went to sea for four years, gathering material for *Typee* (he lived for a month with the Polynesian Typee tribe), *Omoo, Moby Dick,* and *White-Jacket.* Because Hawthorne found a "rag of scarlet cloth . . . the capital letter A" and a related story in a dusty file at the Salem Customs House. Melville and Hawthorne are considered better writers than their contemporary Cooper, whose living was made exclusively by writing. The list of examples is unending. Matthew Arnold's thirty-five years as an inspector of schools formed his social criticism and lent passion to his poetry. Dickens's experience in a blacking factory while his father was in debtor prison made *Oliver Twist* and *Bleak House* as poignant as they are.

"The poet," Edmund Wilson observed, "would do better to study a profession, to become a banker or a public official or even to go in for the movies. What is wrong with the younger American poets is that they have no stake in society." John Grisham continues to do legal work, even though he certainly doesn't need the money. "There's a kind of fear about getting totally cut off from the law because that's where the ideas come from."

"The worse the job is the better it is for your book," novelist Ted Conover told a group at the University of Miami a few years ago. Steinbeck, who worked as a ranch hand, hod carrier, department store clerk, and steward on a ship, wrote movingly about working men and women. It didn't hurt, either, that he wrote his first book, *Cup of Gold*, while a caretaker for two years at a wealthy estate on Lake Tahoe, which had a large library and the added advantage of solitude during the winter months. He believed that poverty fueled his creativity. The subject of money drove him crazy even after money was no longer an issue. When Steinbeck was in reality a wealthy man, a friend once reminisced, "He needed to think he was poor."

Hawthorne sardonically said the customs house was "a good lesson" for someone "who has dreamed of literary fame, and of making for himself a rank among the world's dignitaries by such means, to step aside out of the narrow circle in which his claims are recognized, and to find how utterly devoid of significance, beyond that circle, is all that he achieves, and all he aims at." He was wrong. Too much is made of authors needing to be with other authors.

In *Creating Minds*, Howard Gardner argues that creativity hinges on being marginal. Belonging to an ethnic minority can help. Avoiding peers who hem one in is better. Albert Einstein noted his good fortune in not holding an academic post after graduation from the Zurich Polytechnic and finding a job instead at the Bern Patent Office as a Technical Expert III Class (located in the Postal and Telegraph Administration building!). He worked there for seven years, receiving a promotion to Technical Expert II Class. "A practical profession is a salvation for a man of my type; an academic career places a young person under a kind of compulsion to produce impressive quantities of scientific publications—a temptation to superficiality, which only strong characters resist."

Coda

Poor old Edwin Reardon toils away at the British Museum or, as Jasper Milvain calls it, the valley of the shadow of books. He refuses to write books that will sell and is forced to become a low-paid clerk, a position that saps all his desire to write. As a result he loses his pretty wife who can no longer bear to live pitifully with him, sells off his precious book collection to feed himself, and dies for lack of food and medical care. Milvain, the full-time writer, cares more about being a financial success than producing priceless literature. He builds a reputation by methodical and mechanical writing. He marries Reardon's widow after she comes into a substantial inheritance.

So, what is the lesson? That a writing life must end as inconsequentially as Milvain's if it is to be tolerable? No, the best chance of true success and happiness lies with Reardon. He could have kept his wife, her inheritance, his books, and his writing life if only he had found the right job in the post office.

TWO

The Art of Marketing

In which it is shown that no commodity better lends itself to promotion than books—and that in our market economy we relentlessly market books to sell them and to sell ourselves.

Prose writing has been of great use to me in the course of my life, and was a principal means of my advancement.

—Benjamin Franklin in his modestly titled *Autobiography*

People often say to me, "Ron, how could you invent a Mr. Microphone and a Popeil Automatic Pasta Maker? They're so far apart." The answer is simple. I've always tried to look for needs in the marketplace. The formulas that I use work in any category. Marketing is where it all begins.

—Ron Popeil in his immodestly titled autobiography, *The Salesman of the Century*

Benjamin Franklin had one of our nation's greatest love affairs with words.

His *Autobiography*, historian Carl Van Doren said, "was the first great masterpiece of autobiography by a self-made man." His almanac, *Poor Richard*, is as much a piece of Americana as Plymouth Rock. Franklin published books by other authors and owned one of the finest bookstores in the colonies. He organized Philadelphia's first subscription library and started the Junto, a club that devoted itself to such questions as, "Have you met with anything in the author you last read, remarkable or suitable to be communicated to the Junto?"

The printing trade brought him in daily contact with words and ideas, and they gave him new ideas that often found their way into new words. An eighteenth-century Gutenberg, he improved the printing press and made what may have been the colonies' first decent printing ink. He was the first to show that lightning contained electricity and may have been the first to use *battery, electrical shock, negativity,* and other electrical terms in print.

Franklin was a member of the "Committee of Five" that wrote the Declaration of Independence. As an envoy of the young republic, he became a lion of French high society, particularly feminine society, not only

"I might in this place attempt to gain thy favour by declaring that I write almanacs with no other view than that of the public good; but in that I should not be sincere, and men are now-a-days too wise to be deceived by pretenses how specious soever," Ben Franklin, the original American commercial man of letters, wrote in *Poor Richard*. "The plain truth of the matter is, I am excessive poor."

Benjamin Franklin, painting by Joseph Duplessis, circa 1794–1802, Still Picture Branch of the National Archives at College Park

because of what he had written before, but also because he installed a private printing press at Passy and used it to print charming bagatelles for the ladies.

But a particular story involving his printing business puts his love affair with words into proper perspective. When the proposition of marriage arose with a "very deserving" girl, as Franklin put it, he let the family know he "expected as much money with their daughter as would pay off my remaining debt for the printing-house." When they indicated they did not have that much spare cash around, Franklin suggested that they mortgage their home. Mom and Dad said no, and Franklin's ardor cooled.

Franklin told this love story in his autobiography as frankly as Poor Richard told readers that "I might in this place attempt to gain thy favour by declaring that I write almanacs with no other view than that of the public good; but in that I should not be sincere, and men are now-a-days too wise to be deceived by pretenses how specious soever. The plain truth of the matter is, I am excessive poor."

Almanacs had long been a bread-and-butter product for printers. The second book published in America was a nautical almanac, printed in 1639. Franklin wrote *Poor Richard* himself because he could write well and because writers available for such work charged too much. His first edition, published in 1732, went into two printings and sold an extraordinary ten thousand copies. He wisely called the subsequent compendium of his almanac sayings *The Way to Wealth*. Knowing that he was in the word *business*, he turned production of his improved wood-burning stove over to someone else, but advertised it himself in a paper for the American Philosophical Society, an organization he had started. The advertisement read, "My common room, I know, is made twice as warm as it used to be, with a quarter of the wood I formerly consumed there." On another occasion Franklin wrote a polemic extolling the virtues of paper currency in Pennsylvania; when the legislature decided to have some printed up, he won a contract to do the job. "This," he acknowledged, "was another advantage gained by my being able to write."

"Many heroes," Horace observed, ". . . are oppressed in unending night, unwept, unknown, because they lack a dedicated poet." Franklin was his own poet, although the term today would be marketing consultant. When he invented the lightning rod, he wrote about it. Not long after his paper was read to the Royal Society in London, he was elected a member. When he and some friends came up with the novel idea of start-ing a fire department in Philadelphia, he wrote a letter to himself and published it in his *Pennsylvania Gazette*. He learned as a young apprentice in London that he who writes well attracts influential friends and power.

Franklin was the original American *commercial* man of letters. Well be-fore Oprah touted literature to the masses, Franklin instinctively realized that the word business offered endless marketing possibilities both for his books and for himself. Benjamin Franklin, historian R. Jackson Wilson has observed, was "the first American to gain both wealth and celebrity from his writing."

Perhaps only a single aspect of the marketing power inherent in words lay outside Franklin's range of vision. That is, how far it all would go. Franklin's contemporaries could appreciate *Poor Richard*'s folksy candor about wanting to make money. They had the same goal themselves. Besides, such honesty affirmed the virtuous quality of the work they were buying. But thanks to relentless marketing by Franklin's successors in the word business, honesty no longer pays. After reading Franklin's frank statement of business purpose, many of today's readers would expect a trick. Like today's voters, they assume *only* the worst. And if they don't, they should.

Book publishing, balanced in Franklin's time between literary quality and marketability, is now out of kilter. For a quick example, consider Franklin's modern incarnation, Lester Wunderman. Wunderman recently told *his* story in his autobiographical *Being Direct: Making Advertising Pay*. During World War II, early in his career, Wunderman "found a book few were buying" and marketed it. The book was *I Was Hitler's Doctor*, supposedly written by a physician who had escaped from Nazi Germany. Unanswered questions about the book and its author may have prevented the *New York Times* from reviewing it. Such doubts did not trouble Wunderman. "My job was to sell the books, and I was excited by the prospect of doing so," he recalled. He designed ads that looked like edito-rial copy, used radio spots that sounded like today's "infomercials," and sold by direct mail. At length, he proudly tells us, he drove it onto the best-seller list.

The New Model Is Marketing

Harry Scherman started the Book-of-the-Month Club in 1926. As part of this innovation in book selling, he established an independent book selection committee made up of prominent literary luminaries. The committee was completely free to devise its own selection criteria. If the choices sometimes seemed a bit too middlebrow, the committee at least assured a reasonable level of literary integrity at the BOMC.

Time Warner now owns the Book-of-the-Month Club. Under its ownership, the marketing people for the first time sit with editorial staff to make book selection decisions. Sales have gone up. The same cannot be said for BOMC's literary integrity.

Books have always lent themselves to promotion, as Appendix A shows. But these days, marketing plays an overwhelming role. "The old model was signing big authors," says one management consultant. "The new model is marketing."

The most important book publishers used to be literary gentlemen, who in the words of one of them "were incapable of petty or ostentatious things." While that self-assessment may overstate things a bit, they presided over publishing houses that public relations pioneer Edward Bernays ruefully called "stuffy old firms who treated the business as if it were the practice of a sacred rite." Not wanting their books to seem like other products, they used ninety-five-cent pricing instead of ninety-nine-cent pricing (as in $24.95 instead of $24.99). Although the term *house* lingers, the new breed of publishers manages publishing factories, which are components of larger entertainment conglomerates. Today's publishers have no qualms about tacking on an extra five cents to make the price an even $25.00.

In the mid-1970s, about fifty publishers controlled 75 percent of the adult book market. In the late 1990s, seven publishers controlled 75 percent of that market. "The Literary-Industrial Complex," as dismayed book executive Ted Solotaroff calls it, is nothing if not acquisitive. In 1998, Bertelsmann, a German media company, bought Random House for $1.4 billion to add to its current publishing interest: Bantam Doubleday Dell, which had once been three separate companies. That same year, Random House ranked first among publishers in the number of books on *Publishers Weekly*'s hardback best-seller list, and Bantam

Doubleday Dell ranked second. They were number three and number one, respectively, in paperback best sellers. Bertelsmann's other assets include magazines, such as *Stern* in Germany and *Parents* in the United States; newspapers; interests in AOL, barnesandnoble.com, and other on-line services; music labels, such as RCA; television networks, including Europe's largest; the Literary Guild, Doubleday Book Club, and other book clubs with worldwide membership of more than twenty-five million; and (previously) pig and chicken farming.

With all the trading going on, executives resemble youngsters playing Monopoly on a sugar high. In 1994, Viacom Corporation announced that the publishing arm under Paramount Communications Corporation, in which it had a majority ownership, would take on the name of one of its book entities, Simon & Schuster. The Simon & Schuster stable included its namesake house, plus Pocket Books, Scribner's, the Free Press, Prentice-Hall, Touchstone, MTV Books, Fireside, Macmillan General Reference USA, Jossey-Bass, and others. Meanwhile, the British publisher Putnam Penguin, which combines two separate companies and is owned by media titan Pearson, acquired Viking and New American Library from Times-Mirror and Dutton from a Dutch owner. As the musical chairs continued, Pearson announced that it would buy the educational and reference operations of Simon & Schuster. It has a number of other imprints as well, among them Signet Classics and Dial Books for Young Readers. Keeping up with the trend, The News Corporation, which owned HarperCollins, bought Avon Books and William Morrow & Company from the Hearst Corporation in 1999.

Of course, book company executives are not using play money. They are using shareholders' money, and those shareholders read balance sheets more closely than the books their companies publish. "The biggest thing today is money," Bob Loomis of Random House told C-SPAN's Brian Lamb. "It's what we talk a lot about."

Previously, editors could be satisfied to break even with a promising first-time author; now they feel pressure to make money right away. "There is no such thing as a modest success any more," says Dawn Drzal, a senior editor at Viking Penguin. Bertelsmann executives argue that it has less pressure to make a profit because their company is privately held. Nevertheless, says its chief financial officer, "The market doesn't owe a livelihood to someone who writes books that no one wants to read." He is referring to books that have initial print runs of four thousand or fewer copies, not atypical for significant books on narrow subjects or books by first-time authors.

Bertelsmann, supposedly immune to short-term bottom-line Wall Street concerns, said that it had no intention of taking away the independence of individual book publishing units when it bought Random House in 1998. But by 1999, it announced a consolidation of the units. "This is not a cost-driven exercise," said Peter Olsen, chief executive of Random House. "It's more about marketing effectiveness. We have a lot of publishers competing for limited shelf space and the attention of our buying and reading public. And the question is how can they be most effective. That's what drives it. What we want to do is grow sales."

Holt, the epitome of old-line staid publishing companies, was among the first to fix its sight on Wall Street. Edgar Rigg, its president beginning in 1949, had been vice-president at the Standard & Poor's Corporation, a leading source of financial information and analysis. When he took command of Holt, he remarked that he would run the company "as a modern business instead of a literary tea party." Holt bought Rinehart and Winston in 1959 and acquired an envied listing on the New York Stock Exchange; Holt, in turn, was bought by CBS in 1967.

While Rigg was introducing the idea of department budgets and cash flow forecasts, Doubleday used a formula to help booksellers decide how many copies of each title they should stock. The formula, reported R. W. Apple in a 1960 article for the *Saturday Review,* had been developed by "a German mathematician to predict how many Prussian cavalrymen would be killed by horses' kicks over a twenty-year period." When business formulas like these are brought to bear on the shipping room, Apple noted, "is not the temptation to straighten out the editors, too? To get some fast-moving merchandise to make that shipping room hum?" The answer was yes.

A similar transformation is taking place downstream from publishers. Two companies, Baker & Taylor and Ingram, control book distribution. They direct most of their marketing at the two dominant bookstore chains, Borders and Barnes & Noble. Barnes & Noble sought to make this relationship all the cozier by trying to buy Ingram for $600 million in 1998. When that deal looked like it might run into trouble with the Federal Trade Commission the next year, Barnes & Noble went to "Plan B." Plan B was to enhance its distribution system by opening warehouses

in Nevada and Tennessee and use the balance of its $600 million
acquisitions. More than half of American readers purchase their books ...
these megastores. Independent booksellers are disappearing. From 1991
to 1998, membership in the American Booksellers Association dropped
45 percent.

And don't forget the authors and their agents. Full-time authors whose
names guarantee high book sales behave more like graduates of M.B.A.
programs than like graduates of English or history departments. Indic-
ative of this, many writers workshops have a session on creative contacts
with entertainment executives. "I'm trying to work on what I call the
'Clancy brand,'" Hollywood agent Michael Ovitz said in mid-1998. "I
think there are certain authors that are a brand, and they have to be
treated a little differently than a normal author."

One way that they are treated differently is in the amount of money
they can command. Commercial publishers can't afford not to have
brand-name writers, even if they must pay them high six-figure advances.
It also follows that once Scribner's pays Stephen King a $2-million up-
front fee (which, unlike an advance, is not counted against future earnings) for *Bag of Bones* and shares profits in an arrangement that gives him
55 percent of the loot (much, much better than what the average author
gets), it can't afford not to send out nine thousand advance "readers"
copies and promotional audiocassettes aimed at book clerks, create a Web
site and Bag of Bones refrigerator magnets (refrigerator magnets figure
into the book), and otherwise invest heavily in book promotion.

"Even with the best intentions, impeccable personal taste, and the
highest intelligence," media analyst Leo Bogart points out, "professional
managers pursuing their rational profit goals must regard the actual content of their companies' output as merely instrumental to those goals."
This is to say that in the Literary-Industrial Complex, executives regard
books and their authors as cash cows and create elaborate schemes for
milking them.

Romance houses, which are particularly product oriented, give the authors paint-by-the-numbers instructions for writing books. Editorial
guidelines for Harlequin Romance call for fifty thousand to fifty-five
thousand words emphasizing "warm and tender emotions, with no sexual
explicitness; love making should only take place when emotional commitment between the characters justifies it." The Harlequin Temptation

series is a little longer on words (sixty thousand) and spiciness (it wants "men and women living and loving—today!"). Harlequin Historical "will not accept books set after 1900," and Medical Romance wants at least one of the characters to be a medical professional.

Edward Stratemeyer, the guy mentioned in the previous chapter who manufactured Tom Swift, has morphed into George Engels, who runs Book Creations Incorporated. Engels calls the company BCI, an acronym that seems more appropriate for a bank until you realize that this company is all about money and that it is full-service at that. BCI covers every aspect of the book publishing process. It hires authors to write "from an outline developed with Book Creations and approved by the publisher," designs and processes the printed text, and "develops a publicity campaign to supplement the publisher's advertising efforts." Among BCI's more than four hundred titles is the hugely profitable *Kent Family Chronicles* series by John Jakes. "We prefer to work in the series format," George Engels says in his own promotional materials, "because it establishes a base of faithful readers who keep coming back for the next book." Tom Swift move over. The Airborne Rangers have landed.

"Each book an author writes is potentially a business to be built on," says Robert Gottlieb, a William Morris agent who handles Tom Clancy. Clancy does not write the books for the Op-Center Series, fictional stories about high-tech defense that appear under his name. He provides "executive direction," which doesn't mean much, and has his brand name on the cover, which means quite a lot to a publisher interested in making money.

"You can sell a manuscript as a book," says novelist Olivia Goldsmith; "you can sell in multiple languages, as a movie, serial rights or for books on tape. And just because I don't sell it now doesn't mean I can't sell it later. When a book like *The First Wives Club* becomes a phenomenon, it's a bit like real estate: all my other properties are now in a better neighborhood, so that their value goes up."

"Essentially," she says in an interview in the *New York Times* business section, "I am running my own $1.5 million business."

Edgar Rice Burroughs was one of the first to see the potential for turning a personal writing business into a personal conglomerate. In 1923, this author of twenty-four Tarzan books, as well as fifty other adventure stories, created Edgar Rice Burroughs Incorporated. He made the same bad decisions that many entrepreneurs do, among other things putting his family members on the payroll. And like many successful entrepreneurs, he was constantly on the lookout for new opportunities. In addition to syndicating his writing, he was into real estate, ranching, Tarzan statuettes and bubble gum, and, of course, movies, the financial potential of which was accidentally discovered by a contemporary of his, Lew Wallace.

In 1907, Wallace won a suit against the movie studio Kalem, which put *Ben Hur* on the silver screen without bothering to pay for the privilege. Kalem was forced to give Wallace $25,000. The dirt road that ran from books to Hollywood is now a superhighway. In the race for good movie material, studio executives option books they *might* want to make into movies—and even buy books before the author has finished them or, on occasion, before the author has started to write them. Producers have given a $1-million advance for a nineteen-page book outline, $1.2 million for a sixteen-page proposal, and $1.2 million for a two-page letter. These gambles can pay off as handsomely as a winning lottery ticket. In 1994, three of the top ten highest-grossing movies were based on books: Tom Clancy's *Clear and Present Danger,* Anne Rice's *Interview with the Vampire,* and Winston Groom's *Forrest Gump.*

Over time, publishers have become hypersensitive to movie and television possibilities. As soon as a publisher thinks a book has a chance to go from the page to the screen, the book's value goes up. Random House reluctantly took a chance on John Darnton's book *Neanderthal.* Then came nibbles from Hollywood. Publishers who weren't originally interested in the hardback offered half a million dollars for the paperback rights. Random House correctly guessed that this book would be a best seller— and it hadn't even hit the bookstores yet. It appeared in 1996, and Steven Spielberg paid more than one million dollars for the movie rights, although he didn't seem in any rush to make it into a movie.

Authors often gulp down their pride and let studios alter their books as Louis L'Amour did with his Westerns. "My dad used to say it was like selling a house," his son has commented. "The guy had a right to redecorate it if he wanted." Some movie studios don't stop with the window treatments; they tear down the whole dwelling and start over. The nonfiction book *Sex and the Single Girl* became a fictional movie "with Natalie Wood playing me as a psychiatrist!" said Helen Gurley Brown, who was definitely not a psychiatrist. "Tony Curtis, Henry Fonda and Lauren Bacall also starred. I had nothing to do with the screenplay. Take the money and run, said my smart husband."

Initially, studios made movies based on popular books, because they needed material, because the book had an audience that could be built on, and because buying the book gave cachet and sometimes legal protection to the film. Now the process often is reversed. Television programs and movies lead to books. The three-hundred-plus-page book, *Sotheby's: The Inside Story,* had this announcement on the dust jacket: "As seen on 60 Minutes." Recognizing what a good deal the movie *Titanic* was, HarperCollins came out with:

• *James Cameron's Titanic.* The director's "detailed look at the monumental effort by thousands of artists and craftsmen to accurately re-create the 'ship of dreams.'" With movie-screen–size pages and 175 color photographs, it has the feel more of a movie than of a book.

• A 1999 "Wall edition" Titanic calendar. "I couldn't wait to buy it," a German reader wrote to Amazon.com. "There are interesting facts about the real ship *Titanic* and important dates."

• *James Cameron's Titanic Poster Book.* "Twelve glorious, full-color posters."

• *Titanic: James Cameron's Illustrated Screenplay.*

• And the *Titanic Portfolio.* A "beautifully designed portfolio features cast members and others in a collection of 24 photographs . . . suitable for framing."

The total list of Titanic books has risen like a giant iceberg. There is a culinary item, *Last Dinner on the Titanic: Menus and Recipes from the Great Liner,* and a reprint of the congressional hearings on the sinking of the great ship, *The Titanic Disaster: The Official Transcripts of the 1912 Senate Investigation.* "The Titanic wasn't a total disaster," noted the *Rocky Mountain News* book editor Patti Thorn of the Titanic publishing craze.

Not surprisingly, perhaps, the new chairman and CEO of the venerable publishing house of Penguin Books is Michael Lynton, formerly president of Disney's Hollywood Pictures. He came to Disney with one of those M.B.A.s and a little time on Wall Street as an investment banker. "He appreciates the fact that media drives media," says Jeff Berg, an admiring talent agent, "and if you have valuable properties in one area, like books, you can extend your brand into others." Lynton calls his strategy "books plus."

In a books-plus world, it is harder and harder to tell which came first, the book or the movie. With the release of the 1996 remake of Disney's *101 Dalmatians*, which featured real dogs, publishers also released new books about the old animated Disney movie, as well as new books about the new movie. They also reprinted the original book linked to the original 1961 animated movie. Adding to the confusion, there were several different books claiming to be the original.

A not-too-subtle clue to the way the movie studios view books can be found at Universal City, a movie theme park located on the old Universal film lot outside Los Angeles. Its bookstore displays about thirty titles on a small shelf. The rest of the store is filled with movie-related junk, non-movie-related junk, and candy.

With its ever multiplying channels, cable television offers nearly limitless opportunities for book tie-ins and spin-offs. Simon & Schuster publishes Weather Channel books for youngsters. Pocket Books has a Comedy Central "South Park" book. Pocket Books, an imprint of Simon & Schuster, which is owned by Viacom, which also owns MTV, publishes MTV Books. Black Entertainment Television, which bought Arabesque, publishes a line of African-American romance novels. As of early 1998, Simon & Schuster had published "8.5 million books derived from Nickelodeon programming," according to parent company Viacom. A&E Biography publishes books about some of the people it profiles; its biography of Larry Flynt did especially well, because the movie *The People Versus Larry Flynt* came out around the same time.

Cross-ownership of entertainment properties facilitates these "synergies," a business term that is thrown around boardrooms the way Richard Nixon threw the term "national security" around the White House. For instance, Viacom, which owns all of Pocket Books, also owns 50 percent of the Comedy Central channel. Disney owns Hyperion and ESPN, which have made a similar publishing arrangement.

At the beginning of the new millennium, marketing has become a religion and vice versa. Televangelist Pat Robertson and his Christian Broadcasting Network are selling a new translation of the Bible, in which they have a financial interest. The translation features simplified text and a peppy title, *The Book*. In that spirit, Robertson and his apostles have cranked out some jingles ("Rock me, shock me, turn me, change me, set me free, show me what it has for me, take me to *The Book*"). The advertising budget is seven million dollars, which will cover the costs of promotional calendars and door-hangers with excerpts from *The Book*, with plenty of money left over for music CDs and television commercials. "Communicating with America is very expensive," says a senior vice-president at the religious publishing house that produced this book.

The Celebrity Machine

The rise of movies and television, as everyone knows, has helped create our American celebrity culture, a big break for media-canny, otherwise mediocre authors. One of the first telegenic writers was Jacqueline Susann, author of *Valley of the Dolls*, published in February 1966 and subsequently made into a movie. Susann had worked as an actress, model, and radio personality. If that were not enough to make her aware of the power of stardom, she was married to Irving Mansfield, a former Hollywood publicist and television producer. Susann is sometimes credited with creating the celebrity author book tour. Her first publisher, Bernard Geis, a former Prentice-Hall editor, helped by shrewdly harnessing the marketing power of television. On her whirlwind book tour of *Valley of the Dolls*, Susann did television interviews with Merv Griffin, Mike Douglas, and scores of other network and local hosts. "By the summer of 1966," wrote a biographer, "Jackie was one of the most recognizable women in the United States. She was everywhere—in magazines and newspapers, on posters in bookstore windows and in buses, and, always, on television." Jacqueline Susann's husband described the phenomenon this way: He was selling Jackie, not "a goddam pile of paper."

The trail Susann blazed is trodden today by the likes of Steve Martin, author of *Pure Drivel*. The book, basically a repackaging job, is a collection of the comedian's previously published articles from the *New Yorker*. In an interview, Martin said he mulls over article ideas for a week or so, then writes the essay in half a day. When the essay collection appeared in 1998, Martin made a "surprise" appearance on his old television program, *Saturday Night Live*, and was interviewed on *Charlie Rose, Rosie, Live with Regis & Kathie Lee*, and *The Late Show with David Letterman*.

Just as celebrity authors appear on David Letterman's show, television celebrity Letterman gets contracts to write his own books, which have such titles as *David Letterman's New Book of Top Ten Lists* and *Wedding Dress Patterns for the Husky Bride.* "Celebrities can be incredible publicity machines, with built-in cross promotion," says Mauro di Preta, a senior editor at HarperCollins. "If you can get everyone to cooperate and you have creative marketing, it can really be powerful."

There isn't a celebrity publishers won't sign. To take a random example, Bantam's catalog of summer 1997 books leads with comedian Sinbad's *I Ain't Never Been Cool: The Voyages of Sinbad* and *Saturday Night Live* cast member Julia Sweeney's *God Said, "Ha!": A Memoir.*

The attraction of celebrity writers is not that they can write. It is that they are famous for singing songs, pitching a baseball, or telling jokes—or that they hang around with people who do those things. Because of the O. J. Simpson trial, we have books by a defense attorney, former wife of a defense attorney, prosecuting attorney at the criminal trial, deputy prosecuting attorney, lawyer for the family of one of the deceased in the civil trial, witness, detective, juror or dismissed juror, journalist who covered the trial, friend of the murdered wife, members of the victims' families, friend of the defendant, former girl friend of the defendant, niece of the defendant, and the defendant himself, who by the way declined to testify in his criminal trial. As one wit put it, the jurors selected for the various O. J. Simpson trials faced a really tough decision: Random House or Doubleday.*

Celebrities have such loyal followings that publishers must be careful about letting the matter of quality creep into their relationships. Soap opera star Joan Collins had a $4-million advance from Random House to write two novels. The publisher considered neither manuscript—really two versions of the same book—worthy of publishing and wanted its money back. Random House more or less said in court that they promised

---

*To be fair, O. J. made money for a lot of other people, too. Wasfi Tolaymat, a Jordanian, paid $4,000 for the furniture in the hotel room where O. J. stayed just after the murders; he was later offered $300,000 for the items. Likewise, Mezzaluna, the restaurant where Nicole and her family had dinner on the fatal night and where covictim Ron Goldman was a waiter, sold 240 more meals a day than usual after the murders. O. J.'s sidekick A. C. Cowlings got $2.99 a minute for talking to callers on 1-900-Ask A. C. Cowlings's total take in the first thirty days was $300,000. Of course some publishers bombed on the books they sent forth. Paula Barbieri, former girlfriend of the defendant, received a $3-million advance, but her book sold fewer than 150,000 copies.

to pay on completion of a manuscript, but that implied getting a manuscript with a clear beginning, middle, and end. At verdict time, jurors sided with the lovely Miss Collins. They decided she should at least get her money for one of the awful books. Jurors reportedly left the court clutching copies of Collins's unpublishable manuscript.

In his opening remarks, Collins's attorney had told the jury that the case would show "the proper relationship between an author and her editor and how they collaborate to make that mystical thing called a novel." In shorthand, this means he showed them that it is not the author's fault if she can't write. It's up to the publisher to hire book surgeons, who earn fat fees for operating on manuscripts.

Some celebrities are so busy being famous that even if they can write, they don't want to take the time. Television anchors Tom Brokaw, Dan Rather, and Peter Jennings have recent books under their names that were written with considerable help. "All of these guys think of themselves primarily as journalists, and they want to be recognized as more than just television personalities," said Peter Osnos, a former journalist who is currently publisher of Public Affairs books. "They don't need to cash in, but they like having people acknowledge them as writers." To be acknowledged as a writer, the anchors make a lot of appearances on the morning talk shows aired by their networks. The choice for anchors is to be a writer or to be *seen* as a writer. They are simply too busy to do both.

Once it is established that celebrities don't have to write their own books, it follows that credibility in other respects is not very important either. Traditionally, one writes an autobiography after having lived a long, full life; yet people such as Sinbad and Sweeney have barely begun to live. Furthermore, lack of credibility can even be a selling point. Shortly after Magic Johnson was diagnosed with the AIDS virus, reportedly contracted as a result of promiscuity, he signed a book contract with Random House to coauthor a book with former surgeon general C. Everett Koop about responsible sexual behavior. William Morrow and Company, another publisher, gave Lionel Dahmer, father of serial killer Jeffery Dahmer, $150,000 to write a parenting guide. Friends of Dick Morris observed that he was gleeful after being ousted from his job as an adviser to President Clinton. As a result of his allegedly telling White House secrets to a prostitute, he landed a $2.5-million advance to spill his guts to the entire planet in *Behind the Oval Office*. For her work as the lead prosecutor in the O. J. Simpson case, which she lost, Marcia Clark received a small bonus from the district attorney's office—$14,330—and a big one from Viking—$4.2 million—as an advance for a book on the trial. (The advance was about half what the trial cost the taxpayers.) Clark's cocounsel, who played a secondary role in their botched case, appropriately received $1.3 million.

When recruiting potential authors, superagent Jan Miller says she does not worry about their writing ability; she can hire one of those book doctors. She concentrates instead on whether the authors have television, infomercial, and audiotape potential. Publishers bid on Marcia Clark's book with the recklessness of a runaway jury because she was in demand on television. Television producers seemingly would sell their grandmothers for a celebrity "get." "It's the big interview that causes viewers to find you and watch," says *Dateline NBC* executive producer Neal Shapiro. "It's the difference between a twelve share and a twenty share."

Fabio, the muscular, long-haired guy who appears on covers of Avon Books bodice rippers, is the ideal author. With a sexy author's photo of Fabio for the dust jacket assured, Avon decided to have him write a book of his own. (Well, he supplied the plot, he says.) His celebrity also lends itself to a fabulous array of marketing spin-offs, for which Fabio once again specializes in standing around and looking pretty. There is a music CD, a cologne for Versace, calendars, T-shirts, and so on. On a children's animated television series, *Thor*, he supplies the voice for the Fabio-lookalike hero.

The economics of celebrity books prove the old maxim, the more you have, the more you get. Of the forty people on *Forbes's* 1998 list of highest-paid entertainers, nineteen had at least one book to his or her credit. The list does include two writers, Michael Crichton and Stephen King, but most highly paid entertainers are actors or singers, such as the Spice Girls, who had two books. In 1992, Sam Walton, one of the richest men in America, received the richest advance ever for the memoirs of a businessman, more than $4 million. His contract did not have the usual clause permitting the publisher to reject the manuscript (and recoup the advance) if the work was unpublishable.

Stars know that celebrityhood is like money in the bank. If you are short of ready cash, write a book to make a withdrawal. "As a single mother with few assets and less income than most presumed, I was in deep financial trouble," Sarah Ferguson, the duchess of York, said in her autobiography, *My Story*. She also wrote several children's books and traded on her royal status with a book about Queen Victoria. Marilyn Quayle, wife of the former vice-president, coauthored a terrible book, *Embrace the Serpent*. Later, she reportedly said she wrote it to help pay for her children's college expenses. (Still later, she denied the statement, leaving open the question why she really did write the book.)

Celebrities also understand that writing a book can make them a bigger star. The Washington Speakers Bureau, Incorporated, which arranges high-paid speaking engagements for notable figures, each year assembles an L. L. Bean–type catalog displaying its talent. Like stars in the Michelin guide, the covers of books stud the entry of each personality. In the 1997 edition, weatherman Willard Scott scored three dust jackets; Margaret Thatcher and Marilyn Quayle, two each; Colin Powell, James Baker, H. Norman Schwarzkopf, Bill Bradley, Fran Tarkenton, and Lee Iacocca, one apiece.

Not everyone can be as important to America as Willard Scott or Fran Tarkenton. But most everyone can feel as though he is, and many can make a pile of dough at the same time. All they have to do is follow Franklin's lead and publish their own book, for a book is a great way to market yourself, as the next section shows.

The Ultimate Calling Card

Edward L. Bernays, a founding father of public relations, concocted a creative strategy for promoting reading. As a service to Simon & Schuster, Harcourt Brace, and other publishing clients, he convinced architects, decorators, and builders to construct homes with built-in shelves. "Where there are bookshelves," he said, "there will be books."

The process also works the other way around: books can promote products. Benjamin Franklin's print shop, in addition to books, sold stationery, pencils, ink, and maps. Anticipating the time when Barnes & Noble would integrate cafes into their stores, Franklin also sold coffee, cheese and codfish, patent medicines, fishnets, and lottery tickets. Amazon.com started out selling new books over the Internet. It now offers clients rare books, videos, music CDs, personalized greeting cards, consumer electronics, tools, and toys, and runs auctions. In 1999, it bought a one-third share in HomeGrocer.com, an online grocery-delivery service in the Seattle and Portland areas, and it purchased Drugstore.com Incorporated. It can now sell Prozac along with Balzac.

Before founding the Book-of-the-Month Club, Harry Scherman also saw a lucrative drugstore connection. He joined with Charles and Albert Boni to publish fifteen Shakespearean plays in small, leather-bound books. To promote sales, he convinced the Whitman Candy Company to create the Whitman Library Package: one of the little books of plays together with a big box of candy. Book-and-candy lovers bought 25 million copies of the Little Leather Library by mail and in drugstores.

In the mid-1990s, Northern Trust Corporation, a bank, ran seven not-for-profit book clubs in Florida, as well as one in Chicago and another in San Francisco. The bank found this a good way to attract new customers. Meanwhile, Ernest Hemingway's three sons have authorized the Ernest Hemingway Collection. Built by Thomasville Furniture Industries, it includes nearly one hundred pieces of bed-, living-, and dining-room furniture, plus desk sets, clocks, and other accessories. None of the furniture resembles anything Papa actually had in his home, but is inspired by places Hemingway visited and wrote about.* Avon author Fabio does not monopolize perfume spin-offs. *The Bridges of Madison County* has a perfume of its own, too. And just as Charles Dickens's *Little Dorrit* included advertisements for Persian parasols, smelling bottles, books, and medicines, Whittle Communications in the 1980s published a Larger Agenda Series of short books by big authors interspersed with advertisements from Federal Express and other companies.

Of all the commodities that books promote, however, the one they promote best is their authors. "I was amazed at how much business [my books] brought in," Joe Black says. "Anyone can have a book . . . , it's knowing how to use it [that matters]."

Black dispensed this wisdom to me from his retirement home in Colorado. In his early fifties, he is the beneficiary of a lucrative career that began at Milliken & Company, a South Carolina textile enterprise. After fifteen years at Milliken, Black wanted to go into business for himself, as

---

* "Just as Hemingway inspired his generation," said the furniture maker in a press release, "Thomasville hopes to excite today's customers who desire a similar spirit of individuality in their homes." Here is a hallmark of American marketing, selling individuality to the masses.

his grandfathers had done. His specialty was "continuous improvement processes," or, in common parlance, showing people how to do a better job of marketing, production, and customer delivery. A large part of his consulting business involved lecturing—"something I was pretty good at" — and one day a customer suggested he write down his remarks. Today, Black is author of *The Attitude Connection; Looking Back on the Future: Building a Quality Foundation;* and *Passing Through: Reflections on Life.* He likes to call these books, which he self-published, "bathroom reading for executives."

We have become a nation of Joe Blacks, consultants who live out Franklin's dream of personal independence. The consulting profession grew 52 percent from 1978 to 1992, according to *Money Magazine.* Global consulting revenue is expected to more than double from 1995 to 2000. "Consulting is where the action is," said the chairman of Ernst & Young. Much of that action involves book publishing. "Consulting," in the words of the Fuqua School of Business at Duke University, "is about communication," especially the sort of self-help communication found in *Poor Richard.*

Black brought his books with him to speeches and put them out of sight in the back of the room. At the end of his talk, he made them available. Gauging the audience, he might tell people they could buy a copy at the list price or sometimes he would simply say that people should feel free to pick up a copy and leave however much money they felt was appropriate. Once a man left three hundred dollars. "Some of these guys are so desperate" for help, he said. After a talk to executives at the Sara Lee Corporation, he sold eight thousand dollars worth of books in the back of the room.

The money from direct book sales is nice, but books can pay other even more lucrative dividends. Black used his books like calling cards, giving them first to CEOs or their secretaries, who might pass them on to the boss or, thankful for the gift, be quick to return Black's phone calls. Getting a copy of his book in the hands of a CEO, Black says, was like "getting the sperm to meet the egg." Promotional books—that is, books to promote yourself—account for half the publishing industry, says Jerrold Jenkins, who runs a magazine called *Publishing Entrepreneur.* "If you have a book, your fees go up because you are better positioned."

Books work for spiritual consultants as well. Just as churches have learned that the best way to attract parishioners is to add music, shorten services, and throw in valet parking, T. D. Jakes, a country preacher, uses television, direct mail, the Internet, the telephone, magazines, and books such as *The Lady, Her Lover, and Her Lord* to evangelize. After working with a small publisher, Destiny Image Publishers Corporation, he landed a $1.8-million two-book contract with Putnam Penguin in 1997. A *Wall Street Journal* reporter says Jakes "nurtures, protects and markets his product—himself—with meticulous care."

The *Yearbook of Experts, Authorities, & Spokespersons* shows how the world of consultants and the world of books have slipped into a synchronous orbit. In the *Yearbook's* pages, we have Dr. Brad Blanton, author of *Radical Honesty: How to Transform Your Life by Telling the Truth*. He is director of the Center for Well Being. And there is Dr. Beverly Potter, author of *Beating Job Burnout: How to Transform Work Pressure into Productivity*. And Sheldon O. Burman, M.D., F.A.C.S. from the Male Sexual Dysfunctional Institute. He does not tell us what he has written, but he does advertise himself as "Noted Lecturer and Widely Published Authority." It's just a guess, but if he has written a book, it probably has the word *transform* in its title.

Large established publishers have recognized the profit possible in consultants' books. These men and women come with a venue in which to promote their books, says Kerri Kennedy, senior publicist at Simon & Schuster. Many writers, however, do what Ben Franklin did and publish their own books. This is partly out of necessity. The big book business, with its blockbuster mentality, has made it more difficult for a potential midlist author to get a major publisher's attention. But necessity is not the only reason. Computer technology makes self-publishing much cheaper than it was when professional typesetters and printers had to do the work on specialized equipment. And, there is the little matter of seeking the big chance, as Franklin did so well.

The logic of self-publishing goes more or less like this: If the objective is to make money, then why not make as much as possible. In other words, don't settle for a small royalty from a publisher; publish the book yourself and keep every cent of the profits. Joe Black says New York publishers showed interest in his book. But he figured he would have to promote it himself; and if he was going to do that much work on the project, he might as well do it all. He named his publishing company Life Vision Books. To ensure a profit, he lined up a prepublication commitment for

Global Consulting Industry Revenue

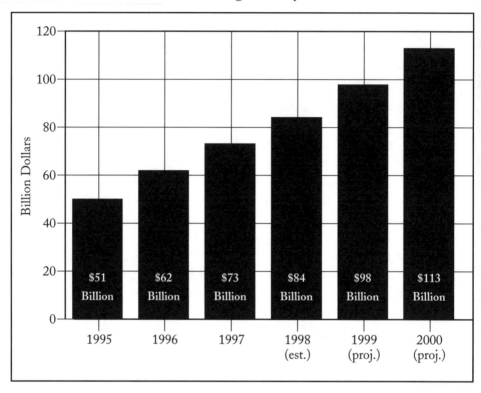

| | $51 Billion | $62 Billion | $73 Billion | $84 Billion | $98 Billion | $113 Billion |
| 1995 | 1996 | 1997 | 1998 (est.) | 1999 (proj.) | 2000 (proj.) |

Source: 1998 Kennedy Information LLC, Fitzwilliam, NH. Reprinted with permission from *The Global Management Consulting Market: Key Data Trends & Forecasts*

his first book from six companies. They agreed to buy twenty thousand copies sight unseen.

It is difficult not to like Joe Black after talking with him and difficult not to admire his professed interest in bettering the human condition through his books. Nevertheless, his homey sayings ("The quality of what goes on around your family's kitchen table is far more important than . . . the quality of what goes on around your boardroom table.") don't rise to the level of Poor Richard's ("Lost time is never found again").*

*Few modern books have the uplift that Franklin brought his readers, providing them with as many enduring practical sayings as Shakespeare did literary ones. As examples, "God helps them that helps themselves," "Eat to live, and not live to eat," and "Where there's marriage without love there will be love without marriage."

Most consultants' books, even when they come out of major publishing houses that ought to care about the quality of editing, are far, far worse. Here is the opening sentence in Bonnie St. John Deane's *Succeeding Sane: Making Room for Joy in a Crazy World,* published by Simon & Schuster: "This book took hold of me like a tree putting down roots and spreading its branches as I watched in awe." Here is the last sentence: "The conclusions of this book are, in reality, up to you." Barbara A. Glanz, billed as "an internationally known author, speaker, and consultant," is author of *Care Packages for the Home: Dozens of Ways to Regenerate Spirit Where You Live,* an Andrews McMeel book. Among her lifesaving suggestions is starting a "Laughter Club" in which friends or family get together once a week to see who has the funniest story. Just as goofy is Michael J. Gelb's *How to Think Like Leonardo da Vinci* (Delacorte Press). His steps to creative brilliance include developing one's senses. "Self-Assessment: Smell" suggests that readers consider if they "can recognize friends by their scent." He includes his address and phone number in the back of the book so that readers can invite him to unburden himself of all this nonsense in person.

The ultimate self-promotional drive that lies behind having a book of one's own is apparent in advice-giver Raleigh Pinskey's *101 Ways to Promote Yourself: Tricks of the Trade for Taking Charge of Your Own Success by Visibility Marketing™ Expert.* His visibility suggestions? Develop a board game (trick number 31), take people out to lunch (trick number 50), and write a book (trick number 43), which he says is "like falling off a log." His rather brief description of how to fall off a log can be condensed further into this don't-worry-be-happy catechism:

• Don't worry about being an authority on a subject. Everyone is an authority on some topic. "A secretary can be an expert in phone etiquette. A high-wire electrician can be an expert in courage and fear."

• Don't worry about having a coherent narrative. Just take stuff you have written before, like special reports and newsletters, "put them all together and have them printed."

• Don't worry if you don't have any scraps of writing lying around and, worse, don't have time to write any at the moment. Talk into a tape recorder while you are driving "to school, to the gym, or shopping." You can hire a secretary to type it all up.

• Don't worry if you don't have time to edit what is typed up. "Look in the yellow pages under Writers."

• And don't worry if no one will publish it. Publish it yourself. "Covers are easy." *

The main thing, Pinskey stresses, is that a book is a ticket to fortune and fame. Some of the benefits of book writing that he lists are credibility, more money, promotions, and "the opportunity to appear on radio and TV programs."

"Write a book to establish yourself as the expert in your field," say Marilyn and Tom Ross, two publishing advisers who have helped Joe Black. (They are given more attention in Appendix B.) As smart consultants who want to drum up business by making themselves well known, the Rosses follow their own advice and write books: *Country Bound!* ("Trade your business suit blues for blue jean dreams"), *Jump Start Your Book Sales: A Money-Making Guide for Authors and Publishers,* and *The Complete Guide to Self-Publishing.* They dedicated this last one, by the way, to Ben Franklin.

The Hegelian Antithesis of Publicity

T. E. Lawrence, better known as Lawrence of Arabia, built interest in his classic *Seven Pillars of Wisdom* gradually. The first edition, privately published, comprised only eight copies, which he sent to Thomas Hardy, George Bernard Shaw, and other famous authors. Next came, in 1926, a privately published, British subscribers' edition of 220 copies, which sold for $150 each. Starting the same process in the United States in 1927, Lawrence authorized an edition of ten purchasable copies priced at $20,000 each. In this topsy-turvy market, someone named Gabriel Wells reportedly paid $1,150 for a copy of the British subscribers' edition at a New York auction and only $1,000 for a rare first issue of the first edition of the King James Bible. Meanwhile, John Q. Citizen cheerfully paid a

---

*Incidentally, consultants' books can be judged by their covers, especially the quotes on them. Typically they have blurbs from people who are far from household names, as in "*The Profit Zone* is by far the best, most informative, and most instructive business book I've read in over a decade"—David L. Sliney, president, Lamco Ventures. My research assistant, Bonnie Bauman, called Lamco, based in St. Louis, and found that it consists of two employees, one of whom is Sliney.

scant $3 for the abridged version of Lawrence's book, called *Revolt in the Desert,* which became a Book-of-the-Month selection. Most remarkable of all, Bernard Shaw said that the retiring war hero cum author did not care about the money. Shaw was writing *Saint Joan* at the time, and the two heroes may have blurred together in his mind. The *New York Times,* with a more steady eye, observed sagely that "It would appear that there can be a modesty so intense as to pass into its Hegelian antithesis of publicity." Lawrence was every bit as sly as he was shy.*

"The public do not accept those who are too openly in the market," said J. G. Holland, a best-selling author in the last century and editor of *Scribner's.* As much as authors may care about money, their seeming to be above remuneration makes for more effective marketing. The parallel in the medical world is that the physician giving you an annual medical exam probably should not let on that he or she is thinking that a few more appendectomies will pay for the swimming pool that the kids keep yammering about. The artistic model, as it were, is Donatello. According to legend, he put his earnings in a wicker basket that hung from the ceiling in his Florence studio. Workers and friends could take what they wanted without asking.

Understanding that his brain should not be preoccupied with "bucksheesh," as Mark Twain called it, Shaw would say things such as "Whenever a publisher gives me literary advice I take an instant and hideous revenge on him. I give him business advice." After Alfred A. Knopf gave Anne Rice a $5-million, two-book contract, the Gothic novelist told a reporter, "The money is lagniappe—that's a Louisiana word for extra." The ideal newspaper profile of an author is one that was done on crime writer George Pelecanos. "If this guy had a theme song," gushed the *Baltimore Sun* reporter of Pelecanos' seeming disinterest in making money, "it would be 'Que sera, sera.'" Buried in the news story were the facts—the significance of which were ignored by the reporter—that Pelecanos went on book tours and asked a local bookstore to hold a signing for him.

Authors can't appear to be fey about money unless they put friends and family to considerable trouble. Washington Irving did not want his publisher to send out copies of his book, *The Sketch Book,* to editors for re-

---

*Lawrence, realizing he was onto a good thing, put an initial $500,000 price on *The Mint,* his study of barracks life.

view; he had influential friends working behind the scenes to get him special attention. Vladimir Nabokov had a dutiful wife who did all the dirty work. Vera drove the car while he wrote *Lolita* in the back seat. She typed his manuscripts and complained that she had to make all the marketing decisions.

Of course, writers who establish an identity as market haters tip their hands from time. "Trade curses everything it handles," said Henry Thoreau. He went on and on about it being "enough if I please myself with writing." At the same time, he dropped notes to James Russell Lowell about coughing up $198 for "thirty-three pages at six dollars a page." Ernest Hemingway wrote in one letter to his editor, Maxwell Perkins, that (1) he was "no actress wanting the name in big electric lights" and (2) that his name on the cover of a new book was too small.

As marketing becomes more pervasive, authors and publishers must market more subversively. No trick is too cheesy. Inspired by his idol, William Elliott Hazelgrove let it be known that he was writing a novel in the attic of Ernest Hemingway's childhood home in Oak Park, Illinois. That ploy, which generated a nice story in the *New York Times*, is reminiscent of Georges Simenon's idea to write a story in a glass cage so that people could watch him in the act. The newspaper that was to publish the story went under, which was just as well. Simenon received a lot of press attention without having to go through with this stunt, which had drawn criticism for being too brazen.

With so many authors appearing in so many cities, publishers have begun to lose interest in standard book tours. Searching for a new approach, they send authors to talk to retailers privately to develop interest in *advance* of book publication. Friends of Edwin Meese, one of Ronald Reagan's presidential spear carriers, came up with a promotional twist for his *With Reagan: The Inside Story.* Saying that good old Ed could not afford a promotional book tour, these chums put together a tax-exempt "Meese Book Fund." A $100 contribution qualified a donor to become a Team Member, $10,000 a Cabinet Associate. Book promotion as a charity! And free-market Reaganites came up with the idea.

We have moved into an age of anti-advertising advertising. There is no official starting date for this trend, but a likely beginning was in 1967. HarperCollins *withheld* review copies of William Manchester's *The Death of the President* by agreement with *Look* magazine, which paid a record sum at the time ($665,000) to serialize it before the publication date. Since then, publishers have learned what every successful stripper knows: The best way to keep customers buying drinks is not to give them what they want right away, but to tantalize. Readers, pounding the table for more, made Manchester's book number one on the *New York Times* best-seller list.

The promotion of Oliver North's book *Under Fire* added a twist to counterintuitive marketing in 1991. Appearing in bookstores without advance publicity, the book's sneak attack became news. *Time* ran a cover story with excerpts, and Ted Koppel did two installments on *Nightline*. North then embarked on a twenty-city book tour.

With praise for books so commonplace, marketing staffs have begun to look for undiluted condemnation. The reasoning, clearly enough, is that anyone can get an upbeat book blurb for the dust jacket. It is more interesting to get a really bad one, as Christopher Hitchens's publisher did for his scathing biography *The Missionary Position: Mother Teresa in Theory and Practice*. Verso sent advance copies "to everyone we could think of in the Catholic hierarchy, to the Cardinal in New York, to the Pope. We figured that anything that upsets the Catholic Church is good news for our readers." No church official took the bait. But Verso managed to find plenty of author-kicks-nun comments suitable for the purpose. "If there is a hell," says a review quoted on the cover of the paperback edition, "Hitchens is going there for this book."

As they get the hang of these techniques, publishers and their henchmen may now look for ways to discredit themselves. The Modern Library assembled a panel of writers to name the "100 Best Novels of the 20th Century." Dissatisfied with the selection process and embarrassed by the list when it appeared in 1998, the judges got down on their knees like repentant Jimmy Swaggarts and apologized to every newspaper and journal that would listen. Modern Library sold more copies of *Ulysses* in several weeks than it had sold in the previous two years, then turned its attention to nonfiction. The pattern repeated with the "100 Best Nonfiction Books of the 20th Century." *The Education of Henry Adams*, which Modern Library happened to publish, was number one. Within two weeks of the announcement, orders for the book equaled ten times its normal annual sales.

*　*　*

I do not suggest that anti-marketing marketing is bad. On the contrary, as the ultimate extension of hype it engenders cynicism, and that is good.

From the moment elementary teachers urge students to read, the message is that books are sacred. No time is spent telling students that many books are awful. As a result, too many youngsters grow into adults who think that anyone who has written a book "must be smart." And, of course, this lack of education plays into the hands of the marketing consultants. The few truly anti-marketing authors out there don't help. Walker Percy refused to flog one of his books on the *Dick Cavett Show*; he said his job was writing books, not selling them. Percy lulls us into putting down our guard.

In our market economy, where books are pumped out like lipstick and pet rocks, we must learn to be ever vigilant for advertising cunning. The reaction to the death of novelist Eugene Izzi in 1996 was as it should have been. When he was found hung to death outside a Chicago office, some suspected that it was a publicity trick that went awry. Savvy literary consumers distinguish between Ben Franklin, the inventor of subscription libraries and improved stoves, and Ron Popeil, who brought us Mr. Microphone and the Ginsu knife and who professed shock that "I could write a book!" about it.

The number of intelligent books rises with the number of intelligent readers. The more that consumers watch for the hand of the publicist, the more likely that they will ask the right questions about the product. Benjamin Franklin, we must remember, was a genius not only because he wrote well but because he read well, too.

THREE

Artless Thank-Yous

—⟨⟨⟩⟩—

In which the reader learns that
authors abuse acknowledgments and
dedications the way they do their
families; and in which the would-be
author learns how to make
the front matter matter.

—∘∅∘—

It is customary for those who wish to gain the favor of a prince
to endeavor to do so by offering him gifts. . . . May I trust, therefore,
that Your Highness will accept this little gift in the spirit
in which it is offered.
—Niccolò Machiavelli, dedication of *The Prince*
to Lorenzo "the Magnificent" Medici

First of panegyric. Every man is honourable . . .
—Jonathan Swift, "How to make Dedications
Panegyrics or Satires; and of the color
Honourable and dishonourable"

—∘∅∘—

To crack open a new book and read its dedication and acknowledgments is typically an occasion for me to relive an experience from years ago, when I was a midshipman. One night I was assigned to stand watch on the fantail of our aircraft carrier with a young enlisted man. While we looked over the inky Pacific, illuminated by a long strip of moonlight, he poured out a story of his sad youth, especially of his unloving parents. Though barely able to make out the sailor's face, I felt a bond born of sincere self-revelation. Then, several days later, we happened to meet in broad daylight. I noticed the sailor had a large tattoo on his arm, a heart with the inscription "Mother."

Authors, whether of fiction or nonfiction, pride themselves on uncompromising honesty and courage, on originality and style. But when the time comes to put the finishing touches on their books, they, like the young sailor, are inclined to suspend judgment; they become perfunctory and reach for smarmy clichés or the trite to decorate their work. The result is that the front of a book is usually a vast literary moonscape not worth exploring.

For proof, consider the fruits of a survey of fifty books taken off several shelves at random.

Half of those dedications in which the relationship to the author was clear were to spouses. This is not only unimaginative; it's not particularly reassuring about the clear-headedness of the writer. More than one-fourth of all homicides involve people who are married or are romantically linked with each other, says one expert on love. About half of all first marriages end in divorce, and people who walk down the aisle a second time are half again as likely as first timers to bomb. If it weren't for the fact that so many people are living together these days, thus avoiding all the annoying paperwork associated with divorce, the norm would be Ernest Hemingway, who dedicated books to four different wives.

Just as troubling, not one of the acknowledgments in these fifty nonfiction books had anything negative to say about anything or anyone. We would be suspicious of an author who showed no generosity of spirit and saw only enemies on every side. But we should be equally suspicious of authors who only see around them unfailingly helpful librarians, cheerful typists, utterly candid sources, and selfless scholars who always make useful comments on time. Praise means nothing if it is not balanced against criticism.

The Perversion of Honest Venality

The front matter of books didn't always seem so fatuous. Not that the panegyrics of early scribes were more perceptive or interesting than they are today. The prose was, if anything, more stupefying. It was also generally more disingenuous. But these faults in days of yore were also merits. Today they are not. Unlike today's writers, who spread honeyed words for no apparent good reason, early writers slathered praise on the opening pages of their books out of shrewd self-interest. They either sought to parry the mailed fist of authority or hoped to court a wealthy patron who would subsidize their work—or, if possible, both.

Niccolò Machiavelli, who specialized in thoughtful political manipulation, dedicated his book on the subject, *The Prince*, to Lorenzo Medici,

In this detail of an oil painting by Santi di Tito, Niccolò Machiavelli has the expression of a man who has dreamed up yet another trick. Maybe it has to do with his latest book, which could be that volume in his right hand. Has the master manipulator come up with an inspired, self-serving dedication?

Courtesy of the Palazzo Vecchio, Florence

whose family ruled Florence financially and politically. Henry Fielding's *The History of Tom Jones* is dedicated to "the Honourable George Lyttleton, Esq.; one of the Lords Commissioner of the Treasury." Lyttleton, a patron of literature, helped Alexander Pope and others besides Fielding. So entrenched was this concept of patronage that Fielding boldly wrote, "Sir, Notwithstanding your constant refusal, when I have asked leave to prefix your name to this dedication, I must still insist on my right to desire your protection. . . ."

Authors occasionally strayed from the norm, but even those exceptions could prove the general rule. Francisco de Quevedo y Villages dedicated *Toys of Childhood* in 1641 to "no person at all. . . . I have considered that all writers dedicate their books with two purposes, which are seldom separated: one that such person should aid the publication with his blessed almsgiving; the other, that he should shield the work from critics."

Crafting these paeans was tricky business, requiring keen political instincts, if not literary skill. Persons considered suitable for dedications were limited to the royal family, church leaders, and the wealthier, more powerful nobility. As suggested by Machiavelli and Quevedo y Villages, these limitations applied not only in England but in other lands as well, including Japan where authors dedicated books to shoguns and daimios. In these small, inbred worlds, the master bedrooms of castles and their dungeons were filled with treacherous rivals. The clever queen on the throne today might tomorrow change place with an idiot cousin in chains. Knowing they could hang for a misguided dedication, authors devised clever stratagems to protect themselves.

Like a general holding back his main forces until their deployment was absolutely necessary, Voltaire did not at first dedicate *Fanaticism, or Mahomet the Prophet.* But when the supposedly sacrilegious play closed after only three performances, he hurriedly dedicated it to Pope Benedict XIV. When the pope then gave it his warm blessing, the author happily observed that the bishop of Rome was infallible in literary judgment as well as matters of faith.

Fear proved a generous muse. Nicolaus Copernicus's radical theory that the sun, not the earth, was at the center of the planets put him at odds with the benighted but powerful church. Frightened—but not frightened out of his wits—he dedicated his treatise on the subject to Pope Paul III. The result is one of the cleverest dedications of all time: "I have dedicated these lucubrations of mine to Your Holiness . . . because, even in this remote corner of the world where I live, you are considered to be the most eminent man in dignity of rank and in love of all learning and even of mathematics, so that by your authority and judgment you can easily suppress the bites of slanderers, albeit the proverb hath it that there is no remedy for the bite of a sycophant."

Tom Paine, who also stirred things up from time to time, took the same approach with *Rights of Man*. He thought the book might cause a sensation, which it did. Within ten weeks of its publication in 1791, it sold 50,000 copies. The typical novel at the time sold 1,250 copies and general works averaged 750 copies. The book was highly critical of despotism, including that of his own British sovereign. To protect himself from arrest for sedition, he shrewdly dedicated it "To George Washington, President of the United States of America, Sir, I present you a small Treatise in defence of those principles of Freedom which your exemplary Virtue hath so eminently contributed to establish. . . ." Paine was counting on the fact that the government of King George III was eager for better Anglo-American relations. Paine's ploy proved awkward for Washington, who wanted to improve relations. He responded coolly to Paine when news of the dedication and fifty free copies of *Rights of Man* arrived.

When nervous authors could not be certain whom to target for a dedication, they often tossed bouquets to everyone in sight. The savvy Sir Balthazar Gerbier put forty-one dedicatory letters in his *Counsel to Builders*, published in 1663. These encomia encumbered one-half his book. Alexander Politi, editor of *Martyrologium Romanum*, had a dedication for each day of the year. Others have divided books into separate volumes to create more opportunities for dedications.

Quick-witted authors who penciled praise out of self-interest hastily erased it for the same reason. George Chapman dedicated his translation of Homer's *Iliad*, completed about 1600, to Queen Anne; the duke of Lennox; the lord chancellor; the earls of Salisbury, Suffolk, Northampton, Arundell, Pembroke, Montgomery (and his wife), South-Hampton, and Sussex (and his wife); lord of Walden; Lord Lisle; Lady Wrothe; the countess of Bedford; and Sir Thomas Howard. He also included Lady Arabella Stuart—initially. Lady Arabella, whom he described as "our English Athenia, chaste arbitress of vertue and learning," subsequently became involved in plots against the king. For this she went to the Tower of London, where she died insane and with her name lopped from Chapman's dedication in subsequent printings.

With every other author heaping it on, faint praise was worse than none at all. Robert Loveday's translation of a French work in 1736 (*Hymen's Praeludia; or Love's Master-Piece*) included a dedication to "The Right Honourable, His Ever Honoured Lady, the Lady Clinton" typical of many of the time. Laden with bowing, scraping, genuflection, and prostration, Loveday's dedication prose ended in a tangled heap with ". . . as the sun (who is the clearest Emblem of your Virtues) when mounted to his meridan, does not disdain to look downwards, so if you vouchsafe to let fall the beams of a smile upon this piece and bid it live, how unkindly others may use it, shall never be placed among the fears of, Madam, Your Honour's most Humble, and ever Obedient Servant, Loveday."

The marketplace for dedications worked like all marketplaces do. Looking for fairness and rationality, there was an attempt to standardize pricing. Isaac D'Israeli tells us that the price of a dedication to a play was fixed "from five to ten guineas, from the Revolution to the time of George I, when it rose to twenty." Famous authors could command twenty or thirty pounds.* Also, as in all markets, there were dedication con men. The falconer and the mongrel, as they were called, hawked books that were complete in every respect except one. The name on the dedication was not filled in. That was done by the mongrel on a hand press when the duo arrived in town and spotted a likely patron. The falconer presented the book supposedly written in the noble's honor. Flattered, The Right Honourable would reciprocate with a financial favor. An early seventeenth-century description of this trick, in a book called *O per se O*, advised that "If a gentleman seeing one of these bookes dedicated onely to his name, suspect it to be a bastard that hath more fathers besides himselfe."

Gradually, the state became less frightening to authors, who were far more beholden to bookstore proprietors than to nobility for their welfare. This occurred about the time of Samuel Johnson, whose eventual disenchantment with traditional dedications shows how the power of noble patrons waned. Dr. Johnson was famous for the high quality of dedications he was commissioned to write for the books of others. He was not above

---

*A guinea is worth a little more than one pound.

the practice under his own name either. He dedicated the plan for his famous dictionary to Lord Chesterfield, then secretary of state. Chesterfield gave Johnson a little time and ten pounds, but afterward ignored him until the *Dictionary of the English Language* appeared. Then Chesterfield wrote two letters, published in *The World,* in support of the soon-to-appear book. Angry to receive help when it was no longer needed, Johnson wrote Chesterfield that he would have no dedication this time. "Seven years, My Lord, have now passed since I waited in your outward rooms or was repulsed from your door, during which time I have been pushing on my work through difficulties of which it would be useless to complain, and I have brought it at last to the verge of publication without one act of assistance, one word or encouragement or one smile of favor." Johnson realized he did not need a patron, which he defined in his dictionary as "a wretch who supports with indolence, and is paid with flattery."

During the transition to market-based authorship, writers without imagination perfunctorily continued to dredge up lords and ladies for dedications, while the more creative honored their new patrons. Fanny Burney, later Madame d'Arblay, dedicated *Evelina* "To the Authors of the Monthly and Critical Reviews. . . . Without name, without recommendation, and unknown alike to success and disgrace, to whom can I so properly apply for patronage, as to those who publicly profess themselves Inspectors of all literary performances?" Samuel Foote began *The Englishman in Paris,* published in 1753, thus:

> My Bookseller informs me, that the bulk of his Readers, regarding in a work of this kind the quantity more than the quality, will not be contented without an additional half sheet; and he apprehends that a short Dedication will answer the purpose. But as I have no obligations to any great man or woman in this country, and as I will take care that no production of mine shall want their patronage, I don't know any person whose good office I so much stood in need of as my Bookseller's. Therefore, Mr. Vaillant, I think myself obliged to you for the correctness of the Press, and the beauty of the Type, and the goodness of the Paper with which you have decorated this work of, Your humble servant, Sam Foote.

Unfortunately, this creativity wears thin quickly. You can dedicate every book to your terrifying sovereign and not discredit yourself. You cannot dedicate every book to your publisher without raising a question about the value of your work (is the publisher doing this book as a favor or because it is good enough to pay for?). "All this [dedicating] is perhaps harmless," William Makepeace Thackeray wisely counseled in the mid–nineteenth century, "but it would be better to allow the system of dedicating—now so enfeebled and spiritless—to die out and be forgotten."

Dedications became as extraneous to writing as moats and drawbridges had become to nobility. But like nail-biters, authors compulsively kept at the habit anyway, dedicating books to loved ones and friends and, imbued with the teamwork mentality of the Industrial Age, listing everyone from librarians to shoe clerks in acknowledgments to nonfiction books. (Fictional books rarely contain acknowledgments, for the simple reason that fiction is supposed to be imagined and to say that you can't do that yourself discredits the book.)

Dedication writing remains so mindless in execution that virtually no one has stopped to think up a decent reason for continuing it or at least rules for how it ought to be done. How-to books for aspiring writers say plenty about choosing typefaces and fashioning bibliographies; acknowledgments and dedications are treated as if they were naughty activities best left out of polite conversation. "If the author wishes to have a dedication page," advises one writing guide, "he should phrase the dedication as simply as possible." *The Chicago Manual of Style* deems dedications "matters for the author to determine," though, disappointingly, it discourages the unusual or interesting: "Extravagant" dedications are "things of the past"; humorous ones are "inappropriate in a serious book." The how-to book *Writing for Love or Money,* edited by Norman Cousins, didn't say a word on the subject, even though love has become a common theme in dedications. Things are so confusing that acknowledgments now appear in the back of books, or are woven into prefaces, forewords, and introductions.

"It's one of those things that you are supposed to know how to handle, like your wedding night," essayist Joseph Epstein said when I asked if it was true he had written about the topic. He had, briefly, in *The Middle of My Tether,* noting in his choice comments that the most fitting acknowledgment he ever received was "I am indebted to Joseph Epstein for (among other things) directing me to Alexander Herzen."

Perhaps the only other person I have found to say something useful was journalist Richard H. Rovere in *The American Scholar* some thirty years ago. The appropriate tone of acknowledgments, he appreciated, is best understood through satire. Rovere began his parody this way: "Like the six that preceded it, this seventh volume in my life of *Raison d'être* owes its existence to many people besides its author. As *d'être* himself once said, slightly paraphrasing his great contemporary, Washington Irving, *E pluribus unum* is a motto that could be as aptly applied to the work of scholars as to the young Republic to which both *d'être* and the incomparable creator of the Leatherstocking tales made such signal contributions."

If literary critics would give more attention to dedications and acknowledgments, authors might think about improving them or having none at all. Even if authors didn't change their ways, the reviewers at least would nourish us with abundant, easily picked fruit for ridicule. Gore Vidal, one of the few such harvesters, said this in his review of Robert Calder's *Willie: The Life of W. Somerset Maugham*: "To Mr. Calder's credit, he does his best to show the amiable side of the formidable Mr. Maugham—the side that Mr. Calder terms 'Willie,' as he was known to friends. But our school-teacher [Calder's job] also distances himself from 'nastiness' in his acknowledgments where he notes 'the unqualified encouragement of my parents, and my children—Alison, Kevin, Lorin, and Dani.' (Did they pipe 'What's rough trade, Daddy?' with *unqualified* encouragement?) No matter. By and large, children, your Daddy has done the old fruitcake proud."

The Unwritten Rules

Although there aren't any rules governing acknowledgments and dedications, authors gravitate toward rigid patterns of pretense, hyperbole, and banality. It is as if each one wanders alone, aimlessly, into lush mountains and by some miracle ends up at the same run-down shack on the other side. Because authors thrash around a good deal before finding their dedications and acknowledgments, it may be an act of mercy to give them a map for this simple journey. These four unwritten (until now) rules will, if nothing else, save time.

Rule Number One: Call into question your way with words.

At the very beginning, suggest that your debts are beyond your capacity to describe. "It would be impossible to acknowledge adequately all the assistance I have received from scholars, libraries, and editors." Or, "I have accumulated more debts than I can possibly repay here." Or, "The fact that I did write such a book is nothing short of a miracle." All of these have been used by actual authors.

Any glossary for acknowledgments features two words, "indebted" and "invaluable," as in "I'm indebted to ——— for invaluable help photocopying the manuscript and coping with the many paper jams we encountered along the way." The phrase "constant encouragement and advice" is essential; "deeply grateful" is a must. Use "cheerful" to describe those who did the most menial chores for you.

At its height, a dedication or acknowledgment should demonstrate that your trouble with words originates in murky thought. Thus if you must venture out on your own, say something incomprehensible. Here we should acknowledge William Shatner's acknowledgment in *Tekwar*: "Ron Goulart, a wonderful writer, showed me the way out and showed me the way in to completing the novel."

Equally effective, state the obvious as if you believe it is an original idea, as did Paul C. Light in *The Tides of Reform: Making Government Work, 1945–1995*: "Writing the acknowledgments is always the most enjoyable part of a book project. Because I write mine only at the end, it is time to remember all the people and institutions who made the endeavor possible." In this way he has distinguished himself from all the authors who get the acknowledgments out of the way before doing any research.

Rule Number Two: Say something about the family, taking care to make it meaningless or patronizing.

Never mind, first, that you will appear to be worried that this is the only book you will ever do and thus have to get all your dedicating/acknowledging in right now and, second, that the original idea of acknowledgments was to thank people who had some connection with the book. Mention your relatives, even if those uncles, cousins, and brothers-in-law who watched football on your television and sucked up your beer never read anything more demanding than the *TV Guide*.

As an example, there is Danny Schechter's *The More You Watch, the Less You Know*: "Where should thanks begin and where can they end in a career that has been so collaborative, a life that has been so collegial?" He thanks his parents, his brother and his brother's "partner Sandy, my incredible daughter Sarah Debs, her mother Valeria, Denzel McKenzie and family, my Aunt Dana and Uncle George, and cousins Marc and David. And rippling out from that circle, there were neighborhood childhood cronies . . . ," arriving at last at "Nelson Mandela and my many friends in South Africa."

With really close relatives, such as your wife or kids, suggest that writing is an ordeal inflicted on the innocent by the crazed. "Most of the time my dedication to *Whistled Like a Bird* has left little of me to give back to them [i.e., the husband and kids]. . . . For two years Jack was 'Mr. Mom,' and rarely enjoyed a homecooked meal." (Obviously he wasn't much of a Mr. Mom.) Or, "Thanks for cooking dinner for yourselves when I was too caught up in my writing to stop long enough to feed you." Or, "Our children . . . I hope are unscarred by this endeavor."

The reader will want some explanation why your spouse hung around such a demented household. Accordingly, he/she should be made to seem quite passive, satisfied with mindlessly cleaning household toilets and, yet, brilliantly editing your copy. Thank your spouse, therefore, "for gentle admonitions and for patient and sympathetic support." Or, "I pay tribute to the patient forbearance of my wife during the long period of gestation and birth of this book."

From time to time, authors strike a different note to make a politically correct point. Eugene D. Genovese dedicated *Roll, Jordan, Roll* to his wife, who "did not type the manuscript, do my research, darn my socks, or do those other wonderful things one reads about in acknowledgments to someone 'without whom this book could not have been written.'" Similarly, James Scott in *The Moral Economy of the Peasant* said, "I wish to report that my wife and children, who have their own scholarly and other concerns, had virtually nothing to do with this volume. They were not particularly understanding or helpful when it came to research and writing but called me away as often as possible to the many pleasures of life in common. May it always remain so." Albert Paul Malvino has made a habit of tacking such dedications on his books, which deal with such energizing subjects as *Electronic Instrumentation Fundamentals*:

> To Joanna,
> My brilliant and beautiful wife
> without whom I would be nothing.

> She always comforts and consoles,
> never complains or interferes,
> asking nothing and endures all,
> and writes my dedications.

I have found this gambit tempting myself ("Regina N. Hamilton, who had other things to do . . ."). But don't become enamored with it. It is as trite as dedicating to your publisher and lacks adequate pretentiousness.

For models of pretentiousness, by the way, none is better than Simon Schama. Few historians can equal his affected writing. Characters in his books don't fall out of bed and *hit* their heads; they *concuss* themselves. He brings these prodigious skills to his book openings, a good example of which is *Citizens: A Chronicle of the French Revolution*: "Throughout the writing of the book my children, Chloë and Gabriel, and my wife, Ginny, endured far more in the way of uneven temper, eccentric hours and generally impossible behavior than they had any right to expect. In return I received from them love and tolerance in helpings more generous than I deserved. Ginny has throughout offered her infallible judgments on all kinds of questions about the book, from its argument to its design. If there is any one reader to whom all my writing is addressed, it is to her."

On reflection, you would think that such a dedication would prompt the family to concuss Schama. But no one seems to mind, including readers who apparently think that this demonstrates that Schama is a genuine writer.

Rule Number Three: Make the reader suspicious of your character.

Suggest that you are pushed around like a flabby sack of meal and could never amount to much on your own. "I might not have undertaken [or, finished] the project without the encouragement of ——." Or, "If I have been a stubborn and obtuse student at times, the fault has not been theirs." Or, thanks to my agent "for tracking me down and handing me an opportunity that rescued me from delusion and despair." I believe the book was dedicated to her psychoanalyst.

Sound defensive, hinting that you may be guilty of something. "The authors of this book were at primary school during the second World War," say the two German authors of *Hitler's Airwaves*, Horst J. P. Bergmeier and Rainer E. Lotz. "We had no direct experience of the operation of Nazi propaganda, nor of Germany's English-language radio propaganda more specifically." Besides, they were just taking orders.

Even better, show that you know the proper thing to do, but aren't going to do it. Marcella Hazan acknowledges that her husband's "name really belongs on the title page" of *The Classic Italian Cookbook*.

Rule Number Four: Appear to take responsibility for the book, then pass the buck.

Somewhere near the end of your acknowledgments you want to say that "The mistakes in this book are my own." Ensure, though, that everything that comes before buries the confession with the overwhelming impression that you had almost nothing to do with the contents of the book.

The formulation here is: "This book could not have been written without the help of my large family, including our distant Kentucky cousins who offered insights I had completely forgotten, and all the comrades who served with me in the Fifth Marine Regiment during the confusing final years of the Pacific Campaign."

For models, you could look to Kay Jane Holtz, who said, "It took a village—a village of colleagues, friends, and family—to raise this book from conviction to finished work" (*Asphalt Nation*). Or, Neal Ascherson, "Many people, living and dead, helped me to write this book" (*Black Sea*). It's always good to blame the dead for mistakes; they tell no tales. Or, copy James Michener, whose extended acknowledgments in *Iberia* concluded with a nod to fifteen people to whom he owes a "debt which can never be repaid." Or, Richard Whately, author of *Elements of Logic*, who in 1870 thanked the Right Reverend Edward Copleston, lord bishop of Llandaff, although "You yourself also, I have reason to believe, have forgotten the greater part of the assistance you have afforded in the course of conversations on the subject; as I have found, more than once, that ideas which I distinctly remembered to have received from you, have not been recognized by you when read or repeated."

Consider blaming God. Philip James Bailey offered his poem "Festus," published in 1839, to "My Heavenly Father, without whose inspiration this book could never have been written." The Reverend George M. Horne wrote that "Segregation is not only sanctioned, but demanded by both Old and New Testaments," then covered himself by dedicating *The Twentieth*

Century Cross to God. And the discredited Bible-thumper Jim Bakker seemed to admit he had sinned when he entitled his book *I Was Wrong,* but then incriminated "my best friend who never left me . . . (Jesus!)."

The Front Matter Hall of Fame

Authors come along from time to time who actually say something in the front matter that elevates the book. These are as rare as Umbrian white truffles.

The most common trait of these true literary geniuses is their search for the relevant and meaningful. Rather than awkwardly grafting a few words on the book, they shape it to the text as T. S. Eliot did in *The Waste Land*: "For Ezra Pound *il miglior fabbro* [the better craftsman]." Pound worked hard on Eliot's poem, reducing it to half its original length. Catholic Hans Küng underscored the ecumenical message of his book *The Church* by dedicating it to the archbishop of Canterbury. Journalist Vincent Sheean dedicated his "autobiography of a listener," *First and Last Love,* to opera star Madam Lotte Lehmann. Bernard Fall gave his *The Two Vietnams* "to the valiant and long-suffering Vietnamese—North and South." *The Secrets of Long Life* by pollster George Gallup and Evan Hill was "Dedicated to the 29,000 Americans Who Are Older Than 94 and to the 179,971,000 Who Hope to Be."

Graham Greene's lovely dedication to Réné and Phuong in *The Quiet American* did double duty. It remembered "the happy evenings I have spent with you in Saigon," the setting of the novel; at the same time it gave the author an occasion to protect his friends by disclaiming their similarity to characters in the book.

Antoine de Saint-Exupéry's *The Little Prince* is a book for youngsters and adults, vastly different audiences. But his charming dedication bridging the gap suggests that both generations can read it with pleasure.

> To Leon Werth
> I ask the indulgence of the children who may read this book for dedicating it to a grown-up. I have a serious reason; he is the best friend I have in the world. I have another reason: this grown-up understands everything, even books about children. I have a third reason: he lives in France where he is hungry and cold. He needs cheering up. If all these reasons are not enough, I will

dedicate the book to the child from whom this grown-up grew. All grown-ups were once children—although few of them remember it. And so I correct my dedication:

> To Leon Werth
> when he was a little boy

My friend Joel Swerdlow prosaically dedicated his first two books to his grandparents and parents. Then he read John Steinbeck's page-long dedication to *East of Eden*. It told a story, complete with dialogue. Swerdlow now tries to craft relevant dedications, as he did in *To Heal a Nation: The Vietnam Veterans Memorial* (written with Jan Scruggs). The long dedication to his brother, dying of leukemia, harmonized with the book. Here is the close: "His courage reaches out to all those who still endure the pains of war, to those whose lives will bear the burden of future wars, and to everyone whose life may be threatened by circumstances such as serious illness. 'Love each other now,' this courage says. 'Enjoy each day, and remember that acts of kindness and loyalty, no matter how small they may seem, can defeat life's most dirty devices.'"

Striving for relevance can spill over into those clarifying notes sometimes placed at the beginning of a book. Arthur C. Clarke's first major novel, *Childhood's End*, opened with "The opinions expressed in this book are not those of the author." He put this in because he did not agree with the book's premise that the stars are not for man.

Humorous books should have humorous front matter. Isaac Asimov and J. O. Jeppson understood this when they dedicated *Laughing Space* to the sense of humor. Mark Twain, who may have been the best of all at dedicating, knew how to put a sharp edge on the funny. He dedicated *Roughing It* to one of the characters in that autobiographical account: "To Calvin H. Higbie of California, an honest man, a genial comrade, and a steadfast friend, this book is inscribed by the author in memory of the curious time when we two were millionaires for ten days."

Twain lost money through foolish investments, but the experiences gave him grist for his lucrative writing. He wrote *Following the Equator* during an especially rocky financial time. When Standard Oil kingpin Henry Rogers helped him out, Twain repaid this kindness by dedicating the book to Rogers's son "with recognition of what he is, and apprehension of what he may become unless he forms himself a little more closely upon the model of the author."

Humor should not be so obscure, though, that we don't get it. Helen Cathcart, a well-known biographer of the British royals, frequently acknowledged "the help given by Harold Albert." In fact, there was no Mrs. Cathcart, only a Mr. Albert, who did the real writing. Unfortunately, we did not know this until Albert died in 1997 and his friends revealed it. Inside jokes are not polite.

Worse is the silly notion of dedicating the book to yourself, thinking that this is witty when in fact it is a tired trick. Charlotte Charke's *Narrative of the Life of Mrs. Charlotte Charke, Written by Herself* (1775), for instance, is "to herself. Madam, Tho' flattery is universally known to be the spring from which Dedications frequently flow, I hope I shall escape that odium so justly thrown on poetical petitioners, notwithstanding my attempt to illustrate those wonderful qualifications by which you have so eminently distinguish'd yourself, and give you a just claim to the title of a nonpareil of the age. . . ." It is far better to dedicate your book to your dog as E. H. H. Green did in *The Crisis of Conservatism, 1880–1914.* The dog, he pointed out, was more helpful and made more sense than any education minister in the previous fifteen years.

One of the most humorous specimens of front matter belongs to *1066 and All That,* by Walter Carruthers Sellar and Robert Julian Yeatman. Among other things it has this item: "Preface to Second Edition. A first edition limited to 1 copy and printed on rice paper and bound in buckboards and signed by one of the editors was sold to the other editor, who left it in a taxi somewhere between Piccadilly Circus and the Bodleian."

It also has an appropriate dedication: ". . . their thanks are also due to their wife, for not preparing the index wrong. There is no index."

As noted earlier, authors who use acknowledgments and dedications to please a spouse take a big chance. "Don't ever dedicate a book to your wife," some wag supposedly said. "The lead time getting it into print is too long." An author can wait patiently to be sure the marriage works out, but belated dedications lack enthusiasm. How happy could the wife of F. Marion Crawford be with his *Casa Braccio*: "This story, being my twenty-fifth novel, is affectionately dedicated to my wife"?

No one likes to hear someone rant in a dedication about a marriage that went bad. Baseball player Jim Bouton dedicated *Ball Four* to his wife ("For Bobbie, Thanks, coach"). Then divorce. With Nancy Marshall, the estranged wife of another jock, Bobbie Bouton wrote *Home Games: Two*

Baseball Wives Speak Out. Utterly fed up with men, they dedicated the book to their daughters. Marshall had no boys; but Bouton had two, to whom she said in the acknowledgments "may you someday understand."

The best solution to affairs of the heart that do not involve the author's spouse is to leave out names, suggesting the truest intimacy of all. Jack Higgins's dedication in *Memoirs of a Dance-Hall Romeo* belongs to this genre: "In grateful remembrance of all the girls of those far-off days, but especially the ones who said yes. . . ." Stephen M. Silverman dedicated *The Fox That Got Away: The Last Days of the Zanuck Dynasty at Twentieth Century-Fox* "to 'R,' a married woman. She knows who she is."

While it is smart to be cryptic when a suit for alienation of affection lies around the corner, it is otherwise bad form to give only the honored person's first names or initials, or to obscure his or her identity entirely. The person receiving the dedication cannot enjoy the full measure of presumably deserved glory. After all, if anonymity is so satisfying, why don't authors ask that book awards be given in secret?

Initials would not have worked with Kurt Vonnegut's *Welcome to the Monkey House,* dedicated to his friend and former editor "Knox Burger, ten days older than I am. He has been a very good father to me." (Mary Higgins Clark went one better in naming her child after her agent, Patricia Myrer.) Likewise, J. D. Salinger's dedication of *Franny and Zooey* is in top form for its sweetness and artfulness in honoring a named colleague: "As nearly as possible in the spirit of Matthew Salinger, age one, urging a luncheon companion to accept a cool lima bean, I urge my editor, mentor and (heaven help him) closest friend, William Shawn, *genius domus* of the *New Yorker,* lover of the long shot, protector of the unprolific, defender of the hopelessly flamboyant, most unreasonably modest of born great artist-editors, to accept this pretty skimpy-looking book."

Dedications and acknowledgments are also fine places to settle scores. One of the most famous examples of political score settling is in Edward Sexby's 1657 pamphlet, *Killing Noe Murder Briefly Discourst in Three Questions.* Tongue in cheek, it is "To his Highnesse Oliver Cromwell," whose assassination Sexby advocated: "To your Highnes justly belongs the honour of dying for the people, and it cannot choose but be an unspeakable consolation to you in the last moments of your life to consider, with how much benefit to the world you are like to leave it. . . . [Y]ou will then be indeed the deliverer of your country."

While treason works quite well for dedicatory invective, gratuitous nastiness can seem, well, gratuitous. Allen Drury's novel about Washington newspaperwomen, *Anna Hastings*, was too mean-spirited about what was then budding feminism: "Dedicated to all those vigorous, determined, indomitable and sometimes a wee bit ruthless Bettys, Barbaras, Helens, Nancys, Kays, Marys, Lizes, Deenas, Dorises, Mays, Sarahs, Evelyns, Mariannes, Clares, Frans, Naomis, Miriams, Maxines, Bonnies and the rest, who never cease to amuse, annoy and quite often out scoop their male colleagues of the Washington press corps. They've made it in a tough league—at a certain cost, of course; but they've made it."

The best victims for the dedicatory strappado are literary enemies or others associated with the book trade who have done harm. Lord Byron cheerfully dipped his pen into poison and dedicated *Don Juan* to a literary enemy, "Bob Southey! You're a poet—Poet-laureat . . ." In this seventeen-stanza dedication, he also mocked Coleridge and Wordsworth. In his *Veritas Inconcussa, or, A most certain Truth asserted that King Charles the First, was no Man of Blood, but a Martyr for his People*, Fabian Philipps made special mention of Henry Bell, who put out a pirated edition of the same book. (This was around the same time as Sexby's call for Cromwell's head.)

> For though you acknowledged to me and Mr. Newcomb the printer that you were not the author of it and understood not *Latine* and that other men of your trade can tell that you understood so little of English, as that you were formerly only a *Press-man* and had not abilities enough to be a Compositor; yet you could have the impudence in the printing and publishing of my book, to leave out half the Title and make some additional title of your own or some other man's composing and dedicate it to his Majesty as a mite of *Your* loyalty and say *that it was written in the midst of his and our sufferings*, and to make the book and price the bigger you had bound up with a list, very often before printed, of the names of the late Kings Tryers, yet, adding to that also as short history, as you call it, of his now Royal Majesty Charles the Second, you are found in the beginning thereof to use these words, *Having, I hope, sufficiently cleared his late Royal Majesty from that execrable sin of Blood guiltiness.*

Fourteen publishers turned down a book of e. e. cummings's poetry in the 1930s. Desperate, he borrowed three hundred dollars from his mother to subsidize its publication by printer S. A. Jacobs, a friend who owned a small publishing operation called the Golden Eagle Press. Tipping his hat to the houses that had rejected the book, cummings entitled the book *No*

Thanks. He repeated the title on the dedication page, listing below it the names of the fourteen publishers, set one below the other, to make a column of type that outlined a funeral urn. Withal, a fitting tribute to those who gave him grief.

Here is another archly worded acknowledgment: "Let me note, finally, that most of the research for this book was done in the libraries of Harvard University, the size of whose holdings is matched only by the school's determination to restrict access to them," wrote Alfie Kohn in *No Contest: The Case Against Competition.* "I am delighted to have been able to use these resources, and it hardly matters that I was afforded this privilege only because the school thought I was someone else."

In *The Silver Bullet,* a scholarly study of the martini, author Lowell Edmunds blames the editor of the *New York Times* book review, among others, for failing to run his author's query: "May these editors find that their gin has turned to gasoline or may they drink too many Martinis and then swallow a toothpick, as Sherwood Anderson is said to have done."

The author of *George Washington's Expense Account* strikes just the right balance. He notes three professors who were supposed to read the manuscript, but didn't. Then he does the supreme favor for his research assis-

NO
THANKS

TO
Farrar & Rinehart
Simon & Schuster
Coward-McCann
Limited Editions
Harcourt, Brace
Random House
Equinox Press
Smith & Haas
Viking Press
Knopf
Dutton
Harper's
Scribner's
Covici-Friede

e. e. cummings could have called his book of poetry *Thanks* and dedicated it to his mother. She gave him three hundred dollars to subsidize its publication. He chose instead to call it *No Thanks* and dedicated it to the fourteen publishers who rejected it. The publishers' names are arranged in the shape of a funeral urn.

"Initial Dedication to No Thanks," copyright 1935, copyright 1963, 1991 by the trustees for e. e. cummings Trust. Copyright 1978 by George James Firmage, from *Complete Poems: 1904–1962* by e. e. cummings, edited by George James Firmage. Reprinted by permission of Liveright Publishing Corporation

tant (and for fellow authors who may need research help): he gives her phone number.

The most felicitous openings, however, are those that conform to the original idea of front matter, to wit, to do yourself some good. The trick, of course, is to seek advantage without repeating tired phrases as if they were fresh.

Desmond Bagley plowed no new ground with *Landslide*, dedicating it to "all good booksellers," but did with *The Vivero Letter*, dedicated to two pubs he seemingly frequented. Charles Dickens singled out an unusual, but no less important friend of writers when he dedicated *The Pickwick Papers* to Thomas Talfourd. Talfourd had worked to strengthen the copyright laws. Louis L'Amour dedicated *The Iron Marshal* to the entire Bantam Books sales force, listed alphabetically. Lawrence Block dedicated *The Topless Tulip Caper* to the Edgar Allan Poe Award selection committee of the Mystery Writers of America and to three specific book reviewers—Barbara Bannon of *Publishers Weekly*, Newgate Callendar, the pseudonym of the *New York Times* mystery reviewer, and John Dickson Carr, whose reviews appeared in the *Ellery Queen Mystery Magazine*.

In *Lifemanship*, one of his books on clever ways to put the other fellow at a disadvantage, Stephen Potter paid just attention to "dedicationship." He favored such dedications as "To Phyllis, in the hope that one day God's glorious gift of sight may be restored to her." Never mind that Phyllis is the author's ninety-six-year-old great-grandmother and only short-sighted. Here is a way to win the hearts of reviewers.

In a handful of cases, authors have exercised their dedicatory privileges for unselfish ends. Sir Simon Degge dedicated *The Parson's Counsellor* to Bishop Woods of Lichfield, praising the cleric's restoration of a church. Woods had not yet done so, but apparently took the hint. After the book appeared, the work was done.

But authors should always prefer self-interested practicality and measure it out in dollars and cents. Thus, while authors are ill-advised to dedicate their books to extended families, it makes great sense to emulate Mary Stott's *Before I Go*, which lists 200 friends. Ditto Brian Lecomber's *Talk Down*, dedicated to 399 people whom he had apparently instructed in flying. Here we move from insecurity to brilliant marketing. Everyone likes to see his or her name in print. And dedicatees constitute an eager market for the book.

FOUR

A Guide to Good Book Behavior

—⟨∾⟩—

In which the author illuminates the
finer points of etiquette for those
who wish to go by the book.

—⟡—

Do Not make any undying promises [when writing love letters
to a gentleman]. . . . Do Not write anything that could be
personally—or legally—embarrassing. . . . Do Not write flowery words
that might confuse him. . . . Do Not make him feel guilty
for not writing; he probably hates the pen.
—ANNE OLIVER, A TYPICAL ETIQUETTE EXPERT
OFFERING TYPICAL LITERARY ADVICE.

—⟡—

Over the years, the Emily Posts of this world have told us how to manage the most minute aspects of life. Just look at the indexes of their books. Here are instructions on "cherries, eating"; "guest, breakage by"; "life-threatening disease, development of"; "napkins, blowing nose in"; "hugging, kissing, and air-kissing in greeting"; and the always troublesome "bug, handling appearance of, at table." But even though advice-giving has made prolific authors of these matrons of manners, they seldom comment on etiquette for writers and their readers. Judith Martin, better known as Miss Manners, occasionally drops in a few words about books in her books, but like the rest she mostly treats literature as if its only connection to the social graces comes in balancing volumes on one's head to develop good posture. Her *Miss Manners' Basic Training: Communication* is devoted almost exclusively to such topics as chain letters and "call waiting."

The etiquette people are unlikely to turn their attention to this void anytime soon. They are fully occupied instructing parents on dealing with their kids' live-in lovers, devising rules for the proper placement of tattoos, and reconsidering all the old guidelines on wearing baseball caps.

On the theory that someone has to do it, I volunteer. For while it is not yet apparent, books probably will become the number one social problem of the twenty-first century. Car manufacturers, linebackers, and movie stars—and their children who want to get even—are writing books, and so is virtually everyone else. They do not have the slightest guidance. So, as someone who knows as well as Emily Post does that the proper way to eat cherries is to stick your head in the bowl and chew, here are my definitive rules for polite writers and readers.

Parties, book celebration*

Book parties have all the potential of any decent wedding for happiness, bad feelings, and mayhem. You can be certain those on the fringes of friendship will feel insulted if they aren't invited and mildly irked if they are, for that means they have to waste a couple of hours and wrestle with

*Although etiquette authors say nothing about book parties, Anne Oliver in *Finishing Touches: A Guide to Being Poised, Polished, and Beautifully Prepared for Life* advises young ladies to use libraries for parties.

the question of bringing a present—in this case, cash to pay for the book. Close friends, many probably writers or would-be writers, will wish it was *their* party.

Book celebrations differ as widely as a wedding in Yankee Stadium does from a wedding in Saint Patrick's Cathedral. Many book signings are informal, often held in bookstores during the lunch hour. Bookstore parties held at the end of the day frequently have food and invitations, but also welcome browsing customers. Publishers who want to give a newsworthy send-off to a book stage gala get-togethers with star-studded guest lists. When Random House hosted a bash for Nobel Prize winner Toni Morrison's *Paradise* in 1998, 350 people attended, many of them celebrities. At the other end of the spectrum are private parties. While most authors welcome the opportunity to glorify themselves and their literary offspring, some authors actually throw parties for other people. William J. Caunitz, author of *One Police Plaza,* gives parties for his publisher's staff, including the receptionist. The cost of parties a publisher gives for an author typically runs from one thousand to five thousand dollars.

The most common book party calamity is low turnout. On one occasion, a bookstore manager recalls, the only people to show up were the author's wife and the publisher's representative, whom the author had not met. Feeling sorry for the writer, the rep posed as a guest.

Like Christmas parties, book parties lend themselves to morning-after regrets. Susan Richman, former vice-president and director of publicity at Macmillan, recalls getting caught up in a festive party she arranged for Ken McAuliffe's *The Great American Newspaper: The Rise and Fall of the Village Voice.* Although she could have all the free copies of the book she wanted, Richman bought one. McAuliffe autographed it with "Dear Susan, you'll regret it in the morning, but I love you tonight."

"You know what?" Richman says. "It was true."

To keep regrets and misunderstandings to a minimum, remember:

• If you are an author, you don't put on a book party for yourself anymore than you would give yourself a surprise party. Normally your publisher does it. But if that isn't possible: "Find someone else to throw it for you," says Nancy Kahan, "It could be your mother." A former nun with the Sisters of Charity (she thought about missionary work), Kahan has been called the Pearl Mesta of books. "The week after I left the convent I gave a party," she says.

• Protect yourself from your fans. Everyone is supposed to kiss the bride, but a few admirers always want more. They back the author into a corner, out of reach of guests who want to give quick, polite congratulations and then head home. When books are for sale, the author can sit behind a table. A publisher's or bookstore representative should stand guard, and if necessary the author can follow the example of crime novelist Patricia Cornwell. When big crowds come, she has half a dozen bodyguards to keep order.

As always, there is room for exceptions, especially for exceptional people such as the legendary Kiki. A French celebrity in the years between World Wars I and II, she acted in films, painted, posed nude for her lover, the photographer Man Ray, and wrote her memoirs. At a Saturday night signing event in a Paris bookstore on Boulevard Raspail, Kiki gave autographs and kisses to all who purchased a copy.

• Feel free to build a party around a theme in the book, no matter how tacky. To celebrate the publication of *The Encyclopedia of Bad Taste*, the HarperCollins publicity director staged a bad taste party at the American Booksellers Association in Las Vegas—a city that epitomizes bad taste. The director rented Caesar's Palace and filled it with Fuzzy Dice, Archie Bunker look-alikes, and Spam hors d'oeuvres. To celebrate Jon Krakauer's *Into the Wild*, its publisher erected a climbing wall that guests could scale. Anne Rice works hard to develop her persona as a Gothic novelist. Her New Orleans home is decorated with skulls, and she sells T-shirts stamped with a scan of her brain. In keeping with her image, she arrived at a book party in a coffin carried by a hearse.

Be careful of theme parties getting out of hand. One cautionary tale is a party for Jack Hanna and his *Monkeys on the Interstate: And Other Tales from America's Favorite Zookeeper*. Hanna brought two baby orangutans, a baby wallaby, an enormous toad, and a number of giant African cockroaches. The monkeys preferred the bookshelves to the jungle gym that had been provided. Their diapers leaked.

Yet another cautionary tale involves Michael Moore's book *Downsize This!* Moore, famous for his hilarious anti–General Motors movie *Roger and Me*, said he was looking forward to promoting his anti–

corporate America book in Borders Group megastores across the country. Things went sour when he turned signings into theme parties: He told bookstore employees they should unionize and, according to Borders executives, advised patrons to buy his book elsewhere.

• Don't forget how you got to the party in the first place. Naturally you want to celebrate your new book. And party hopping is thrilling and ego boosting. But this is only one aspect of your business. If you write full time, get back to the typewriter. No new books, no new parties. If you write on the side, remember where your bread is buttered.

Albert "Chain Saw Al" Dunlap is an object lesson in what happens when one forgets these rules. Dunlap, known for his ruthless management style, characterized by the firing of numerous employees, was unhorsed himself as chairman and CEO of Sunbeam Corporation in 1998. His board was unhappy with the company's flagging finances and blamed Dunlap all the more because those woes did not deter him from promoting his new book, *Mean Business.* Dunlap received the pink slip shortly before flying to London for a book signing.

• If you are a guest at a party, don't expect to have intimate conversations with authors, especially when the parties are big. When writers are doing their best to be polite to everyone, they cannot think deep thoughts. Louis D. Rubin, Jr., an author and former publisher of Algonquin Books, recalls a woman who kept asking him at a party, "Who am I?" At length, she explained that they had gone to grade school together. Rubin thought she had changed a great deal. One bookstore proprietor notes that street people often come to book parties for the food. He really doesn't mind (after all, the publisher is paying), but doesn't like it when gatecrashers start an intense, loud argument with the author to convince people they are bona fide guests.

• Finally, on buying and selling books at parties: A cozy gathering in someone's home is no place to sell books—period. Written invitations to parties in public places can note "books will be available for purchase." Only a philistine is surprised not to get a free copy, and only socially stunted authors expect all their friends to buy their books. Do not say, as a friend once did after a celebration for one of my books, "At your party, I bought other people's books."

Dress code, the book jacket and other book garb

For years, the British shaped fashions of the mind. Proper institutions of higher learning had Oxford-like ivy-covered walls. Proper authors seemed to have stepped off some soggy moor. They wore tweeds and, if male, had a pipe. They had perky retrievers close at hand, apparently fresh from pursuing badgers.

That image is passé. The British influence in arts and letters has waned recently. Britain's Margaret Thatcher, who gutted her nation's university system, is not much of a reader, and her successor as prime minister, John Major, never went to college. As a result, Americans have had a chance to think for themselves when it comes to dressing for their books. In the process, they have concluded that smoking is bad for your health and tweeds don't make much sense without moors.

My highly scientific perusal of book jacket photos lying about the office of the *Chicago Tribune* book review editor a couple years ago showed a pronounced tilt toward the come-as-you-are look for authors. A full 71 percent of the men were dressed in sweaters, T-shirts, and sports shirts; one percent were bare-chested. The other 28 percent wore ties, 10 percent of which were loose. Two-thirds of the women dressed casually, one-third dressed for business. The most formal was Judith Martin, who as Miss Manners is supposed to look that way.

The only constant pictorial element seems to be dogs. Anyone inspecting book jackets' photographs of authors for clues as to what lies inside would conclude that the majority of literary output is devoted to kennel management. Which gets us to rule *número uno* for publicity photos: What you wear—and what you have with you in the publicity photo— should reflect the contents of the book or "the real you," which in many people's minds are the same thing. Judy Maguire, a good friend and avid reader of trash, always looks at book jackets. "Hey, does this guy look like a mystery writer?" Or if it is a racy novel, "Okay, how did this woman get her material?"

Danielle Steel understands this point of view. She fancies herself a private person but poses for sexy publicity photos. Basketball star Dennis Rodman's *Bad As I Wanna Be* is a pitiful specimen of a book. But his book signing at a Barnes & Noble on New York's Fifth Avenue was, well, fitting: a lacy white wedding dress and veil over his orange hair. With

Rodman dressed for success, the chain reported a 35 percent increase in sales the week following the event. In a photo for *Nancy Reagan: The Unauthorized Biography*, author Kitty Kelley sat amid rows of files. Obviously she had produced a well-researched, reliable book. Brown-haired Olivia Goldsmith sometimes poses wearing a golden wig, but in a sense, that is honest. Her books, such as *Bestseller*, are to literature what peroxide blondes are to beauty.

Although sexy photos are not a bad idea, authors need to supervise their photos with the same intensity they do the editing of their words. Author Caryl Rivers opted for a black cocktail dress with rhinestones and a décolletage to appear on the dust jacket of her thriller *Indecent Behavior*. The publisher, apparently missing the point, cropped the cleavage. Rivers subsequently decided the original shot wasn't appropriate for magazines

Rule *número uno* for book garb is to wear something that reflects the contents of your book. This rule applies both to the book jacket photo and when you attend you book signing. The book that basketball star Dennis Rodman is signing is his memoir entitled *Bad As I Wanna Be*.

Jim Estrin/NYT Pictures

and other mass media. To correct the problem, she painted a black turtleneck on the photo with water colors.

Jill Krementz, a leading photographer of authors as well as a writer herself, likes the idea of including spouses and children in photos. But my rule is the same for kids, dogs, and other living things. No animal belongs in a picture unless it figures into the book. Ronald Parker was quite right to pose with a sheep in *The Sheep Book: A Handbook for the Modern Shepherd.* You should not show off your new baby unless the book is about pregnancy or childcare.

Krementz is correct in fretting over the artistic quality of book jacket photos. As she notes, spouses, children, and friends often end up taking the pictures. This is sometimes a result of the author's errant desire to give family members a piece of the action. More often, publishers are too cheap to pay for professional photographers. "I think that writers deserve better," says Krementz, articulating rule *número dos:* Polite publishers pay for decent photographs.

A final rule is that you are not obliged to have a photo. Larry McMurtry and Carlos Castañeda avoid them. Publisher Michael Korda says Castañeda "thinks the camera steals your soul." While that sounds a bit primitive, not having a picture does add a certain mystique. Novelist Thomas Pynchon is so reticent that his last known portrait reportedly appeared in his college yearbook. Many years ago, an editor who was unaware of Pynchon's camera-shyness sent a photographer to his seedy dwelling in Mexico City. The photographer found a man in the room who said Pynchon was out and would be back later. When the photographer returned, Pynchon had cleared out. Pynchon, says one of his editors, is "a publicist's dream." *

Autographs, giving and getting

Thomas Hardy considered autograph hunters noxious pests. He tossed the books they sent him into a large room. Mark Twain objected that writing of any kind was work; requesting his autograph was like asking

---

*Still, shy authors shouldn't complain when someone tries to take their picture, as Pynchon did when a surreptitiously taken photo of him and his son appeared in the London *Times Sunday Magazine.* Outraged, his publisher told the *Times* it wanted the negatives. Authors cry out for attention; they cannot complain when they get it.

"a doctor for one of his corpses to remember him by." J. D. Salinger would not autograph a copy of his book for a little girl who also resided in the small town of Cornish, New Hampshire. In one of the few interviews Salinger has ever given since moving to the town, he told a young writer that autographs were "a meaningless gesture."

Edmund Wilson personified the image of the author who is rude and proud of it. Written requests for autographs—and just about anything else—received this pro forma response:

> Edmund Wilson regrets that it is impossible for him to: read manuscripts, write articles or books to order, write forwards or introductions, make statements for publicity purposes, do any kind of editorial work, judge literary contests, give interviews, conduct educational courses, deliver lectures, give talks or make speeches, broadcast or appear on television, take part in writers' congresses, answer questionnaires, contribute to or take part in symposiums or "panels" of any kind, contribute manuscripts for sales, donate copies of his books to libraries, autograph books for strangers, allow his name to be used on letterheads, supply personal information about himself, supply photographs of himself, supply opinions on literary or other subjects.*

Hardy, Twain, Salinger, and Wilson were wrong. Salinger may believe autographs are meaningless, but the little girls who ask for one apparently don't think so. Readers may be strangers to writers; but authors survive by inviting themselves into people's homes. The least they can do is scribble their names in the host's book. Party-giver Nancy Kahan had the right idea about her book, *Entertaining for Business.* "They were paying forty dollars. I was so grateful. I would have written four pages."

Many people buy books as investments. Signing the book can add value. Nixon's *Memoirs* was available in an unsigned $19.95 edition. There also were two autographed editions, one selling for $50 and a presentation copy, limited to 2,500, for $250. No one understood the economics of book collecting better than the New Hampshire bookseller who bought multiple copies of Calvin Coolidge's *Autobiography* when it came out in 1929. During a signing at the book department of Boston's Jordan Marsh

---

*For an example of someone who takes just the opposite approach, there is the late Leon Edel. Edel, the editor of Wilson's papers, provided me with the above quote when he could have been working on his own memoirs.

Company, the entrepreneur kept returning to the line, bringing a fresh copy each time to the former president. "Sir, will you please inscribe it to me? My name is Robert Frost . . . John Steinbeck . . . John Dos Passos . . . etc." He held the books until the early 1960s, when he began selling them.

Of course, some people may not want an author to mark their book. Thus, while authors must sign if asked, they should not grab someone's newly purchased book and say, Here, let me sign that for you. Writers who don't recognize that distinction deserve the comment about the author in the film *Only Two Can Play*: His unsigned books are the rare ones.

The most valuable inscription from a resale point of view is generally the author's autograph sans personal comments. But when more than a signature is requested, a simple "Best Wishes" is always safe. Witty, if brief, is good, too. Late Chicago columnist Mike Royko gave a copy of *Sez Who, Sez Me* to each of his research assistants, each with the identical inscription: "You were the best. Don't tell the others." Trite or smarmy comments are bad form. Richard Halliburton, the giddy 1920s and 1930s travel writer, specialized in these. At a signing for one of his books, attended mostly by local matrons, he wrote, "Here's all that's fine, books and old wine, boys be divine to ———."

Should some presumptuous person request a highly personal inscription, the author—being a writer—should feel free to inscribe something clever, for example, "To Sally, the woman with dreams," rather than "To Sally, the woman of my dreams," as she requested. Book buyers who do not know the author should also be certain that they are asking the right person to autograph the book. A story has it that Spaniards often approached an Ernest Hemingway look-alike living in their country. Always accommodating, he would scrawl the following on the flyleaf of their Hemingway books: "With best wishes, I am not—Ernest Hemingway."

Other dos and don'ts of book signing are:

• When attending bookstore signings, autograph seekers should not bring a book they bought elsewhere or try to get a signature on a photo or some other nonliterary item. When the line of people extends from the store to across the street, autograph seekers should not ask authors for a long inscription.

• Judith Martin, Miss Manners, insists books should be signed on the dedication page. Hats off to her for at least having an opinion on the subject, but lots of authors think any place in the front makes sense.

• Don't ask an author to sign a book if you are particular about handwriting. When Elizabeth Crook came out with a first novel, *The Raven's Bride*, she worked hard on perfecting her inscription, which included the date, the city, and "with my regards." The first woman in line at her first book signing party looked down at the signature and said, "It didn't come out too good, did it?"

• Just because an author has given you an autograph, does not mean he or she wants to become a pen pal or hear about *your* book. Famous authors get more mail than they can handle, much of it from Begging–Letter Writers, as Charles Dickens called them.* If authors don't reply, just be glad they aren't like New York Yankee Don Mattingly, who responded to letters from my young son with an invitation to join his fan club for $12.95, about the same price as a paperback book.

• Don't ask an author who is a close friend to sign a book if you plan to sell it to a used-book store. Writers, like dogs, are always hunting their own scent and are likely to find that you have dumped their book for a few pennies. When Paul Theroux discovered that his longtime friend V. S. Naipaul was selling off autographed copies of his books, he was hurt. In revenge, he wrote *Sir Vidia's Shadow*, relating what a bad fellow Naipaul was.

Conversation, with author

Etiquette is largely devoted to saying things that don't come naturally, unless you are a congenital liar. That's why in the case of "life-threatening disease, development of," one does not exclaim, You look awful! These fictions

---

*The Begging–Letter Writer, Dickens said, hectored him always and for all things. He "has besieged my door, at all hours of the day and night; he has fought my servant; he has lain in ambush for me, going out and coming in. . . . He has fallen sick; he has died, and been buried; he has come to life again, and again departed from this transitory scene; he has been his own son, his own mother, his own baby, his idiot brother, his uncle, his aunt, his aged grandfather. He has wanted a great coat, to go to India in." One supplicant asked him for a donkey.

are essential to polite book conversation, especially when addressing the ever-present, though sometimes unspoken question: "Did you read my book?"

Reading your friend's book is a nice thing to do, but not required. You simply may not be interested in the history of road salt. On the other hand, saying outright that you haven't read the book is a royal faux pas. Ad libbing in hopes the author will be fooled is all right, provided you keep in mind that authors are alert to every nuance. Marcel Proust once lamented "about a book published only a few months earlier, [that] people never speak to me without mistakes proving either that they've forgotten it or that they haven't read it."

For similar reasons, some other comments are also *verboten*. Don't try to get away with "The book was interesting." Car accidents are interesting. Just as bad is, "Hey, I saw your book the other day." One writer I know used to wait for the obvious next line: "I liked it." Now he doesn't bother. He just says, "Thank you."

The best approach is the literary equivalent of air-kissing. You say that you haven't read the book yet, but it's on the top of your list. Or you're saving it for summer when you can enjoy it. Or simply avoid the question altogether. Dianne Donovan, former book review editor at the *Chicago Tribune,* suggests saying: "I understand it's a fine piece of work."

A friend of mine has a particularly clever technique. He buys the book and calls a few days later. "I've just read the first chapter. It's great." Good manners prevent the author from pressing the issue. Authors who keep talking about their books are as bad as parents who talk incessantly about their children.

Finally, don't ask how the book is doing. Authors will feel the need to explain why the book is not a best seller or describe all the wounds inflicted by obtuse reviewers or lazy publicity staffs.

The one exception to this dissembling is when you have gone to the trouble of reading the book. In that case, you are entitled to discuss it critically. If the author doesn't respect that, too bad.

Lying, acceptability of, under certain circumstances

Clare Boothe Luce sent herself flowers at the office and wrote a favorable unsigned review of her first book, *Stuffed Shirts,* for *Vanity Fair.* Walt Whitman mailed copies of *Leaves of Grass* together with unsigned favorable reviews, which he had written himself. This is not bad manners in the way most people are trained to see it. It is quite all right to lie about your book, but, as usual, you should observe the rules.

The preferred approach is to have your publisher lie for you. This is as much the publisher's responsibility as is printing the book. The publisher writes the overblown dust jacket copy, which says this is the greatest book since *Gone With the Wind*. You ensure that you are too busy writing the next book to read carefully what the publicist has drafted and give the copy a hasty approval. This way you have plausible denial.

The publisher should also choose the blurbs for the dust jacket. This is so even when these are solicited from your friends, who cannot refuse to help because they soon may want a few nice words from you.

You, in turn, do not have to read friends' books when it comes time to return the blurbing favor. You are expected to do the lying yourself, however, and the thicker you lay it on the better. (Laying it on is often easier if you haven't read the book, which might allow some doubts to creep in.) This is acceptable because you appear to be lying for someone else. (Of course, you are doing yourself a favor at the same time. An arresting bit of praise is more likely to be used on a book's cover. Getting your name on the back of someone's book is almost as good as getting it on the front of your own—and easier than doing all that research and writing.) The standard approach to blurbing is to write a paragraph or two, heaped with well-turned phrases, and give the publicist permission to use whatever parts work best.

Getting caught in a lie is embarrassing, but does not necessarily ruin the book. Derek Goodwin wrote *Just Killing Time* under a pseudonym (Derek Van Arman) and submitted it along with laudatory, albeit phony, blurbs from the likes of John Le Carré and Joseph Wambaugh. A bidding war among eight publishers ensued, resulting in Simon & Schuster offering Goodwin $920,000. When the putative blurbers denied they had authored the blurbs ("I'd never be that effusive over anything, even my own books," Wambaugh said), Goodwin said he had been set up. Simon & Schuster ducked the book, but Dutton purchased the rights and published it not long afterward, giving Goodwin a $600,000 advance, which was not far below the Simon & Schuster offer. The *Washington Post* reviewer observed that parts of the book bore a strong resemblance to scenes in books by other authors ("Let us simply say that *Just Killing Time* is derivative") and that it was nevertheless "often extremely exciting and considerably better" than other books in the genre.

Putting your name on a book ghosted by someone else is utterly mendacious, pervasive, and also entirely acceptable. Even professional communicators—for instance, television anchors—use ghostwriters to write about their own lives. The practice is so widespread that famous people hire ghosts not only to write their memoirs but also novels and works of history. Ghosts have even been known to hire ghosts.

The public doesn't blink. It doesn't feel cheated when Charles Barkley or O. J. Simpson find it convenient to say they were misquoted in their autobiographies. "I should have been more responsible," Barkley said, "and read it before anything went out." Nor do readers care that Sarah Ferguson, the duchess of York, brags that she could talk knowledgeably about her book on Victoria despite the fact she hadn't read it.

Even so, there are limits. Milli Vanilli, as Rob Pilatus and Fabrice Morvan called themselves, did not get in trouble because they lip-synced their songs. You might even argue that they didn't get in trouble for lying about it. What brought them down was believing their lies. They didn't thank anyone at all when they received their Grammy Award for "Girl You Know It's True." Then they lobbied to do the singing themselves on a new album, after which they went on a 108-city lip-sync tour. Things started to fall apart when, during one performance, the audio equipment stuck.

Maureen Dean, the wife of Watergate figure John Dean, learned a similar lesson. She told a *Washington Post* reporter how her maid sharpened pencils each day so Dean could labor until exhausted on *Washington Wives*. Irritated, her ghost materialized. "I read this," Lucianne Goldberg said publicly, "and I am thinking, I wore a window in the seat of three big flannel mommy nightgowns sitting at my computer in an Upper West Side apartment with kids screaming and a basset hound howling, while she's telling reporters about her pencils and foolscap. Talk about tacky." Ms. Dean should have done what she did so well when her husband was hauled in for the congressional hearings on Watergate: remain glamorously silent.

Acknowledging your ghostwriters feebly is not much better. Lee Iacocca tucked William Novak's name in the end of his thank-yous, calling him "my invaluable collaborator." Iacocca was effusive in thanking the secretaries who worked for him over his thirty-eight-year career. Bill Cosby's first two books, beginning with *Fatherhood*, did not have a word of thank-you to the real daddy of the book, ghostwriter Ralph Schoenstein. By the time book three appeared, Schoenstein received only "warm thanks."

The worst approach to acknowledging those who have helped you is to follow the example of Donald Trump. Trump wanted his ghost to help pay for a $160,000 book party. No one should expect ghostwriters to act as if the book is their own if they don't receive half of everything, including space on the cover.

Bookseller, treatment of

Erik Barnum is the senior member of my informal bookstore brain trust. He formerly managed Sidney Kramer Books in Washington, D.C., but now lives in Vermont, where the air is cleaner and the egos smaller. His tales of impoliteness outdo Homer's *Odyssey*. He vividly recalls one publication party where a guest snapped her fingers and shouted "waiter"; another guest went behind the counter with the cash register, hauled out more wine, and began to serve it.

Bookstore clerks who take low-paying jobs to rub shoulders with writers find themselves instead pouring cheap wine for nonreading party-goers. When authors drop by, it is not to discuss Dante. They want to see how prominently their books are being displayed. A friend of mine remembers seeing Lillian Hellman in Doubleday's bookstore on Fifty-third Street in New York, berating the help for not displaying her books in the window. One Washington, D.C., policy wonk came by Barnum's store to ask why his book was not placed on a higher shelf. Because your name begins with Q, dummy, Barnum thought to himself.

With those episodes in mind:

• Leave the clerks alone. And while you are at it, be nice to the handlers who helped arrange your book tour. This is not only because it is nice to be nice. It is also, as my mother-in-law has pointed out to me, smart to be nice.* Escorts attending the American Booksellers Association annual convention have held their own event on the side to bestow the

---

*The full quote from the mother-in-law, for those who would like it, is "It is nice to be smart, but smart to be nice."

Golden Dartboard Award to the worst author clients. Past winners include Shirley MacLaine, Jeffrey Archer, Martha Stewart, and Faye Dunaway. Naturally, this little gathering has generated unfavorable press attention.

• If you don't like placement of your book on the shelf and you are a name author, just tough it out. A British friend of mine once spotted James Clavell in a New York City bookstore, moving his book to a different location. My pal thought that unsporting, and it lowered his estimation of the man. If you are a no-name author, feel free to sneak in and move it quietly to a better location. Or change your name to A. A. Aaron.

Books, giving as gifts

If you wonder why Americans seem so unread, look no farther than those etiquette manuals' advice on gift giving.

The Amy Vanderbilt Complete Book of Etiquette, revised by Letitia Baldridge, only gets excited about giving books to babies, who can't read. This enthusiasm is born in the idea that the infant will wreck pages (rather than destroy something truly valuable "like ashtrays and ornaments"), providing parents with an excuse for meting out firm injunctions against destroying property.

Only occasionally do the others mention books as suitable presents for children out of the toddler stage. An even more recent version of Amy Vanderbilt's etiquette book, by Nancy Tuckerman and Nancy Dunnan, recommends "an array of bright-colored socks" and ankle weights. Nothing is said about books. Emily Post likes video games and posters as birthday presents for teenage boys. When daughters and sons graduate, you might give them a book, but stay away from history or literature. The preferred book, we are told, is *Black's Law Dictionary,* or some other professional volume that will help them acquire property they won't want *their* kids to deface.

For someone in the hospital, Tuckerman and Dunnan recommend, along with worry beads, "a current best-seller." A book on the subject of a person's favorite sport is a possible gift, Vanderbilt-Baldridge say, although they seem partial to "a golf utility brush." Ms. Post says that full-fledged adults might receive a book, but again, nothing serious. For nuns, light novels are okay, but Ms. Post's preferred present for women of the cloth is "a check, cash, or a gift certificate to a local department store."

I protest. For this I blame my family, starting with my grandfather, an eccentric Englishman who invented a version of the modern golf-tee though he never swung a golf club. He didn't wrap presents at Christmas; he just sent me down to his book-packed basement to pick out an armful. My father followed the tradition of giving books. He gave me a book the day I was born. That leather-bound copy of *The Three Musketeers*, beckoning from the shelf as I broke ashtrays, was an incentive to learn to read.

So, give books whenever possible. Normally, you should give a book someone else has written, but there are exceptions. You should give *your* book to people who gave you useful criticism or wrote a dust jacket blurb. You may give your book to someone who asks for it—but then there's another regulation: Readers don't ask for an author's book. If you aren't willing to buy it—and make both of you happy—then stick to golf utility cleaners.

Book promotion, by friends and relatives

While you do not have to buy your friend or relative's book, it is nice if you do, and even better if you help promote it a bit. Like all matters of etiquette, of course, this is not as straightforward as one might think. The aunt who says that she buys two copies of your book, one to keep and one to lend to friends, is hurting sales. She should shame her chums into buying the book themselves.

Robert Cullen is the author of *Soviet Sources*, a thriller about a Moscow-based foreign correspondent, which he once was. He proudly tells people what his sister did to mobilize support for his book. The sister, who had worked in the book publishing business, sent a note to all their siblings in North Carolina, Philadelphia, and Washington, D.C. She instructed them to buy six copies of the novel to present to friends and libraries, purchasing each at a different store. While in the store, they were to make certain that each book was displayed face out, not spine out. If the book was not available at a bookstore, they were to urge the clerk to stock copies. They were not to use credit cards, she warned, which would reveal they were related. Finally, they should carry the book at all times on public transportation with the cover showing.

Authors, would-be, asking for help

You may send a copy of your manuscript to a famous writer in hopes he or she will take the time to read it and give you free advice. But how much work are you doing for free these days? "If authors read all the manuscripts sent them, they would never be able to do anything else," Edmund Wilson said. "The author of a manuscript who desires advice should send it to a publisher or an editor: they pay people to do this kind of work." Wilson was correct about this.

Thank-you notes, to reviewers

Whenever it occurs to you to thank a reviewer for doing you a good turn, think of this story.

In the early part of the century Arthur Hungerford Pollen invented a superior gunnery control system for the British navy. He did not get the Royal Navy to use his system until he had won over Frederick C. Ogilvy, one of the most respected gunnery officers in the navy. Pollen, wanting to express his thanks, sent Ogilvy a basket of oysters. Unfortunately, the oysters were tainted. Ogilvy died a few weeks later.

As noted elsewhere in this book, critics are inclined to write nice reviews. Nevertheless they fancy themselves independent. They don't like it when someone suggests they are pussycats, and they become self-conscious when a grateful author sends them a case of Châteauneuf du Pape. So, don't kill off their kindness with some of your own.

Illness, development of

No list of dos and don'ts can cover every eventuality. But if there is any cardinal rule for authors, who spend large portions of their life alone with their thoughts, it is this: Worry constantly that your public is watching. That might possibly prevent the embarrassment that befell novelist Kaye Gibbons.

During a public reading in Anson County, North Carolina, Ms. Gibbons began to feel queasy. She politely excused herself from the warm auditorium and retreated to the washroom. Most would agree that she should have taken off her portable microphone before throwing up.

FIVE

Inglorious Employment

———◈◈◈———

In which it is shown that book
reviewing is so bad because so many forces
drive so few critics to be so nice.

We may go so far as to say that, while the critic is *permitted* to play, at times, the part of the mere commentator—while he is *allowed,* by way of merely *interesting* his readers, to put in the fairest light the merits of his author—his *legitimate* task is still, in pointing out and analyzing defects and showing how the work might have been improved to aid the general cause of Letters, without undue heed of the individual literary man.

—Edgar Allan Poe

The new generation isn't really critics. They're literary reporters.

—Robert Straus

In fact, "greatness" is so common in current reviews that the only way left anyone to become a distinguished writer is to be a bad one.

—James T. Farrell

The nineteenth-century poet Thomas Moore challenged a critical reviewer, Francis Jeffrey, to a duel with pistols at dawn. It probably would have come to nothing even if the police had not arrived in time to arrest them. Both authors were unskilled in the use of firearms. Besides, as rumor had it, the duelists had taken the sensible precaution of showing up with unloaded pistols. All of which is as it should have been. The weapon of choice for authors and their critics is the pen. Blood flows copiously without anyone dying. The quarrels may rage for years as one adversary and then the other sallies forth to strike a blow that enriches literature.

There was no greater master of insult and injury than Lord Byron. While writing a satire of contemporary poets to be called *English Bards,* he spied a sour review of one of his earlier poems in the *Edinburgh Review,* edited by the ever-provocative Jeffrey. Seeking revenge, Byron expanded his work to *English Bards and Scotch Reviewers.* Rather than using words derringer-like to take out the reviewer, he sprayed his anger around like a machine-gunner in a gangland shoot-out. Among "the scribbling crew" he wounded were Samuel Coleridge ("To turgid ode and tumid stanza dear") and William Wordsworth ("The meanest object of the lowly group"). He ridiculed the Moore-Jeffrey duel. ("Can none remember that eventful day / That ever glorious almost fatal fray / When LITTLE's leadless pistols met his eye, / And Bow-street Myrmidons

"An author's works are public property," Lord Byron said in the preface to his scathing *English Bards and Scotch Reviewers;* "He who purchases may judge, and publish his opinion if he pleases; and the authors I have endeavoured to commemorate may do by me as I have done by them." Knowing that critics would, indeed, settle scores with him, Byron left England. Safe in Greece, he bought a fancy Albanian get-up, and Thomas Phillips painted him in it.

Portrait of George Gordon Byron, Sixth Baron Byron, by Thomas Phillips, Courtesy of the National Portrait Gallery, London

stood laughing by?")* In one small section of the poem, he mowed down more than a half-dozen fellow writers, including the earl of Carlisle, who had been his guardian and to whom he had dedicated *Hours of Idleness.* Byron's change of heart stemmed from the earl's declining to present Byron when it was time for the young poet to take his seat in the House of Lords.

> Let Moore still sigh; let Strangford steal from Moore;
> And swear that Camoëns can sing such notes of yore;
> Let Hayley hobble on, Montgomery rave,
> And godly Grahame chant a stupid stave;
> Let sonneteering Bowles his strains refine,
> And whine and whimper to the fourteenth line;
> Let Stott, Carlisle, Matilda, and the rest
> Of Grub-street, and of Grosvenor-place the best,
> Scrawl on, till death release us from the strain,
> Or Common Sense assert her rights again.†

"An author's works are public property," Byron said in the poem's preface; "he who purchases may judge, and publish his opinion if he pleases; and the authors I have endeavoured to commemorate may do by me as I have done by them." In other words, he knew that the fight had only begun. To avoid the scathing reviews of *English Bards and Scotch Reviewers,* Byron left for Constantinople.

"Nothing is so exhilarating as being shot at without result," author and prime minister Winston Churchill once observed. Not only do literary shoot-outs give authors an exciting diversion from the daily solitude of writing; readers have a good deal of fun as well. Feelings are hurt, but as Lady Sneerwell said in *The School for Scandal,* "There's no possibility of being witty without a little ill nature." Besides, such quarreling is more than mere mud wrestling. It has a higher purpose.

---

* Moore once used the pen name Thomas Little.

†He also noted of reviewers:

> And shall we own such judgment? no—as soon
> Seek roses in December, ice in June;
> Hope constancy in wind, or corn in chaff;
> Believe a woman or an epitaph,
> Or any other thing that's false, before
> You trust in critics, who themselves are sore.

Reviewers cannot single-handedly change the course of civilization. Negative reviews for Karl Marx's *Das Kapital* did not forestall the Russian Revolution and the Cold War. Nor did his collaborator, Frederick Engels, ensure the rise of communism by writing positive reviews.* That would be too much to expect from a reviewer and, really, not in our best interest. Ideally, we do not want critics to command. We want them to have the power of suggestion. Every good work of nonfiction presents arguments that are best understood when critics tell us what other explanations exist and where the explanations at hand fall short. Similarly, every work of fiction lends itself to interpretation. The critic, in H. L. Mencken's words, "makes the work of art live for the spectator." Half the fun of a good book is talking about it afterward. With a nod to Marx, the dialectic in vigorous criticism sets standards for excellence and brings progress.

Unfortunately, we today are making little progress, as precious little passionate book analysis and evaluation occurs now. In 1986, Bill Henderson published *Rotten Reviews*, a compilation of negative notices of the classics. When it sold well, he brought out *Rotten Reviews II*, scathing reviews of more recent works. But these were slim books, with large type and generous white space between the excerpts, many of which appeared in a much earlier time. The norm for literary criticism and reviewing today is far less Byronesque.

"Sweet, bland commendations fall everywhere upon the scene; a universal, if somewhat lobotomized, accommodation reigns," wrote Elizabeth Hardwick, an essayist and novelist, in a famous 1959 *Harper's Magazine* article. "Simple 'coverage' seems to have won out over the drama of opinion; 'readability,' a cozy little word, has taken the place of the old-fashioned requirement of a good, clear prose style, which is something else."

Critics of the critics have echoed these sentiments regularly in the years since. Book reviews rarely tell us "how to think about books," says Victor Navasky, publisher and editorial director of the literary-minded

---

* "As long as there have been capitalists and workers on earth, no book has appeared which is of as much importance for the workers as the one before us. The relation between capital and labour, the hinge on which our entire present system of society turns, is here treated scientifically for the first time and with a thoroughness and acuity possible only for a German."—Engels in the Leipzig *Demokratisches Wochenblatt*, March 21, 1668.

Nation: they are book reports, de facto public relations services for publishers. Perhaps some reviewers want to be "critical agents of natural selection in our cultural evolution," as one publisher surmised after calling a few. But they can't. Our modern mass media system won't let them.

Reviewing, the nineteenth-century poet William Wordsworth said, was "inglorious employment." It still is.

Books as News: Why Balance Is Bad

Margaret Fuller, often considered America's first full-time book reviewer, became literary editor of the *New York Tribune* in the mid–nineteenth century. Books, she said, are "a medium for viewing all humanity, a core around which all knowledge, all experience, all science, all the ideal as well as all the practical in our nature could gather." In the interest of doing justice to literature, she criticized the corrupt practices that prevailed at the time. Publishers bought good notices and traded review copies for advertising space. Reviewers often used reviews to help friends and damage enemies. "No reviewing medium appeared to be entirely free of corruption," said book historian John Tebbel of the times. Fuller's vision, in contrast, was to tell "the whole truth, as well as nothing but the truth."

Fuller appeared at a time when this seemed possible on a grand scale for the first time. The American newspaper, traditionally the province of special interests, was reinventing itself as a medium for the masses. Journalists would not be special pleaders for narrow interests; they would be independent. As it turned out, however, newspapers would never achieve Fuller's vision. The structure of modern journalism ultimately enshrined the uncritical review. Publishers no longer had to spend the money to buy favorable reviews; they got them free.

Adolph Ochs, a newspaper trendsetter, introduced a special Saturday book review section shortly after he bought the *New York Times* for $75,000 in 1896. (Beginning in 1911, the review section appeared on Sundays.) Paying attention to literary matters brought prestige and additional ad revenue to the newspaper, but he was not keen on sponsoring aggressive criticism. In keeping with his general, profitable philosophy, Ochs wanted to treat books as news. This meant fair, dispassionate, unoffensive reporting, a kind found neither in the muckraking journals proliferating at the time, nor in highbrow literary journals. Opinion, Ochs thought, should appear only on the editorial pages. "It always pained him," observed Gay Talese, a historian of the newspaper, "when a show was panned or a writer was condemned."

The tradition continued with Arthur Hays Sulzberger, Ochs's son-in-law and successor. In response to a complaint over a negative review, he confessed "to the feeling that if the author of the review in question felt as irritated as apparently he was, he should have returned the book stating that he was not the proper person to do it justice."

The *New York Herald Tribune,* the *Times*'s rival, created a special Sunday book review section in the mid-1920s. Irita Van Doren, who oversaw it for thirty-seven years, was well connected: her husband was historian Carl Van Doren; after a divorce, her lover was presidential aspirant Wendell Willkie. She was witty: Her dissertation at Columbia was titled "How Shakespeare Got the Dead Bodies off the Stage." And she was of the same general mind as Ochs when it came to book reviewing. "If there was a weakness to her book section," wrote a biographer of that newspaper, "it was in its civility and reluctance to pass negative judgment. A certain lack of critical rigor resulted."

A study in the mid-1930s asked thirty-five book review editors how they viewed their mission. More than three-fourths said that they served as a guide to book selection; 13 percent said they aimed to shape readers' tastes. "Mass production journalism is doing much to lower the status of reviewing," wrote historian James Truslow Adams in a 1931 essay in *The Saturday Review of Literature* (which no longer exists). "From the standpoint of the American daily, a book is merely 'news.'"

The canons and routines of reporting militate against the canons and routines of criticism. A report is objective, at arm's length from the news. A review is biased and makes news about the book. Reporters use formulas to fill the news pages on a rigid deadline day after day. Critics abhor the thought of forcing words into a few simple shapes. Stamina is essential in the reporter, but merely nice to have in the reviewer, whose chief virtues lie in thoughtfulness and perspective. Fuller irritated Horace Greeley because she preferred working at home. She didn't appreciate the bustle around her in the *Tribune*'s third-floor editorial offices on Nassau Street.

Newspapers, which seek to conserve space, have been prime agents in the killing of the essay, a highly creative form of expression that flourished in literate periodicals of the nineteenth century and has all but disappeared in our age. The *New Yorker*, one of the last popular publications welcoming the long discursive article, capitulated in the 1990s. The ideal reviewer from the point of view of the newspaper is one who works as Lewis Gannett did. Irita Van Doren brought the newspaperman to the *Herald Tribune* in 1928 as a daily reviewer. Over the next twenty-seven years, he wrote some eight thousand reviews. He could read a book in three hours and report on it in his "Books and Things" column by deadline. "A daily newspaper can seldom wait for true critical appraisal, which involves comparison, reflection and unhurried judgment," wrote Gerald Johnson in his biography of the *Times;* "but the news element in the publication of a book—its author and publisher, its theme, and at least a rough approximation of its literary quality—can be covered as rapidly as any other news event."

The *New York Times Book Review* remains the most influential source of book criticism in the country. In addition to including it in its Sunday paper, the *Times* sells seventy-seven thousand copies of the supplement separately, and syndicates reviews through its news service. The *Times* review has sought to be more critical since Elizabeth Hardwick wrote her scathing attack, and today book publishers are heard more often to complain that it is too harsh and elitist. Still, progress has been limited. Three issues of the *Times* review from 1997, which I chose at random, contained forty-three substantial reviews of adult fiction and nonfiction. Of these, thirty-four were positive and only four truly negative. Two offered equal doses of poison and elixir. Three were entirely descriptive, with no discernible judgment, although this could be said about most of them.

While many of the positive reviews pointed out failings, reviewers offered these discreetly, the way one friend tells another of bad breath. The Fallacy of the Penultimate Paragraph, as we might call this technique, buries the criticism far down in the story, then immediately contradicts it.

• "The novel has its wrinkles. With no strong antagonist . . . Yet the reader can overlook such flaws, thanks to the book's . . ."

• "Every scholar could complain of some topic omitted or inadequately treated. But few would ever be able to match this achievement."

• "———'s hyperbole, straying from satire to earnest social message, begins to verge on overstatement. . . . Still, that's not to take away from what —— has pulled off here."

• "If the novel has a weakness . . . Yet, the permutations and ghoulish nuances of his sound explorations offer such disquieting food for thought that any doubts . . ."

• "This is an exciting and important story—and I wish it had been told more swiftly and economically. . . . On balance, however, there is *everything* to applaud." (Emphasis added.)

The *Times* is not alone in this. Here is a nice example of the Fallacy of the Penultimate Paragraph from the *Washington Post:* "The book does have its gaps and irritating quirks. . . . These are quibbles. Overall, —— is magnificent."

Our modern reviewer is like a counselor at a self-esteem camp, Sylvia Frank, the editor of this book has suggested. This reluctance to criticize, however, is not simply a manifestation of the all-embracing, nonjudgmental, politically correct society in which we live. As Ochs understood, balanced, dispassionate writing attracts more readers than highly opinionated coverage. More readers means more advertisers, who want to reach large audiences. More advertisers means more profit for the newspaper. All of which is fine for book publishers. It's in the publishers' interest for newspapers to treat their books as news.

Not surprisingly, the few outstanding organs devoted to criticism relish opinion and do not aspire to mass audiences. The foremost is the *New York Review of Books.* It has established itself as a vigorous authority so full of opinion that some consider it an embodiment of the famous and variously attributed statement, "I never read a book I must review, it prejudices you so." It has a circulation of only 125,000. The quarterly *Hungry Mind Review,* from St. Paul, and the *Village Voice Literary Supplement* count for far less. The regular *Voice* has only 36,000 subscribers; the *Hungry Mind* 40,000.

A couple other opinionated publications offer vigorous reviewing, only this is an ancillary activity for them. The *New Yorker* publishes a few reviews in the back of each issue and has special literary sections from time to time. So does the *Nation,* which has one of America's most glorious records of reviewing. In its early days, it concentrated on literary matters, including among its regular reviewers Henry James. For a time the *Nation* appeared as a weekly cultural supplement to the *New York Evening Post*. Although its agenda is now left-wing political commentary, it has kept its interest in books and aggressively reviews the publishing business as well. Its circulation, sadly, is also low, only one hundred thousand paid subscribers.

Academic publications might be expected to offer advantages similar to the specialized organs of opinion mentioned above. They suffer from no injunction to be balanced. As it turns out, the best characteristic academic publications have in common with the opinion organs is low readership. H. L. Mencken rightly noted that professors must have theories the way dogs must have fleas; worse, it might be added, professors are always trying to give them to someone else.

When professors aren't trying to show off, they are trying to get even. Two reviews appearing side-by-side in the same issue of the *Journal of American History* a quarter of a century ago illustrate what is wrong with such reviewing. David Quentin Voigt of Albright College described Harold Seymour's *Baseball: The Golden Age* as "turgid" and not the definitive work it promised to be. Seymour of West Newbury, Massachusetts, called Voigt's *American Baseball* "a slipshod piece of work." Not much help here, although one allows that these two reviews taken together provide a little entertainment. Anyone going through academic reviews quickly discovers that they are worse than the mass media at distinguishing which books are important and which aren't.

What of that great gizmo of popularization, the television? The klieg lights have created a few literary bright spots. C-SPAN's "Booknotes" program is a thoughtful literary forum. The moderator, Brian Lamb, gives authors plenty of time to talk about their work. And there is Oprah Winfrey. No television personality could be less like the laconic Lamb than she. While he seems barely to breathe, she hyperventilates. She is also more powerful. When she mentioned that reports of mad cow disease had scared her away from hamburgers, terrified Texas cattlemen sued her under the state's False Disparagement of Perishable Food Products Act. Now that she has made a big production of having authors on her program, which is broadcast in more than 130 countries, she is the most important literary trendsetter on the planet. After Oprah boosted Jacquelyn Mitchard's *The Deep End of the Ocean,* the first-time author had enough royalty money to buy a Cape Cod retreat house and hire a personal trainer. "A look at the charts for just one week," said *Publishers Weekly* in a wrap-up on 1996 book selling, "indicates her colossal impact on a book's ascendence: back on November 11, all of the number one titles on *PW*'s four lists were there because of Oprah." Oprah tells authors ahead of time that she has chosen one of their books. Their publishers put the presses on high speed to meet the demand that is certain to follow.

Both Lamb and Oprah are missionaries for books. Lamb's conversations with authors about writing are assembled in two worthwhile volumes. Oprah urges viewers to replenish destroyed libraries and send volumes to state prisons. Yet neither is a critic in the sense that term is commonly understood. Many of the books they review are good, but they are not telling us which books are bad or what is bad about the good books they have on the program. Although Lamb will probe in a conver-

Oprah Winfrey approaches books with all the critical faculties of a cheerleader hopping up and down for the school's football team. Here Ms. Winfrey roots for author Toni Morrison. I hoped to get a photo like this from Oprah herself, so I wouldn't have to pay for it. Possibly wary that others will not be so kind to Oprah as she is to authors, a staffer said that they would have to know first what my book would say. I paid for this Reuters picture so I could say what ever I pleased.

sation, he is still chiefly an interviewer. Oprah is a book cheerleader. An effervescent everywoman, she gushes "wow" over and over as the author talks, and she asks people in the audience how they feel about the book. The audience, likely more thrilled to be with Oprah than the author, clap on cue. In close-ups they have the eerily glazed looks one expects to find among Branch Davidians. While the cattlemen were suing Oprah over her disparaging comments about beef, their wives invited her to meet with their book club.

Who can blame Oprah for doing handstands? Why be a detached critic when you can make yourself into a home entertainment center? Oprah has her own book club and film production company, Harpo Productions. After plugging Toni Morrison's *Paradise*, she bought the film rights.

Radio has one serious, influential book reviewer, tough-talking Don Imus. Imus reaches more than ten million listeners on more than one hundred radio stations, as well as on MSNBC-TV. Simon & Schuster publisher Jack Romanos believes that Imus increased the print order for Howard Kurtz's *Spin Cycle* from 25,000 to 200,000. Imus also made a best seller out of Jane Mendelsohn's *I Was Amelia Earhart*. To further his influence, he started the Imus-American Book Awards in 1998. Each year he gives one award for $100,000 and three for $50,000 each. The National Book Award, in contrast, comes to a piddling $10,000. It is difficult to be neutral about Imus. Perhaps the closest thing we have today to the acerbic Byron, he has called Simon & Schuster's Romanos a "beady-eyed little weasel." He pointed out that Oprah would never put Kurtz's book on her program: "If you said, 'Have you read *Spin Cycle*?' she would have thought it was a washing-machine manual!"

It is hard to escape the view, so powerfully expressed by media critic Neil Postman, that serious discourse is almost impossible over the airwaves and, when it does occur, is still bad because people may acquire the false hope that broadcasters can do better routinely. As a reviewer on public radio for "Marketplace," I tried initially to treat books the way a print critic would, with a coherent narrative. These reviews sounded like the oral book reports that third-graders give to their classmates. ("If you want to know how the story ends, read the book!") The solution was to have a dialogue with the program host. While this worked better in the sense that it was more entertaining, it was hardly serious literary criticism. In any event, that format was dropped and replaced by the old book report format. The producers preferred this approach because it used less air time. The center of gravity for electronic book reviewing is the QVC shopping channel. On Valentine's Day, that network trotted out romance writer Janelle Taylor to stump for *My Reckless Heart*. The author of a self-help finance book sold 160,000 copies. The producers do not select books based on their literary quality. In an effort not to offend, which can get people out of the buying mood, the producers reject books that have off-color titles.

Winfrey, Lamb, and Imus are the best you will find over the airwaves. They read the books discussed on their program. A National Book Critics Circle survey reported in the late 1980s that more than one-third of all reviewers think it is occasionally ethical to review a book they have not read completely. But electronic media are the worst offenders. In most cases, an author shows up at the radio or television station, is hustled in front of a studio audience, and is asked, profoundly, "so tell us what this book is about."

In 1998, *Boston Globe* columnist Mike Barnicle found his job on the line over George Carlin's *Braindroppings*. It appeared that Barnicle had lifted portions of the book to use in one of his newspaper columns. He responded by denying having read the book. Subsequently, someone found a clip from a local WCVB-TV program on which he recommended it as summer reading. Faced with choosing between admitting that he had plagiarized the book in print or lied about reading it on the air, he did not hesitate to say that he had lied. He was fired anyway—by the newspaper. Months afterward, he still appeared on WCVB as well as MSNBC, where he had also been a regular on Don Imus's program.

This leaves the Internet. Amazon.com and barnesandnoble.com provide in-house or commissioned reviews of books. "The merchandising teams are not pressured to promote a specific title," the barnesandnoble.com director of communications said. "But if I was responsible for a page, then why would I feature a book that I don't like?" In 1999, *New York Times* reporter Doreen Carvajal revealed that publishers could buy Amazon.com listings under categories as "New and Notable" and "Destined for Greatness." "The rapidly growing company began charging publishers modest fees last summer [1998] in a limited experiment," Carvajal reported. "But this year, Amazon increased the offerings to publishers so that now $10,000 is the price tag for a premium package for a newly released computer book." Amazon.com's management defended itself by saying that it rejects advertisements for books that did not meet its standards. Nevertheless, the online bookseller quickly announced that it would identify when a publisher had purchased nice words about its product.

It is equally difficult to be enthusiastic about Amazon.com's invitation to customers to "review" books. Book authors can disguise their names, type in a few choice words about their books, punch the send button, and no one knows the difference. There are no standards. Just as bad, one can imbibe, for hour after hour, honest reviews written by readers without getting much nutrition. Do you care that some guy in Cincinnati thinks *Undaunted Courage,* Stephen Ambrose's story of the Lewis and Clark expedition, is "overall mildly interesting; no sex and the violence seems mildly antiseptic"? Or that a couple recommends *Possession: A Romance* by A. S. Byatt as "totally awesome . . . Her English is excellent!"? Or that somebody in Portugal thinks *The Bridges of Madison County* is the best book he has ever read? How many books has he or she read? We don't know. Just punch the buy button on your computer.

Absolute Power Corrupts Absolutely

Who should review? "The unusual mind, capable of presenting fresh ideas in a vivid and original and interesting manner," as Hardwick suggested? Or the expert in the subject of the book, who is best qualified to assess its originality and importance? George Orwell tried this rule: "Books on specialized subjects ought to be dealt with by experts, and on the other hand a good deal of reviewing, especially of novels, might well be done by amateurs."

Any approach is bound to be wrong. The generalist knows too little about a subject; the expert too much and is more likely to have a vested interest in one argument or another. Review editors find it difficult to apply any rule to novels. Doing a little background reading, the editor can guess fairly accurately how a particular historian is likely to react to one point of view or another. But how well can one predict if a fiction reviewer will favor one plot or literary style over another? "When it comes to a book he cares about positively or negatively," observed the authors of *Books: The Culture and Commerce of Publishing*, a review editor's "choice, in the last analysis, is a political act."

These imperfections, however, would not be a liability, and could be a plus, were it not for another, greater problem: the paucity of book reviewing. Lord Acton's oft-quoted epigram about power corrupting, and absolute power corrupting absolutely, works counterintuitively with reviewers. With little reviewing going on, individual reviewers have much more power and, wanting to be fair, pull their punches.

A truly astonishing imbalance exists between the number of books published and the amount of book reviewing that goes on. The *New York Times, Chicago Tribune, Washington Post, Los Angeles Times,* and *San Francisco Chronicle* have substantial stand-alone Sunday sections. A handful of other daily newspapers have slimmer, precarious review sections. Both Denver's *Rocky Mountain News* and the *San Diego Union–Tribune* launched tabloid sections in 1997; they do about six full reviews in each issue, plus roundups. The *Boston Globe* has what it calls a books section, but it is really three or four pages deep; the rest of the section deals with other news.

The norm—reviews buried in arts/entertainment sections—is not particularly secure either. In 1987, according to one study, 52 percent of all Sunday papers did some book reviewing, down from 61 percent twenty years earlier. These reviews tend to be short and favor authors or subjects of local or regional interest. The 1987 study also found that 3 percent of papers ran book reviews or columns every weekday, compared to 29 percent who ran reviews of television programs.

Magazines are no better. "Of the 100 top magazines (the smallest of which had a circulation of about 800,000 in 1993), no more than half a dozen review books on a regular basis," notes Leo Bogart, a media analyst, "and most of them review no more than a single book per issue."

With so few people assessing books, individual reviews carry more weight. This has a chilling effect on reviewers; and when it doesn't, it should. *Times* reviewers in the 1930s knew that their critical comments (circulated to some 700,000 readers) could be offset by a favorable review in the *Herald Tribune* (circulation nearly 500,000). There is no *Herald Tribune* today, and across the country one-newspaper towns have become the norm. Knowing that their judgment is as imperfect as it is powerful, responsible reviewers have every reason to feel obliged to err on the side of being fair and restrained, rather than critical. They do not want to be like Pancho Villa, who, when asked what to do with a prisoner, said, "Shoot him for the time being."

Not everyone likes to acknowledge the power reviewers have. Elizabeth Hardwick argued that *Times* reviews "do not affect the sales of books one way or another," and the editors of the *New York Review of Books*, who include Hardwick among their ranks, take the same line about their supercritical publication. It is doubtful, though, they really believe this. More likely this is a sign that they know how much power they have and feel guilty that they use it anyway.

Although it is impossible to say exactly how much sway a given review will have, most everyone knows that a bad *New York Times* notice can kill a book, especially when the author under review doesn't have a wide following. It is no secret that publishers will sometimes cancel promotion for a book panned in the *Times*. And who would gainsay the marketing value of a good review in the *Times* or in any other major daily? After all, if publishers and bookstores think it worthwhile to send out all those free books to reviewers, shouldn't reviewers surmise that their independent vote in favor of a book will help even more?

Of course, a name writer can withstand a bad review. If the review whips up enough controversy, it can even sell more books. Readers often want to know what all the fuss is about. What's more, prominent writers occasionally can bully publications into giving them equal time, as Norman Mailer did when John Simon panned *Harlot's Ghost* in the *New York Times*. The *Times* provided Mailer with an entire page to review Simon as a person, to wit: "John Simon was in a rut . . . John, who knew that his faculties of review were inferior to no one's in the land, was nonetheless becalmed in a sea of mediocre status."

No such luck for people like poor Dan Moldea and his book *Interference: How Organized Crime Influences Professional Football*. The *Times* reviewer said some positive things, while noting "there is too much sloppy journalism to trust the bulk of this book's 512 pages." Not able to get a retraction, Moldea filed a ten-million-dollar defamation suit against the *Times*. He said the review unfairly damaged his reputation and ruined sales. He had as much chance of winning the case as the handicapped writer who sued the *Washington Post* under the Americans with Disabil-

ities Act. The disabled plaintiff claimed that the *Post* had published reviews of similar books by nondisabled writers and therefore was obliged
to provide "public accommodation." What publicity Moldea generated
probably didn't do him much good with either publishers or reviewers.
Instead of giving his next book a bad review, newspapers might think it
best to give it no reviews at all.

Times book editor Rebecca Sinkler's public explanation/quasi-apology
for the Simon review revealed the corruption that comes from literary
power. "Normally," she said, "*The Book Review* would not assign a book to
a critic who had frequently disparaged its author's work." Sinkler also
confessed that she instructed her editors to ask potential reviewers, "Is
there any reason the author would object to you?" Expressed another way,
the *Times* assigns reviews to people who like the author's work or haven't
given it much apparent attention.

Henry VIII understood the function of good reviewing. When he did not have enough
royal time on his hands to read a book, he gave copies to two people with warring
points of view, heard them out, then drew his own conclusions.

Painting after Holbein in the Royal Collection at Windsor Castle, the Royal Collection, copyright Her Majesty Queen Elizabeth II

How much better it is when book reviews wound, not kill. Should someone misjudge from time to time, so what? Other reviewers would serve as a corrective. Henry VIII, a king, and Walter Kerr, once a king of theater criticism, had the right idea. When Henry did not have time to read a new book, he would give copies to two people with warring points of view, hear them out, then draw his own conclusions. Likewise, Kerr did not want to review plays twice, once for the daily paper and then on Sunday. He preferred to leave daily reviews to others and do his criticism only on Sundays. "I wanted the vote split," he said. Good criticism runs on the same principle as our legal system. Attorneys on each side make the best case they can. The reader judges. While imperfect, this is better than the alternatives.

The Dainties on Reviewers' Plates

Fairness is not the only reason for self-censorship among members of the literary bar. The piddling amount of reviewing available reminds writers there is no future in being a literary critic. This makes their instinct for self-preservation all the keener.

Few writers can seriously aspire to a career as a full-time reviewer. Jonathan Yardley, one of a handful of book reviewers who truly deserve the title critic, is a staff member at the *Washington Post.* The *Times* is unusual in that it uses a small group of in-house staffers for almost all its daily reviews. But these are exceptions. Outsiders who have other jobs write virtually all of the Sunday reviews in the *Post* and the *New York Times.* The *Wall Street Journal* does one daily review Monday through Thursday and runs several in a Friday weekend section that includes advice on wine buying and showcases a house a week. It has no full-time reviewers. In only a few places, for that matter, do book review editors concentrate on reviewing alone. More typical is Michael Deeds of the *Idaho Statesman,* who is responsible for books, food/home, travel, entertainment/amusements, science/technology, women, and fashion/features. Arthur Salm, the book editor at the *San Diego Union-Tribune,* does all the book review editing, writes a book column, is back-up movie critic for the paper, and writes occasional features.

Free-lance writers cannot live off the money they make from reviewer's fees. The *Chicago Tribune,* which uses outsiders on Sundays, pays $250 to

$450 for a review; the *Rocky Mountain News* pays $20. "We're thinking of raising it to thirty dollars," said editor Patti Thorn with a laugh. *Kirkus* and *Publishers Weekly,* two leading trade publications for booksellers and libraries, pay about $40 for a review. Their reviewers range from struggling writers to schoolteachers who want to earn a little money on the side. Review editors toss in a free copy of the book provided by the publisher.* Under these circumstances, editors find it difficult to develop a trustworthy stable of talented writers. "If they have something else going on," Thorn said of her ill-compensated critics, "they drop out for a while."

The pay does not inspire a reviewer to dig into a book to find its weaknesses. Rather than seeing themselves as part of a profession of critics, they are more likely to see themselves as writers who will someday be at the mercy of a critic. Reviewers learn that it pays to hug the shore, as John Updike puts it, and not venture out with a review.

For their part, book publishers, who have come to expect favorable reviews, reward friendly reviewers by quoting their words—if they are nice—on the covers of subsequent editions. (If they are not especially nice, the publisher sometimes covers the offending comments with ellipses.) This leads reviewers to practice the equivalent of grade inflation in our universities. "There is a bad trait in a reviewer," Frank Swinnerton, a well-known English reviewer, said in a 1939 lecture, "that he likes to see himself quoted—and he will never be quoted unless his words have a blaze and lustre beyond those of other reviewers." The crafty reviewer throws around phrases like "long overdue," "penetrating and insightful," "brilliant," "moving." "Reviewers are commonly believed to use the word 'masterpiece' by rubber stamp," Swinnerton added. "A whispered word of praise is unheard amid the bawling of 'stark,' 'glorious,' 'stupendous' and the like."

Edmund Wilson had the self-confidence to write a lengthy review of a book that he said was "as synthetic, as arbitrary, as basically cold and dead, as a scenario for a film." But most writers, intent on a by-line in the *Times*'s book review, understand that the editors are not as troubled by

*"One starts reviewing books when young for the vanity of being asked to review them and of seeing one's name on the review," Geoffrey Grigson wrote. "One continues it for money, one persists in it as a way of acquiring books one wants very much which are too expensive to buy."

what Margaret Fuller had called the "system of mutual adulation and organized puff." Editors, for their part, don't want to waste precious space on inferior books. What's the point of saying something awful about a book no one is talking much about anyway? Naturally the editors don't come right out and say this to the reviewer, even when the stakes are especially high—as when they are assigning a book written by a reporter on their own papers. Over a pleasant lunch one day, Rebecca Sinkler confided to me the newspaper's approach to selecting reviewers for books written by *Times* men and women: "We hope they understand."*

The critic, Byron noted, is "grateful for the dainties on his plate."

Galley Slaves: Rowing for the Publishers

Every week, usually on Thursdays, daily newspapers run a food section. Every Sunday, they review a few books. Both operate on the same philosophy. In one, editors profile accomplished cooks and print yummy recipes next to advertisements for ground chuck. In the other, they publish book reviews and author profiles next to ads for best sellers. Your paper has more food stories than book reviews because Piggly Wiggly does more advertising than your local Barnes & Noble. Remember, the *Herald Tribune* did not launch a book review section in the 1920s simply because it wanted to promote culture. It wanted to capture some of the advertising dollars going to the highly profitable *New York Times* Sunday review section.

The place to start exploring the implications of this cozy relationship is with the timing of a book's publication. Publishers want to have books available for sale at bookstores when book reviews appear. That way, books aren't sitting in warehouses, which costs publishers money, or on stores' shelves, which costs both the publisher and the bookstore money. To help regulate this process, publishers fabricate publication dates for new books, that is, a date when the book is officially available.

*Similarly, Harcourt Brace Jovanovich withdrew an unflattering biography of Katherine Graham, *Katherine the Great*, by Deborah Davis, which it was planning to nominate for an American Book Award. Some thought a letter from *Post* editor Ben Bradlee was one of the reasons. When Graham came out with her memoirs, *Personal History* generated a cover story in the *Post* Sunday magazine, a positive review, and excerpts in the newspaper's Style section, not to mention attention in the *Post*-owned *Newsweek*.

Editors, always looking for a clear-cut event on which to hinge a story, happily play this dating game. They accept bound or even unbound galleys from publishers, instead of waiting for finished books. Galleys usually have a simple paper cover and are printed on inexpensive stock. They generally do not contain many items that will be included in the finished books: photos, index, numbered pages. The publisher gets the final volume ready for distribution while the reviewer is reading the galleys and writing the review.

As a result, reviewers do not review the book, only the bones of the book. They can say little, for instance, about the quality of the printing job. If this seems a trivial matter to most readers, it may be because no reviewer has encouraged them to think about the implications. A well-designed book is easier to read. A well-made book is worth keeping. (And who wouldn't want to keep a twenty-five-dollar investment instead of seeing it fall apart after one reading?) Also, it is helpful to know whether the index is useful, or if the photos are any good. A reviewer of an art book may get the real thing to review, but even that is not guaranteed. I have reviewed the galleys of a biography of an artist that had large blank spaces where his art would appear in the final edition. The less that reviewers say about such matters, the less likely publishers will pay much attention to the quality of the printing or the CDs that are now occasionally issued with books but not available to the reviewer.

"I love books physically," Alfred Knopf said. "And I want to make them beautifully." Admirers in the book business credited Knopf with setting high publishing standards. Frequently, Mencken said in praise, "the format of one of his books got as much attention in the reviews as its contents."

The only person I know today to take this aspect of reviewing seriously is Paul Lukas. An eccentric who started the self-published *Beer Frame: The Journal of Inconspicuous Consumption,* Lukas reviews products and their packaging. He is proud to have written reviews "based exclusively on the book's physical properties." Unlike Knopf, his literary interests run to *Erotic Sexual Positions from Around the World,* which a friend of his spotted in a vending machine in a women's rest room in Rodeo, California. ("I'll gladly wade through piles of novelty midget rubbers and garishly decorated French ticklers if I can land even one more condom-machine product this entertaining.") As is typical of people in 'zine work, as his type of publication is called, Lukas's career is not stable. A new editor killed Lukas's "Inconspicuous Consumption" column in *New York*. He is now doing a travel column, published on the Web, called "There in Spirit," in which he writes each week about places he did not visit. It won't be Lukas who arrests the decline in the art of making books.*

Another problem with working with uncorrected galleys is that the reviewer does not know precisely what the final text will say. The galleys typically have a warning on the front like this: "NOT FOR SALE. FOR PROMOTIONAL PURPOSES ONLY. These are uncorrected galleys. Please check all quotations or attributions against the bound copy of the book. We urge this for the sake of editorial accuracy as well as for your legal protection and ours."

I once noticed a review copy of a book that announced "Unrevised and unpublished proofs. Confidential." How, I wondered, could a review copy be confidential?

Review editors check any direct quotes that a critic uses against the finished book, which generally arrives at the newspaper's offices soon before the review is to appear. This ensures that the review does not misquote the final text. As a practical matter, the galley is usually close to the final product. Nevertheless, reviewers can never be certain that a book they judge to be full of sloppy writing and errors of fact will end up that way. Reviewers usually don't see the finished book until the editor sends a copy after the review appears.† A process that keeps finished books out of the hands of reviewers until their review is published does nothing to discourage shoddy editing, a problem examined in Appendix C.

The book selection process is also flawed, as any visitor to a book review office quickly discovers. Here one does not find editors leisurely contemplating which books to let through the sluice gates and into our culture. Editors live precariously under the cresting waves of books that crash in on them relentlessly.

Kirkus and *Publishers Weekly*, the trade publications keeping bookstores

---

*Lukas has a healthy reaction to reviews of his own book: "Most people either totally love what I do or else they just don't get it."

†Ironically, publishers generally send only finished books to radio and television stations. As noted earlier in the essay, these media outlets are less likely to read the book at all before interviewing an author. *Publishers Weekly* is highly responsible in noting in its short reviews whether or not it has seen photos to be used in a book.

and libraries up to date, each review about five thousand books annually. Their reviews, crucial to deciding what gets reviewed by the major mass media reviews, cover about 10 percent of the books published by the major houses and a much smaller share of the total number that come out in a given year. The *Times* itself can only review two thousand or so books annually. That includes brief reports on books. There isn't enough room for all the worthy ones—and what is worthy anyway? Books people want to read? Or books that people ought to read? With so many authors and book publicists hectoring them, review editors usually throw up their hands and try to do a little of everything.

Because they cannot possibly read every new book before deciding which ones to assign for review, editors develop crude decision-making rules, not unlike procedures used by battlefield medics to sort out who will be treated and who allowed to die. The *Times* favors books that come out initially in hardcover; those that have single authors; those that are published by larger houses. The *Times* does not review the romances sold in supermarkets. ("You have to draw the line somewhere," says the current editor, Charles McGrath.) *USA Today* will review romances, as does the trade magazine *Library Journal*. The *New York Review of Books* reviews government reports from time to time, which none of the above does. When he was a book editor at *Time,* Timothy Foot developed a quick process for deciding if he would review a book that seemed a likely prospect. He would read the last chapter; if it was interesting, then the first. If the book was still interesting, he would read the middle ones. I once visited a review office in which the editor pointed to a stack of recently arrived books piled high on her desk and revealed part of her sorting strategy. "I will assign these to reviewers tomorrow," she told me, "— or just dump them and move on."

The safest selection strategy is to turn to the familiar. "We are journalists, we're in the magazine business, and we want people to buy our magazine," said a book editor of the *New Republic* in the 1980s, explaining why he chose books by writers "who have visibility, who have a public. . . . Our prejudice is not only for talent but also for people who are well-known."

The book reviewing process is best summed up as a "pseudo event," a term Daniel Boorstin coined to describe the modern penchant to manufacture reality. The ultimate book pseudo-event is the best-seller list.

There is no industrial standard for these lists. The *Washington Post Book World* surveys local bookstores to see what is hot in two categories: hardcover (fiction and nonfiction, ten each) and paperback (ditto). The *New York Times*, which has a national ranking, compiles best-seller lists for fiction and nonfiction (fifteen books in each), paperbacks (again, fifteen in each category), and "Advice, How-to and Miscellaneous" (four books). *USA Today* lumps books of all types—ranging from self-help to serious literature—into one list of fifty.

Some lists use data compiled within the week; some have a longer lag time. Some use only bookstores; some include online booksellers. The *Wall Street Journal*'s list does not include book club, drugstore, or airport sales. *Publishers Weekly* excludes book clubs, but not drugstores or airports. The *Village Voice* has twenty-five stores in its national survey. *USA Today* has some three thousand independent, chain, discount, and online booksellers in its national survey. The *Times* says its rankings reflect sales figures "at almost four thousand bookstores plus wholesalers serving sixty thousand other retailers, statistically weighed to represent sales in all such outlets nationwide." It does not, however, actually follow every book; it tells bookstores which ones should be tracked as potential best sellers. Not surprisingly, these lists come to wildly different conclusions. It is not unusual for a book that is number 9 on the *Times*'s list to be number 150 on *USA Today*'s and not on *Publishers Weekly*'s at all.

The *Times* claims that its survey bookstores are a secret, but publishers know where many of them are. In 1995, *Business Week* reported that two marketing consultants may have boosted their standing on the *Times*'s best-seller list by buying large numbers of books from stores in the newspaper's survey group around the country. The book, on the *Times*'s list for fifteen weeks, was aptly titled *The Discipline of Market Leaders*. At first, *Times* book editor Charles McGrath denied that list tampering was possible. He later conceded that the book may not have belonged on the list at all some weeks.

Buying your way onto the best-seller list is the literary equivalent of salting, a mining trick in which a seller puts gold in a shaft to convince a buyer that there is much more to take out. In the case of consultants, the scam involves not only additional book sales, but also more invitations to speak. When an author-consultant can command speaking fees of thirty thousand dollars per appearance and is giving eighty speeches a year, as was the case of one of the authors of *The Discipline of Market Leaders,* it is no big deal to spend lots of money buying one's own book.

A book that sells a lot of copies quickly has a better chance of becoming a best seller than one that sells the same number of copies over a long period of time. Time of year also makes a difference. "While a novel selling 1,500 copies a week might qualify in the dead of summer," *Wall Street Journal* reporter Joanne Lipman noted, "a novel selling five thousand copies a week might face a tough battle during the hyperactive week before Christmas."

So ubiquitous are these lists, and so different from one another in how they are derived, "best seller" has become meaningless. The term, which did not come into use until the turn of the twentieth century, is thrown around with such abandon that we think nothing of describing a book written in the sixteenth century, when no such concept existed, as a best seller. Publicists called *Inside Intel* by Tim Jackson a "National Bestseller." It appeared on the best-seller lists of the *San Francisco Chronicle* and *Business Week.* The former was based on reports from some fifty local bookstores (in an area quite interested in Intel and other high-tech companies); the latter publication appeals to a narrow audience. Ads for the autobiographical *Sam Walton: Made in America* said "America's #1 Merchant Just Became American's #1 Bestseller." In fact, it was the number one seller at Sam's Club, the Wal-Mart founder's discount chain. HarperCollins advertised Paul Johnson's *The Birth of the Modern* as a national best seller when it had only appeared on the *Washington Post*'s locally derived list.

The *New York Times* started its best-seller list in 1942 at least in part because of "the poor showing the [review] section was making on the company's accounts," expecting the list to improve revenues. Whatever the list has done for the *Times,* it certainly has promoted best sellers. Best-seller lists are self-fulfilling prophesies. Not wanting to be left out of cocktail party conversation, people buy best sellers (although, like reviewers, they don't always read them). Giant bookstore chains help out by discounting the prices of books as soon as they become best sellers. Amazon.com started an online price war on best sellers in mid-1999, when it took 50 percent off the standard price. Amazon also deeply discounts titles that Oprah selects for her book club. Such Internet-based services have made it so much easier for people to jump on the latest book craze that bookstores report problems keeping hot titles in stock. The *Times* links its Web page to Barnes & Noble's. Click on a *Times* review or best seller and Barnes & Noble will get a copy of the book in the mail pronto. "Since Barnes & Noble has had a link on the *New York Times* Web page, books [with positive reviews] are immediately out of stock," one bookstore owner told *Publishers Weekly*. Authors often have clauses in their contracts giving them bonuses if their books become *New York Times* best sellers.

This explains why a best seller remains a best seller. Only two of the fifteen nonfiction books on the *New York Times* list in mid-January 1998 had enjoyed best-seller status for fewer than two months. Five had been on for a year or more. In the words of Boorstin, "A best seller is a best seller is a best seller."

Expect to see this phenomenon become more pronounced as electronic scanning of book sales makes national recordkeeping easier. As it is, you can dial in to Amazon.com to see how your book is faring against the competition at any given moment. Every hour it ranks sales of its top ten thousand best-selling books; it updates rankings for the one hundred thousand best sellers daily. Jeff Bezos, Amazon's CEO, calls this the "literary stock market." An enterprising writer for the *New Yorker*, Jamie Malanowski, found that she could move Thomas Carlyle's 1837 *The French Revolution* thousands of places on the Amazon.com list by buying one or two copies. Consider what that can mean when someone is determined to build up momentum for his or her book. The tracking system also allows publishers to gauge how well an appearance on NBC's *Today* show increases sales. When a book does well after an appearance, the publisher has reason to pump more money into promotion. Meanwhile, specialized software of growing interest to booksellers profiles individual consumers (what books do you like, how much are you spending on books, and so forth) and analyzes the data to decide what books to recommend to you.

If you think best sellers have any relationship to reality or quality, remember that the *New York Times* is proud that it does not review all the books on its best-seller list.* Its editors are mindful of the fate of books such as Monroe Sheldon's *In His Steps: What Would Jesus Do?* That book

---

*In one issue taken at random, five of the fifteen nonfiction books and seven of the fifteen fiction books on the *Times*'s best-seller lists had never enjoyed a Sunday review. The review gave three others only brief notices.

was possibly the best best seller at the turn of the century, a judgment that stands up after discounting the Reverend Sheldon's gross overstatements about selling thirty-three million copies worldwide. A better guess by a historian of best sellers, Frank Luther Mott, is about six million, which is nevertheless astronomically high by the standards of the time. More significant, though, is that fact that no one remembers the book today unless they collect book curiosities.

Good-bye to Byron

Reviewing offers endless opportunities for creativity. J. Edgar Hoover's Federal Bureau of Investigation had a Publication Section, later named the Book Review Section, to track subversive writing. Luis Borges critiqued a book that did not exist except in his mind. Umberto Eco reviewed two brief works, the fifty-thousand- and one-hundred-thousand-lira bank notes.

Authors who fight against troublesome reviewers can be equally creative, as well as entertaining. James Russell Lowell wrote that "Nature fits all her children with something to do / He who would write and can't write, can surely review." What fun to know that Charles Dickens did not read reviews of his work in his later years, or that Harold Brodkey protects himself another way. He has his spouse read the reviews. And we relish stories like the one best-selling novelist Marcia Davenport tells. She was on a radio panel with Alexander Woollcott, who had little good to say about her books in his reviews and was ridiculing them before the program began. Just as the microphones switched on, he keeled over and soon after died. "I used to say not very nicely," she commented later, "that it was I who killed Woollcott."

For all the drama nasty reviews generate, however, we cannot look forward to enjoying a resurgence of them. Of course, there will be a little unpleasantness from time to time, but book reviews and book reviewers won't change their ways. If anything, book reviewers will come to sound more and more like Boy Scouts who have pledged to be trustworthy, loyal, helpful, friendly, courteous, kind, obedient, cheerful, thrifty, brave, clean, and reverent.

The first requirement for the return of nastiness is a proliferation of book reviews. The potential for developing more advertising, necessary for a resurgence in critical reviewing, is significant. The book industry currently accounts for only 1.16 percent of all newspaper advertising. Large newspaper organizations, such as Knight-Ridder and Gannett, are in the best position to attract new ad dollars, as book critic Carlin Romano has observed. They could create stand-alone review sections that would appear in each of the Sunday papers in their groups. (Gannett owned seventy-four daily newspapers in 1997; Knight-Ridder owned thirty-one.) In addition, large newspaper companies might be persuaded to run more reviews, even if they don't attract advertisers, for the same reason that they subsidize foreign news bureaus. It is a sign of superiority.

Unfortunately, book publishers don't have much interest in buying ads. In the late 1980s, the *New York Post* created a sixteen-page book review section. To be economically viable, it needed eight pages of advertisements. "Yet we rarely sold *any* book ads," said Steven Cuozzo, a long-time editor. When the *San Diego Union* merged with the *Tribune,* the *Union* dropped its stand-alone, bimonthly book review section. After intense public pressure and "Yes, we'll advertise" assurances from book publishers, the *Union-Tribune* launched a weekly Sunday section in February 1997. Publishers ran half a dozen advertisements, *total,* in the first year. In that year, Crown bookstores bought a full-cover, back-page advertisement each week. In the second year, it contracted for only fourteen weeks of back-page ads. Pat Holt, editor of The *San Francisco Chronicle* review, says the Bay Area is the number one per capita book market in the nation; the area "is also the center of independent book publishing and of independent bookstores." Yet the section barely breaks even. One issue I happened to pick up had one ad, a box one inch high by one column wide.

As for the notion of increasing reviewing as a public service to enhance a media operation's prestige as foreign coverage does, don't hope for that either. Foreign news coverage is decreasing.

Meanwhile, newspapers become more bland by the day. As the number of dailies has decreased, so has their willingness to be controversial. They censor themselves the way reviewers do when they are afraid of abusing power. The economic basis for this is so sound that, even where competition exists, a newspaper's inclination is toward conflict avoidance. The *St. Paul Pioneer-Press,* which competes with its twin city rival the *Minneapolis Star-Tribune,* has dropped editorials all together.

As in so much else, *USA Today* epitomizes the trend in journalism. It runs editorials that say nothing worth saying and only publishes an opinion on its op-ed page if an opposing view is hitched to it. To make doubly certain those opinions don't amount to much, the editors print only sound bytes. The same goes for book reviewing. On a more or less typical Thursday—the day it reviews the most books—*USA Today* ran a story on poet Ted Hughes's hyped book *Birthday Letters,* reporting various other authors' opinions of Hughes. And it ran three lists, always a noncontroversial approach to reporting: A list of the ten worst presidents from a book on the subject, its regular list of the top fifty best sellers, and a separate list of some books selected at random that are farther down in bestsellerdom (one book was number 213).

Some authors and publishers might consider this good. But it is not. A good fight draws a crowd. That is why Britain's *Times Literary Supplement,* which does a good job of stirring up trouble, advertises that its letters columns carry "the usual howls of rage from wounded authors." Bland reviewing, on the other hand, contributes to reader malaise and the decline of reading and literary standards. It also makes the literary world a drearier and, paradoxically, less friendly place. After all, Thomas Moore did not press for another duel to the death with the reviewer who maligned him. He and Francis Jeffrey became friends.

SIX

Literary Luck

———❧❧❧———

In which it is shown that the talent
that best serves a writer is luck and that
sometimes the worst luck, like dropping
dead, can be the most fortuitous of all.

———❧❧❧———

—⁓—

Best sellers, if not written by someone in the news, about whatever
it is that landed him in the news, tend to be accidents.

—Robert Graves

There is a great deal to be said
For being dead.

—Edmund Clerihew Bentley

—⁓—

Writers sweat. They work and rework their prose. They grovel to obtain friendly dust-jacket quotes. They go on long author's tours, answering the same stupid questions on each of the nation's 1,200 talk shows. But authors cannot control what is often the most important factor determining whether a book rises above the publisher's dreary midlist or, worse, heads for the shredder almost as soon as it rolls off the press. That factor is luck. Any kind of luck. It can be dumb luck, even bad luck. A fatal slip on a banana peel can land an author on the best-seller list.

But let's not get ahead of ourselves. We'll save death for its rightful spot, last. The place to start is birth.

Accidents of Birth

Being born in the right family is as much a blessing for would-be authors as it is for those who aspire to be members of the House of Lords. This is not to say authors need *good* parents or even parents who are competent at something besides child rearing. We are talking here about famous parents. The more unlovable they are, the better. We can stomach only so many happy-family books like *Cheaper by the Dozen*. The *Mommie Dearest* genre, named after the get-even memoirs of Joan Crawford's adopted daughter, entertain us endlessly.

Ronald Reagan, who was as disengaged from his children as he was from his presidency, endowed them with a rich supply of material for books, some of which actually ended up as best sellers. In *On the Outside Looking In,* Michael Reagan, an adopted child, recounts his lonely childhood. Patti Davis's *The Way I See It: An Autobiography* told how as a ten-year-old she wanted a psychiatrist for a birthday present. In *First Father, First Daughter: A Memoir,* Maureen Reagan reported that about age nineteen she learned that seven-year-old Patti, her half-sister, did not know they were related. As her father explained, "Well, we just haven't gotten that far yet."

Even if the old man gets on your nerves, you can get a little reflected glory by extolling his nonfamily accomplishments, as son Michael did in *The City on the Hill.* And once you have gotten your anger out of your system, you can write a nice tribute, the way Patti did after her father was diagnosed with Alzheimer's. Always willing to patch things up, Ronald and

Nancy Reagan wrote separate introductions to that book, *Angels Don't Die.*

The Reagan family also understands that you don't have to write directly about your parents to trade on their fame. You can pretend it is fiction. Patti Davis, who can't put her pen down, wrote three novels whose characters include powerful, detached fathers and evil mothers: *A House of Secrets, Home Front,* and *Deadfall.* And once you're launched in the writing business, you can veer away from the family into subjects that really interest you. Davis's fourth book was *Bondage. Publishers Weekly* called it "a smorgasbord of irresponsible, unprotected sex."

Someday, a smart entrepreneur should publish a leather-bound, limited edition set of the Reagan offspring's books under the title *Family Values.* The only Reagan child who apparently would not have a volume in the set is young Ron Reagan, who defiantly said in 1991 that he would not resort to books. This is less a matter of self-restraint than an inclination to trade on the family name in another art, television. On *Saturday Night Live,* he danced in his underwear, and he played himself in a Cinemax comedy special, "Ron Reagan Is the President's Son." Realizing he was a chip off the old block, young Ron called himself a "quasi-entertainer."

Not that children of the famous don't encounter resistance when they try to write about something other than Mom and Dad. One publisher after another rejected the first novel submitted by Victoria Gotti, daughter of reputed mob boss John Gotti. Maybe they worried about the prose (e.g., "His hunger for her had grown like a tumor inside of him") or that they might get cement shoes if the book did not do well. But the absence of a clear tie-in with her father's underworld connections probably presented the greatest problem. She insisted that *The Senator's Daughter* was not a *roman-à-clef* and, anyway, Daddy was in the plumbing supply business. All the same, the mother of three had written a *crime* book, and certain facts about her family could not be refuted. Such as her father being an inmate in the Marion, Illinois, penitentiary. Finally, a small publisher, Forge, decided this was an offer it couldn't refuse. Gotti's maiden name appeared on the book's cover in large letters; the title in small ones—a form usually reserved for famous writers. Sure enough, Victoria received lots of publicity, such as those morning television interviews where she could explain that her father, one, was in the plumbing supply business and, two, read drafts of the book while he was in jail. Perhaps realizing the value of trading on her family's history, she titled her next book *I'll Be Watching You.* The perceptive critic would not miss the point.*

If one's parents don't have high visibility, an author can look to siblings. Buddy Foster wrote about his sister, Jodie Foster. Or you can rummage around in the family's past for someone famous. Thibault de Sade, the great-great-great-grandson of you-know-who, has hit on the idea of writing a biography of his ancestor. No telling when it will be out, but he is already giving interviews. Unlike Reagan's children, he is hoping to improve the image of his famous relative.

If you are a writer and related to a famous writer, it is wise to suggest you share a famous writing gene. In interviews, novelist Joanna Trollope says that she and her famous ancestor, Anthony Trollope, "share a sense of sympathy and forgiveness, a sense that we're all in this together." Since she is the fifth-generation niece of the famous writer, she is really in this together with hundreds of Trollope kinfolk. But she is the one smart enough to stake a claim and receive the headlines that read WRITER JOANNA TROLLOPE DOES UNCLE ANTHONY PROUD.

News Breaks

The public's thirst for books about certain topics is unquenchable. In the early years of this country, the best way—almost the only way, really—to have a best seller was to write about religion. "Of the first twenty best sellers," observed Frank Luther Mott in *Golden Multitudes,* "thirteen were definitely books of religious teaching, and that element was strong in four others." Today, as publisher Michael Bessie once put it, "there are never too many books about Hitler, Lincoln, Napoleon and the Civil War." Or dogs or Marilyn Monroe. Andrews McMeel's publishing list for all 1998, for instance, offered these new doggie books: *The Good Shepherd: A Special Dog's Gift of Healing, What Do Dogs Dream, Dog in the Dunes, Why We Love Dogs: A Bark and Smile Book,* and *Three Dog Bakery Cookbook.* Amazon.com lists more than 150 books about Monroe, including *Marilyn, My Marilyn:*

---

*The *New York Times* reported that in 1980 Gotti's young son "died after his minibike swerved into the path of a car driven by a neighbor, John Favara. It was an accident. Four months later, witnesses saw three men club Mr. Favara on the head and stuff him into a van in a Long Island parking lot. He has not been seen since."

An Anthology of Poems about Marilyn Monroe and *Africa and the Marriage of Walt Whitman and Marilyn Monroe*. That doesn't count the scores of Marilyn videos and calendars that Amazon.com sells.

Before prospective authors jump on the bandwagon with one of these topics, however, they should consider the value of catching the wave of a major unexpected event.* This hope-to-strike-it-rich mentality has many advantages. Thinking about making your book better is hard work; hoping to get a news break is not. Also, because big news is mostly bad news, you can rejoice in the worst kind of occurrence, such as war.

War does as much to glorify writers as it does generals. It took Daniel Yergin seven years to write *The Prize: The Epic Quest for Oil, Money, and Power.* He completed his work a few days before Iraq's invasion of Kuwait in August 1990. While the battle raged in the Middle East, Americans held the television remote control in one hand and *The Prize* in the other. It became a best seller.

The Gulf War also brought good fortune to Albert Hourani, Tony Horwitz, and Samir Al-Khalil. Hourani's long-planned *A History of the Arab Peoples* was coincidentally completed at just the right time. His publisher upped the print run to three times as many copies as originally planned. *Wall Street Journal* reporter Tony Horwitz also had just finished his book. Originally titled "I Never Saw a Fat Man in the Desert," only one of its seventeen chapters was situated in Iraq. Nevertheless, the name was changed to *Baghdad without a Map.* Random House republished *Republic of Fear: The Inside Story of Saddam's Iraq,* written by Samir Al-Khalil (a pen name) and published in 1989 by the University of California.

A number of authors and publishers tried to cash in on the war with instant books: *The Rape of Kuwait* ("Read it and you'll know why we're there," said the television commercial); *Saddam Hussein and the Crisis in the Gulf* (written in two and one-half weeks; well over four hundred thousand copies shipped to book stores), *Desert Shield Fact Book* (a workbook-like volume published by a company that manufactures war games; Dan

*Authors can make their own luck by looking far ahead. Many news events or happenings are tied to anniversaries or events that are planned for a distant date. James Michener, who understood how to tap into the literary market as well as anyone, produced *Hawaii* to coincide with Hawaiian statehood and *Centennial* to coincide with the United States's two-hundred-year birthday celebration in 1976.

Quayle called the publisher twice for copies); *Victory in the Gulf* (written by the staff of *U.S. News & World Report*); *The Gulf War Reader: History, Documents, Opinions; CNN Reports: War in the Gulf* (CNN also produced a video); *How to Defeat Saddam Hussein;* and *Operation Desert Shield: The First 90 Days* (a book of photographs). But while these books enjoyed some financial success, the authors who showed up on the battle lines first with thoughtful books were the most rewarded.

Capitol Hill offers especially rewarding sweepstakes. Upton Sinclair wrote *The Jungle* to reveal the lives of poor urban slum dwellers. Legislators were hashing out pure food and drug laws at the time, and the public was less interested in Sinclair's hero than in his job in Chicago's unsanitary stockyards. "I aimed at the public's heart," Sinclair said later, "and by accident I hit it in the stomach." Although the writing and plotting were far from elegant, the book sold twenty-five thousand copies within the first six weeks of publication in 1906. Similarly, David McCullough's *The Path Between the Seas: The Creation of the Panama Canal* appeared when Congress reconsidered its canal treaty with Panama. I covered Capitol Hill at the time and, as I recall, each legislator received a copy.

But news breaks can come anywhere, anytime. Three different biographies of Che Guevara appeared in 1997. No one could have anticipated that the body of the revolutionary would be found in Bolivia at the same time and moved to Cuba for reburial in the Sierra Maestra. A serious, long-planned book about the Titanic, *Unsinkable,* happened to appear when the movie did. It almost certainly would not have become a best seller under normal conditions. Nor would a 1958 book on the same subject, *A Night to Remember* by Walter Lord, have gone back to press for what is now more than seventy printings in excess of 2.7 million copies. Even a small whiff of news that a movie may be in the offing can be good luck for a book. Budd Schulberg's *What Makes Sammy Run?* did well when it came out in 1941 and was still selling at the rate of about one thousand copies a year in the early 1990s. When people started whispering about a movie possibility in 1998, it became a best seller on the *Los Angeles Times*'s paperback best-seller list.

This type of publishing luck will become all the more powerful now that CNN sends a daily schedule of top news items to Barnes & Noble. This allows the bookseller to promote the most newsworthy books in the ads that it runs over the network for its online book service. Bear in mind, though, that news breaks work the other way around, too. A writer saws away for years on a study of modern Russia. Finally, this exhaustively researched book makes its way to stores and, wham, there is a coup in Moscow. The entire leadership is on its way out. This is what happened to the hapless former Senator Gary Hart and his *Russia Shakes the World: The Second Russian Revolution and Its Impact on the West.* He had done the second revolution. The public was wondering about the third.

Bon Mots and Bonne Chances

The National Book Award in the United States fetches ten thousand dollars and a crystal sculpture. The Booker Prize in England brings more money, twenty thousand pounds. But it is not the prize money that counts most. The winner of France's Prix Goncourt receives only fifty francs, not enough money for a decent meal on the Champs-Elysées, but the real reward comes later. Having garnered a prize, a book almost certainly will enjoy a big boost in sales, and publishers will clamor for the rights to a prize-winning author's next book. Salman Rushdie and Anita Brookner saw their careers soar when they won the Booker for *Midnight's Children* and *Hotel du Lac,* respectively.

It is tempting to think that these awards are based strictly on merit. Don't be tempted. Many books are meritorious. The so-called best books are merely a matter of taste. With judges being quirky, figuring out the next winner is rather like betting at roulette, except the odds are worse. There is always the lingering suspicion that, unlike the literary experts hired by bookies to set the odds for the Booker Prize, judges do not read all the entries all the way through.

Once authors realize that luck determines who wins prizes, they can relax a little and, with this added perspective, wait calmly for lightning to strike not only from some formal literary jury but also from some other authority who happens to like their work and puts in a good word for them with the reading public. The latter, in fact, is to be preferred. A *bon mot,* unlike a book award, is understood for what it really is, a *bonne chance.*

The obvious place to obtain a *bon mot* is from a literary authority. One of the more famous examples occurred with James Hilton's *Lost Horizon,* published in the 1930s. It did not attract many readers until Alexander

Woollcott recommended it in the *New Yorker* and said on his radio program that he "had gone quietly mad" about the book. It sold six thousand copies a week. Shangri-la, the name of the imaginary lamasery in Hilton's book, is now an entry in our dictionaries.

Whether the *bon mot* comes from a literary authority or not is really irrelevant. Personal advice columnist Ann Landers can make the presses run full tilt. Nearly fifty publishers rejected *Staying Dry: A Practical Guide to Bladder Control* before Johns Hopkins University Press agreed to take it. Once the book was published, none of the major bookstore chains would stock it. Enter Landers. When she put a good word about the book in one of her columns, the fortunes of the three authors—Kathryn L. Burgio, K. Lynette Pearce, and Angelo J. Lucco—reversed instantly. The press marketing director at Johns Hopkins said he had trouble finding enough paper clips to attach checks to the letters that flowed in. *Staying Dry* sold more than one hundred thousand copies in a year. It was the 1991 winner of the Golden Fluke Award, presented by the Association of American University Presses.

A generous word from a president is money in the bank. Abraham Lincoln liked the poem "Mortality," which he apparently came across in a newspaper. Lore has it that he did not know who the author was. Still, he memorized the verses and repeated them over and over. Had he not done so, no one would remember the Scottish poet William Knox today. Teddy Roosevelt helped Owen Wister when he said he liked *The Virginian*. Eisenhower boosted Zane Grey, although Grey was well established by the time Ike was in the White House. Malcolm Muggeridge decried the "squalid aspirations" of Ian Fleming's 007 books, which appealed to a public that had an "inglorious appetite for speed at the touch of a foot on an accelerator and for sex at the touch of a hand." John F. Kennedy, one of those readers, helped Fleming when he revealed that he liked James Bond thrillers. (He also did a big favor for Evelyn Wood when he sent a dozen White House staffers to her speed-reading course. After that people flocked to the Evelyn Wood Reading Dynamics Institute.) Reagan put in a nice word for Tom Clancy, although one guesses he waited for the movie to come out. Mystery writer Walter Mosley enjoyed a steep increase in sales when Bill Clinton said he read his books and invited the author to the White House. (A prime minister, or ex–prime minister, is as good as a president. Lord Asquith gave Lytton Strachey's *Eminent Victorians* a valuable boost in an Oxford lecture. "It must be confessed that the lecture was a horribly dull one," Strachey told his mum, "—but one can't be too severe after such a noble piece of advertisement.")

A *mauvais mot* can be as good as a *bon mot*. When Czech President Václav Havel and his young actress wife were given gossipy treatment in *The Seven Days That Shook the Castle,* they sued the author who had to black out some of the juicy contested sections. Sales soared for the book, which now bore a **CENSORED** stamp on the cover. When Abolhassan Bani-Sadr, the former president of Iran, wanted to come to the United States to promote his book *My Turn to Speak: Iran, the Revolution & Secret Deals with the U.S.,* the State Department said no. After officials changed their minds, more than twenty reporters greeted him at the airport. His American publisher quickly printed more books. An angry Mets baseball player generated attention for *The Worst Team Money Could Buy: The Collapse of the New York Mets* when he tried to punch one of the authors. "You can't buy that kind of publicity," said the book's editor.

Ditto for the forty-thousand-dollar full-page ad in the *New York Times* taken out by the attorney for junk bond mastermind Michael Milken. The ad lambasted James Stewart's *Den of Thieves: How Ivan Boesky, Michael Milken, Martin Siegel, and Dennis Levine Plundered and Created Havoc on Wall Street.* Milken can be excused for being irritable at the time. He was appealing a ten-year prison sentence, plus the feds and his old firm, Drexel Burnham Lambert, were suing him for more than one billion dollars. But Milken hardly got even with Stewart. Stewart's book made it to the *New York Times* best-seller list.

There is nothing better than dramatically losing a book award *and* getting a bad word to boot. Federico Andahazi, an Argentine author, wrote a novel about a scientist who made practical studies of the clitoris. No one paid much attention until *The Anatomist* won the Fortabat Foundation prize for the best first novel by an Argentine. When Amalia Lacroze de Fortabat learned that this book had won, she canceled the ceremony and took out newspaper ads attacking the book. The result was booming sales in Andahazi's home country and, thanks to the publicity, a fat contract with a United States publisher who wanted to do an English-language translation. While Señora Lacroze de Fortabat did not give Andahazi the prize, she relented to pressure and gave him the prize money, fifteen thousand dollars.

Devilish Luck

One of the signs of Napoleon's greatness, a writer once told a German publishing house, was that he had a publisher shot. Lafcadio Hearn, a nineteeth-century writer, told his publishing house that its opinion had "less than the value of a bottled fart." One day, Goethe said his relationship with his publisher "could only become more beautiful"; the next, angry that mail from his publisher was delayed, he said publishers "are all fiends, there must be a special hell for them."

Delighted when that first book contract arrives in the mail, authors often view their publishers as saints. Afterward, discontent gradually eats into the relationship like so many termites. As the relationship nears collapse, authors fixate so much on what is wrong they forget that really bad publishers may be the greatest blessing of all.

After handing Hong Kong over to the Chinese, the last British governor of the longtime British colony contracted with HarperCollins to write a book. The hand-over received worldwide press attention, making Christopher Patten a celebrity. "I have never read a book by any modern politician which is so lucid or engrossing," said a HarperCollins executive after reading some of the early chapters from *East and West: China, Power, and the Future of Asia*. To build interest in the book, the publisher held a special dinner at the Savoy.

Having done all these kind things for their author, HarperCollins then did the nicest of all. Rupert Murdoch, who owned HarperCollins, decided to cancel publication of the book. The reason, most thought, was that the media magnate did not want to offend the Chinese, with whom his publishing empire was conducting business. (HarperCollins had published the English-language edition of a biography of Deng Xiaoping by his loving daughter at the same time that Murdoch was seeking a Chinese satellite license for Star TV.) Patten immediately received a new contract, this time with Macmillan in London. In addition to keeping his $200,000 HarperCollins advance, he and his forthcoming book enjoyed more press attention than a battalion of publicists could have generated. When the United States edition appeared, the cover had a large red sticker announcing that this was "The Book Rupert Murdoch Refused to Publish." The press release also took full advantage of Murdoch's generosity: "*East and West* . . . was too controversial for Harper-

Collins to publish." And if this were not sweet revenge enough, there were the reviews that pointed out, often in the first paragraph, that Murdoch welshed on the book deal.

Bret Easton Ellis was just as lucky, though less deservingly so, when he wrote *American Psycho*, a novel about a Wall Street executive who kills women in ghastly ways. In 1990, Simon & Schuster reneged on its agreement to publish the sordid tale. This, too, generated press attention that never could have been bought. Vintage, another publisher, picked up the book. It was a best seller.

Dead Lucky

"Good career move," said Gore Vidal when he learned that Truman Capote had died.

Sure, death presents some problems, especially when it comes just before a book is released. Dead authors sell no tales. No autographing parties. No talk show appearances. And SADS, Sudden Author Death Syndrome, is particularly bad when the author is: Jim Fixx, author of *The Complete Book of Running*, who died while jogging; Joseph E. McEvoy, who had a heart attack shortly before publication of *Swim Your Way to Fitness: A Lifetime of Exercise Programs;* or Jerome Rodale, a publisher of organic food books who bragged "I'm going to live to be 100 unless I'm run down by a sugar-crazed taxi driver" and then keeled over while taping a segment for the *Dick Cavett Show.*

Still, when beloved authors die, as happened when J. Anthony Lukas committed suicide shortly after completing *Big Trouble,* literary friends can do the book tour for them. And an author's death is news. Obituaries sell new books and resuscitate old books that everyone has forgotten. You can't be rediscovered until you have died.

A few years ago I read an obituary for Eleanor Clark, a writer with whom I was not familiar. The death notice reported that her *Rome and a Villa* was a minor classic. Interested, I called a used book service looking for a copy. The clerk told me that since the obituary, people were bombarding them with requests for the book.

Seth Morgan died in a motorcycle accident shortly after *Homeboy* came out in 1990. "Alive, we sold maybe two copies a week," said a bookstore owner in New Orleans, where Morgan lived. "But the day he died, we sold out our last twenty signed copies. It's crazy. Strangers still offer us eighty dollars for them, but we sold the ones Seth signed a long time ago."

"You don't want to be out of stock when an author dies," says Les Phillabaum, director of Louisiana State University Press. Publishers, however, are leery of taking on a book written by an unknown who has just passed away. The book is not only subject to the usual marketplace vagaries; certain long-term rewards are also more limited. Publishers want sustained relationships with talented writers. That is why they try to put clauses in book contracts that give them options on the author's next book. As publishers see it, the publicity dollars spent on the first book build an audience for subsequent books.

But the tragic death of an author also heightens the mystique of a book, especially if it, too, has tragic elements. Phillabaum learned this firsthand. John Kennedy Toole, another young man from New Orleans, committed suicide after writing *A Confederacy of Dunces.* Toole's mother convinced Walker Percy to read a smudged carbon of the manuscript. He passed it on to Phillabaum at LSU Press, which decided to take a chance. The book won a Pulitzer Prize and twenty years later continued to sell in excess of a hundred thousand copies annually. It is a comic novel and sad. "The tragedy of the book," Percy would later say, "is the tragedy of the author."

Many dead authors are like a mummy I used to see at a local run-down museum when I was a boy. Its hair, according to local lore, kept growing some years after the body was dead. The prolific Victor Hugo died in 1885, and, as his biographer notes, the posthumous publication of new "important works . . . retrospectively changed the landscape of nineteenth-century French literature and increased the size of Hugo's *Oeuvres Complètes* by about a third. . . . Unknown fragments have been emerging ever since. It will be a long time before any edition of his correspondence can be described as 'complete.'" As Isaac Asimov said, "Why should a little thing like death put an end to my writing."

Ernest Hemingway has not rested in peace since his suicide in 1961. As the chart on page 171 shows, his posthumous work includes previously unpublished novels as well as collections of his correspondence, newspaper reports, and short stories. Much of this material he did not think worthy of publication, and he left explicit instructions that some should not be published. Loved ones, however, figure it is none of his business anymore; it's theirs. Hemingway remains one of Scribner's top authors. A 1999 book by Hemingway is *True at First Light*, an unfinished autobiographical novel that was condensed and edited by one of his children. "This is it," Charles Scribner III has said; "there are no more books." But don't believe it. The offspring who edited this book is in his seventies and may not have any more of Papa's books in him. But Hemingway's kids have kids, and they likely will find something to condense and edit, even if it is an old Hemingway laundry list.

When profitable authors die and leave no unpublished work, publishers scare up ghosts. V. C. Andrews, author of horror books directed at the teenage market, died in 1986. She had written seven books. By the end of 1998, twenty-four new books had appeared under her name. The ghostwriter, Andrew Neiderman, created new characters, and the books sold better than Andrews's had. This inevitably led to disputes with Andrews's heirs. Neiderman felt that his $1.75-million take on the fifth book was too small considering that it made $4.5 million for the Andrews's estate. On the other hand, Neiderman admitted feeling "a second presence" when he was writing the books, and all parties agreed that Andrews's name needed to stay on the books for marketing reasons. Said the publisher, "The intent of the estate is to continue to publish books that are imbued with Virginia's spirit."

There are many others who publish from beyond the grave. In 1998, thirty-eight years after Richard Wright died, *Haiku: This Other World*, the last book he wrote, appeared for the first time. Jules Verne's rejected futuristic novel, *Paris in the 20th Century*, did not appear until the twentieth century was virtually over; it was a best seller anyway. Louis L'Amour died in 1988. Bantam has kept all his old books in print and introduced new ones year after year. Each book has a previously unused jacket photograph of the immortal author. "To his readers," one Bantam executive says, "Louis is still around. We still speak of his work in the present tense."

John Gardner has written Ian Fleming–James Bond books, and Robert Goldborough has written Rex Stout–Nero Wolfe books. Alexandra Ripley wrote a sequel to Margaret Mitchell's *Gone With the Wind*, and St. Martin's Press paid $4.5 million for the rights to write another sequel. The sequel to the sequel has not yet materialized because of protracted and broken-off haggling with the first prospective author, Pat Conroy, but it will in due course.

Perish and Publish
Posthumous Books by Ernest Hemingway

ERNEST
HEMINGWAY
1899–1961
WIP*

*Write in Peace

1964
A Moveable Feast (nonfiction)

1969
The Fifth Column and Four Unpublished Stories of the Spanish Civil War (story collection)

1970
Islands in the Stream (novel)

1972
The Nick Adams Stories (includes eight sketches or rejected story fragments)

1982
Ernest Hemingway: Selected Letters

1985
Along with Youth: Hemingway, the Early Years (biography by Peter Griffin contains five fragments and unfinished sketches by Hemingway: "The Ash Heel's Tendon: A Story," "Crossroads: An Anthology," "The Current: A Story," "The Mercenaries," and "Portrait of the Idealist in Love")
The Dangerous Summer (autobiographical nonfiction)

Ernest Hemingway: Dateline Toronto (journalism articles from the *Toronto Star*)

1986
The Garden of Eden (novel)

1987
The Complete Short Stories of Ernest Hemingway: The Finca Vigía Edition (extracts and manuscript fragments, none of which was intended for publication as a complete story)

1994
Hemingway: The Toronto Years (biography by William Burrill that included twenty-five previously unpublished journalism articles by Hemingway)

1998
The Good Lion (children's book)

1999
At the Hemingways: With Fifty Years of Correspondence between Ernest and Marcelline Hemingway
True at First Light (novel)

Compiled by Bonnie Bauman

Anne Frank noted in her diary that she wanted to be a famous writer and "go on living even after my death!" Her name is now a registered trademark. Royalties go to Anne Frank nonprofit organizations, not only from *The Diary of Anne Frank*, but from "I Am Anne Frank" musical compact disks. There have been suggestions for the manufacture of Anne Frank blue jeans.

The death of the principal character in a nonfiction book also presents life-after-death opportunities. When Princess Diana died in a car accident, old biographies appeared bearing new titles. *Diana: Her Life in Photographs* became *Diana, Princess of Wales: A Tribute in Photographs*. *Diana: Her True Story* came out as *Diana, Her True Story—In Her Own Words*. The author of this last work, Andrew Morton, admitted for the first time that he had worked closely with Her Royal Highness in preparing the first book. Random House published *Diana: A Tribute*, an updated version of an earlier book published in Britain.

Capote's death not only enhanced the value of his books. "It turned out to be a bigger boon to Capote's friends. There have already been three books about him since his death thirteen years ago," said Julia Reed, who was reviewing George Plimpton's 1997 book, *Truman Capote*.

Near death—as in being sick or really, really old—is sometimes as good as death itself. Shortly before Dr. Spock died in 1998, his wife said that she needed financial help to keep him alive. She staged a series of fund raisers to coincide with the release of the seventh revised edition of his baby book.

People who stave off death fascinate us. We give them special parking places and suspend judgment when they write books. The Beardstown Ladies, celebrated for their putatively brilliant investment club, sold eight hundred thousand copies of their first book, success that led to other books. Nothing much changed when a mean-spirited little whippersnapper in Chicago reported that their investments really weren't that good and neither was their math. The little old ladies had not known the right way to calculate annualized returns; the proper calculations showed their returns fell far below the market annual averages. They were sorry. "We're saddened by the people who judged us guilty and suggested we were in it for the money," said Betty Sinnock, the lady who can't add. "I feel like [the reporter] really didn't relate what the Beardstown Ladies were all about." Accepting the apology, the public keep buying the books, in which the publisher didn't work too hard at inserting correction slips. Sinnock remained on the individual investors committee to the New York Stock Exchange. The reporter attended a speech for which Sinnock received a standing ovation. "They got away with it, and more power to them," one of the members of the audience told him. "Look at how many books they've sold."

Helen Hooven Santmyer's *And Ladies of the Club* attracted extraordinary press attention that would not have come if the novelist hadn't been an octogenarian (eighty-eight years old, to be exact). Ohio State University Press, which dared to publish all 1,344 pages of its rambling prose about daily life in a small Ohio town, won the same Golden Fluke Award once received by *Staying Dry*. The book hit the best-seller lists; after the venerable Ms. Santmyer passed away, she spawned another book: *Early Promise, Late Reward*, a biography drawn from five hundred letters she had written to family.*

Similarly Jessie Lee Brown Foveaux got lucky when a *Wall Street Journal* feature reported that she had written a memoir while in a writing program for senior citizens. She was nearly ninety-eight. Some thought her memoirs in the same vein as *The Bridges of Madison County*, hugely popular at the time. Within minutes of the *Journal* article, publishers, literary agents, and Hollywood producers were calling her in Manhattan, Kansas. After reading the book, several publishers lost interest because they thought the writing "boring" and, perhaps, because the bidding was steep. Warner got *Any Given Day: The Life and Times of Jessie Lee Brown Foveaux* with a seven-figure offer. If boring, the book was at least charmingly short (287 pages) compared to Santmyer's hefty tome. "Not only has this woman's life spanned the whole century," said one bidding enthusiast, "but it has elements of every part of life—marriage, divorce, alcoholism, children. It also has incredible commercial appeal."

Scanning the sea of used books in his Dublin store, Fred Hanna once told a visitor, "Once these people die, they come into vogue. That's a sad thing." But Walt Whitman also understood that death can take authors to their true reward. As he put it in *Song of Myself,* "Has any one supposed it lucky to be born? / I hasten to inform him or her, it is just as lucky to die and I know it."

*Anyone looking for lucky patterns may wish to note that the first two Golden Fluke Awards went to a book on bladder control and to a book by an old person.

Whitman, by the way, could also speak to the good fortune that comes with a *bon mot* from the nation's First Reader. Kenneth Starr's aggressive investigation of President Clinton revealed that the president gave *Leaves of Grass* to Monica Lewinsky. A few booksellers said sales bumped up a little.

Whitman would have been even luckier, of course, if he had stayed away from poetry. Sales of *OY VEY! The Things They Say! A Book of Jewish Wit* shot up 250 percent when Starr reported that Lewinsky gave a copy to Clinton.

SEVEN

Best Stolen Books

—◊◊◊—

In which it is shown that we are
born with the urge to steal the books
that mean the most to us.

—◊◊◊—

—◦◈◦—

Never lend books, for no one ever returns them. The
only books I have in my library are books that other folk
have lent me.

—ANATOLE FRANCE

—◦◈◦—

The New York Public Library, true to the spirit of a knowledge-propagating institution, irrepressibly provides all sorts of facts about itself. Speaking about the Central Research Library on Fifth Avenue and Forty-second Street, staff reel off statistics on the length of the book stacks (132 miles) and the number of inquiries to the library's Telephone Reference Service in the 1997 fiscal year (118,236). They can even tell you some of the typical questions people ask: what is the word for fear of the number thirteen (triskaidekaphobia), and is the country of Rwanda for sale (no). But ask one certain question and the first reaction comes from another great library tradition: Shhhhhhhh!

The question? Which books are most frequently missing—you know, disappear from bookshelves or never seem to be returned? Or, less delicately phrased: Which books do people steal most often?

Librarians are not the only ones troubled by the question. All guardians of books are: bookstore proprietors, the nice attendants in Christian Science reading rooms, and you and I, who loan our dearest books to our dearest friends knowing but not admitting that the volumes are gone forever.*

Yet, for all the angst the question causes, it is worth asking. The answer tells us as much about our intellectual lives as Alfred Kinsey's studies did about our sex lives.

A General History of Book Theft

Best-seller lists are supposed to be a barometer of our tastes. Really, they reflect the capacity of affluent Americans to throw down twenty-five or thirty dollars for a thin diet book they don't have the will power to use or for a fat, everybody-is-reading-it tome that they won't ever get around to reading. The best-stolen list, in contrast, tells us which books people really want—want so much that borrowing them for a week or two is not enough. For these books, people risk public humiliation or arrest.

*Many of us keep a mental ledger of what we have gained and lost. A friend wrote me about the books missing from his shelves. "The one book in my library that I believe was stolen from a library is Vol. 1 of *Kapital*, 331.01M392, stamped L.A. Public Library, but I inherited or stole this book from a post-college roommate, ————. It's okay, though, because he was a YPSL [Young Peoples Socialist League]."

Everybody steals books. In 1992, the Library of Congress apprehended three aggressive thieves—a doctor, a government lawyer, and a book dealer, the latter a great-great-grandnephew of Robert E. Lee. About the same time, a British constable was sentenced to eighteen months for book theft. While investigating a murder, he stole three Waverly novels, a set of encyclopedias, and a set of sacred texts from the victim's east London flat. "People who steal books are some of the best people in the world," says Allan Robbins, now retired from the Alexandria, Virginia, library system. Certainly, they are the people who love and use books the most—the people, you might say, who are most likely to be angry when they visit a library and find the volume they want is missing.

One class of especially prime suspects includes the likes of the former Groton instructor found in 1931 with more than 2,500 volumes from the Harvard library. He said he was preparing for a college professorship. The academic book thief most often cited is the notorious Italian Count Guglielmo Libri-Carucci. He started out in the mid–nineteenth century as a professor of science at the University of Paris, edited the *Journal des Savants*, and at length secured an appointment as secretary of a commission responsible for cataloging important historical manuscripts in French libraries. He traipsed from library to library, using his specialized knowledge to identify the best books. Many of these he stuffed

Pope Not-so-Innocent X. Is that a book he is holding in this famous painting by Velázquez? If so, he probably lifted it from someone else's library.

Pope Innocent X, portrait by Velázquez, 1649, courtesy of Galleria Doria Pamphili, Rome

under his cloak when he left town. As a result of selling his literary loot, he was found out and fled to England. He took eighteen crates of books with him.

Thou-shall-not-steal types have been among the most brazen biblio-klepts. As a middling prelate, Giambattista Pamfili came to inspect a well-endowed private library in Paris with a group assembled by one Cardinal Barberini, who had vouched for all of them. Nevertheless, Pamfili tucked a history of the Council of Trent inside his robes. When the library's owner realized a book was missing, Barberini shut the door and insisted that everyone undergo a search. Pamfili protested, a struggle took place, and the volume dropped from his robes to the floor. As Pope Innocent X, Pamfili drove the Barberini family out of Rome and had generally terrible relations with the French. He paid for his sins, too. People stole books from *his* library.

Cardinal Domenico Passionei, while Vatican librarian, stole the books he was supposed to safeguard. He was not inclined to take a holiday from book theft when he was away from the office, either. When visiting an abbey, Passionei would enter its library, ostensibly to do research, lock the door, and throw rare volumes out the window so that he might easily pack them off when his visit was over.

Nor is book theft the exclusive province of the Church of Rome. Leaders of other denominations were every bit as zealous. At the turn of the century, Boston book dealers reported that local Protestant ministers were stealing sermon pamphlets.

Governments regard book pirates the way Queen Elizabeth regarded Francis Drake's privateering, as patriotic. The Alexandrian Library, the greatest of its time, had a section called "Books from the Ships." The Alexandrians confiscated volumes from voyagers who pulled into port, copied each, and returned either the original or the copied version to the ship and kept the other for themselves. Roman generals considered books legitimate spoils of war. Emilius Paulus, for one, claimed the entire Royal Macedonian Library as a prize; Sulla claimed the collection of Apellicon of Teos, which held books that had belonged to Aristotle. (Cicero, who complained about his trusted slave Dionysius stealing precious manu-scripts from *his* private library, used Sulla's purloined books.) From their raids of England, the Vikings took books back in their ships. During the Thirty Years' War, the Swedes collected treasures for Stockholm's Royal

Library from Germany, Denmark, Poland, Bohemia, and Moravia. When French revolutionaries toppled Louis XVI, they stole books from the First and Second Estates (the nobility and clergy) and eventually placed them in public libraries for the Third Estate (the common people). It was these books the good Count Libri appropriated for himself.

After World War II, the Red Army carted entire German libraries back to Moscow. Some stayed there (the Lenin Library received 760,000 volumes) and millions of others ended up in provincial libraries. The Germans are still trying to get the books back, a daunting task since no decent records exist on where all the books ultimately went or, if found, where they should be returned. "We are not even concerned with books from the eighteenth and nineteenth centuries," a leading German librarian has commented. "What we want are the main collections of libraries from the early sixteenth and seventeenth centuries."

The United States did not sign the international copyright convention written in Bern in the late nineteenth century. This, too, was a type of theft. American publishers did not want to relinquish their ability to re-publish foreign books without paying for them. The East Asians have been particularly aggressive in carrying on this tradition. "To steal a book," according to a Chinese saying "is an elegant offense." Years ago, I picked up several pirated editions of English-language works in Taipei. The Taiwanese publisher brazenly had reproduced the original copyright notice. More recently, a Chinese publisher wrote to Joseph Stiglitz, who served on President Clinton's Council of Economic Advisers, asking if he would write a special preface to his economic textbook, which they were pirating.

Book theft is an integral part of the lifestyles of today's rich and famous. Gustav Hasford, an Academy Award nominee for his work on the screenplay for *Full Metal Jacket,* was convicted of stealing thousands of books, many from overseas libraries. According to a 1960s study, a high school educating children of wealthier parents experienced more than twice as much library theft as a school serving the poor. The Waldorf-Astoria, whose presidential suite goes for as much as seven thousand dollars a night, buys about two hundred used books a year, its manager told me a few years ago. The hotel puts these on shelves in the rooms and along the hallways so wealthy guests can steal them.

Less pricey hotels, by the way, also treat books like soap, towels, and the mints that they put on your pillow. Rome's cozy Hotel Olympic, a short walk from the Vatican, is my favorite. In my room, I found a paperback with the hotel's name on the cover and short stories by Paul von Heyse, Leo Tolstoy, and D. H. Lawrence inside. A quote on the flyleaf, from Cicero, read, "A room without books is as a body without a soul." The idea, the management made clear, was that guests should feel free to take the room's soul home in their luggage.

Much further downscale are Hilton hotels. When Conrad Hilton published his autobiography in 1957, the *Library Journal* said it was "well recommended, but may have a limited appeal." They could not have been more wrong. Management puts a copy in each of the chain's 102,232 rooms. Once a year, each hotel tells headquarters how many copies it needs. The turnover is nearly 100 percent a year, says public relations senior manager Kenra Walker. This means that the publisher, Simon & Schuster, has a guaranteed sale of about 100,000 copies a year. If you have an old copy of Hilton's life in your library, be certain to spend a night at a Hilton. Simon & Schuster published a new edition in 1994, and you'll want to pick it up.

Apparently, the only thing that keeps people from stealing books is that the thought hasn't yet occurred to them. "I have to tell you I don't enjoy talking about this subject," said one librarian in a typical statement. "I don't want to give people ideas."

The Criminal Book Mind

In 1992, looters of a Sunset Boulevard strip mall had their way with Circuit City and Trak Auto. They did not touch Crown Books. Which proves that the primordial urge to pilfer books originates in a different part of the brain than does the inclination to swipe a television. Librarians admit as much when they refrain from using words like "stolen" and talk about long overdue books not having been "returned yet." They obviously wouldn't be so charitable about someone who had hot-wired their cars.

The difference between books and cars is that books deal in ideas, and ideas are supposed to be free. New York City law recognizes this distinction. The city fathers require street vendors, who often sell stolen goods, to acquire licenses—unless they are book peddlers. Book peddlers/thieves are protected from licensing by New York's free speech laws. The man who turned in mega–book thief Stephen Blumberg told an interviewer afterward, "I *am* a bad guy."

No one with any sense would ever ask a barber for a free haircut. Perfect strangers ask writers and publishers for free copies of their books all the time. One colleague of mine, an occasional writer, proudly told me that she wheedled *two* free copies of one of my books from the publisher on the pretense that she was a reviewer. (Posing as a reviewer is a common book theft ploy done through the mail. It's essential if one already is in prison and can't drop by the local bookstore for a little stealing. But academics have been known to do this with impunity, creating fake journals and asking publishers for books to review.)

French writer Tallemant de Réaux said book stealing is not a crime if you do not sell the book, but merely want to keep it. Bookstore clerks see this attitude among "customers" every day. One tells me about a man in a three-piece suit who left with two books for which he had not paid. When the clerk chased him down, the thief made no apology. Instead, he tried to strike a bargain: He would pay for one book if the clerk gave him the other free. Others treat bookstores as if they were circulating libraries. They buy a book, read it, then return it. This can go on forever.

How many books are missing? In 1978, Princeton found that more than 4 percent of its library holdings were lost, along with about 10 percent of the books in the branch libraries. Ten years ago, the director of collection development for the Chicago Public Library system guessed that as many books are stolen each year as they buy. In the 1990s, the New York Public Library inventoried its 132-mile-long research collection, from which books cannot be checked out. About 1.5 percent of the books were missing, says Caroline Oyama, manager of library public relations.

But who knows for certain? Just as it is difficult to find a needle in a haystack, it is difficult to know if one is missing. The whole idea of theft is to avoid detection. Besides, when juggling thousands of books, librarians can inadvertently misplace a few, so that something by L. Ron Hubbard ends up next to Dante's *Inferno*. It's not always easy to distinguish between what is overdue, what is lost in the system, or what is stolen, librarians often say. Moreover, with the costs of books and periodicals increasing, libraries have less money to conduct inventories. And librarians don't like to count missing books anyway. The experience is too painful.

"Everybody is still making up the numbers," says Katherine Leab, editor of *American Book Prices Current,* which is of use to rare book dealers and to dedicated criminals who want to steal only the best.

The American Top Ten

Any book is vulnerable. Not long ago, someone lifted the reservation book from one of New York City's more elegant restaurants, La Côte Basque. This probably will never happen again. But some books are stolen every day. Despite imperfect statistics and the reticence of most in the know to talk, it is possible to piece together a plausible best-stolen list in somewhat the same way police artists sketch a criminal's face from fragmentary recollections. Here is the result:

Number One: The Bible

From a marketing point of view, the Bible is, truly, the Good Book. Almost 80 percent of Americans in one study ranked it the most influential book in history. (Second was *Dr. Spock's Baby and Child Care,* selected by only 4.7 percent of respondents.) Bookstore shoppers spend an estimated $400 million a year on Bibles. And when the devout are not paying for them, they are stealing them.

Stealing the Bible might seem to defeat the purpose of wanting it in the first place: salvation. Yet we can take it as an article of faith that the Bible is the number one best-stolen book of all time. To most people, the word of God bespeaks a merciful supreme being, not one who will hurl lightning bolts out of the skies at those who ignore the Ten Commandments.

One ploy when stealing in a bookstore is to take an expensive Bible out of its case and put it in the case of a cheaper Bible, thus getting a better price and perhaps a venial instead of a mortal sin entered in the Big Card Catalog in the Sky. The easiest way to get a free Bible, though, is to check into a hotel. Bibles are considered housekeeping items, like soap and towels, says a spokesperson for the American Hotel & Motel Association. The Bible moves as quickly out of foreign hotels as it does out of American ones. A cleaning lady in Singapore's Meridian Hotel told me that rooms lost more Bibles than *The Teaching of Buddha,* which is written in English and Japanese and has an explicit note inviting people to steal it. The Nashville-based Gideon Society doesn't invite people to steal the

Bibles it places in hotel rooms. It just leaves them temptingly tucked in a drawer within easy grasp of the bed. Not wanting to be weighed down with as much guilt as the converts they are creating, the Gideons are heavy into denial. Ask Jerry Burden, the Gideons' executive director, if he knows how many Bibles are stolen each year by budding Christians, and his response is "That's one of those things we don't comment on." The society doesn't distinguish between books that are stolen and those that are defaced or worn out, another staff member said defensively. The Gideon Society simply replaces books as necessary. It does this on a colossal scale. In 1997, it distributed forty-five million Bibles in seventy-seven languages in 172 countries. This is a sharp increase over a decade ago, in large part because the Gideons have expanded their entrapment scheme to formerly communist countries that have opened themselves to salvation.*

Number Two: The Joy of Sex

Sex books fill a special, high-volume niche in book crime for several reasons. First, everyone has doubts about his or her sexual prowess, sexual attractiveness, etc. How could it be otherwise? Advertisers link sexual themes to the purchases of cars and bathroom cleaners. Second, as much as they think about sex, most Americans think they are doing something wrong when they search out a book telling them how to get more out of

---

*Can one truly steal the Bible in as much as it is God's word and God gave it away free? This matter was resolved in *Urantia Foundation v Maaherra.*

In this case the Urantia Foundation, which claimed control over the *Urantia Papers,* sued Kristen Maaherra for reprinting the book and giving it free to friends. Maaherra argued that the foundation could not own the *Papers,* which originated, as the book put it, with "planetary celestial supervisors." These supervisors included the divine counselor, the chief of the Corps of Superuniverse Personalities, and the chief of the Archangels of Nebadon, all of whom spoke through the patient of a Chicago psychiatrist. The foundation argued that it owned the copyright because its members had assembled the teachings, which was a creative process.

The court, ill-equipped to determine the existence of the chief of the Corps of Superuniverse Personalities, sided with the foundation. It said that the *Papers* "did not belong to that narrow category of works in which the creative spark is utterly lacking or so trivial as to be virtually non-existent."

Message to God: If he wants to ensure *His* Word is free for all to take, he should file for a copyright or hope he does not end up in the U.S. Ninth Circuit Court of Appeals.

it. "People are a little ashamed, like buying a condom," said the late Dr. William A. Moffett, a leading authority on book theft and director of the Huntington Library in San Marino, California. "'I'm not getting this book for myself; I'm getting it for a friend.' The druggist didn't believe that either." The only convenient solution is to steal the book.

While all kinds of sex books have appeal, *The Joy of Sex* tops the list. According to a *Library Journal* survey, seventy-four public libraries reported that it and its sequels were the most-stolen books. It would probably beat out the Bible if hotels would put it in rooms, too.

Another book that does well is the one turned to when marital sex becomes joyless: the do-it-yourself divorce book. There is an edition for each state, so that readers can understand the particular laws that will lead to their sexual liberation. "We almost treat it as a commodity," one Maine librarian commented. "We buy multiple copies for multiple locations, and it's consumed."

Number Three: Practice for the Armed Services Test

Ask librarians from Ogden, Utah, to Towson, Maryland, which how-to books are the most popular, and they instantly think of a book that never makes it on the best-seller list: *Practice for the Armed Services Test.*

Runners up are *Practice for Promotion to Supervisory and Administration Positions in the Civil Service* and manuals for college entrance exams. A few years ago, the *Washington Post* reported that half the car repair manuals were missing from the Library of Congress. The library's inventory showed twenty-six copies of the *Joy of Cooking*, a book that has been revised over and over again. The staff could find only five copies. My guess is that *Constructing and Maintaining Your Well and Septic System*, published in 1984 and still on *Publishers Weekly's* "Home Repair Best Sellers" list in 1990, is missing as well.

Subtle regional tastes appear in this category. The citizens of Los Angeles apparently like to steal interior design books, according to press reports. Gardening books and car repair manuals go in Staten Island, say New York Public Library officials. Books on diagnosing medical problems, managing stress, and getting rich in real estate are in demand in Manhattan. New Yorkers generally are interested in stealing *How to Hypnotize Your Friends* and *How to Raise and Train Pigeons.*

As conditions change, so does the value of how-to books. One story that comes to mind is of the pregnant woman who checked out a book of baby names and kept it until her offspring was old enough to return the book for her.

Number Four: Curses, Hexes, and Spells

With good reason, the movie *Ghostbusters*'s opening scene was in a library. Books about the occult, demon worship, spiritualism, witchcraft, black magic, and other forces of darkness and light are regularly spirited out of libraries and bookstores. According to one British survey, books about the occult are more in demand in that country than are sex books. Bookstores also report that tarot cards frequently disappear.

Number Five: Steal This Book

Abbie Hoffman's *Steal This Book* is probably the most stolen of the anti-establishment books, which by definition invite theft. The beat writers Jack Kerouac, Charles Bukowski, Allen Ginsberg, and William Burroughs are in demand by nonpaying customers. Much of the black literature that is stolen seems to fall into this antiestablishment category as well. The autobiographies of Malcolm X and Angela Davis are difficult to find on library shelves.

The message of Hoffman's book so distressed publishers, he had to publish it himself. (The logo for his Pirate Press was a long-haired youth blowing up the Random House Cottage.) The book sold well. It appeared in April 1971, and by July sales reached one hundred thousand copies, according to a *New York Times* reviewer. "It's embarrassing. You try to overthrow the government and you wind up on the Best Seller's [*sic*] List," said Abbie Hoffman. The book also seems to have stolen well. When researching the subject of stolen books for an article, I could not locate a copy anywhere, including the New York Public Library and the Library of Congress.

A used paperback edition of *Steal This Book* goes for as much as $125— when you can find one. Hoffman's book is now out in new editions, not that you have to pay to get a copy. Before Hoffman died, he gave a copy to a friend who put the book on the Web. Readers can find it at http://tenant.net/Community/steal/index.html.

Number Six: Standard Federal Tax Reporter

This loose-leaf book, as well as other legal volumes, has as much chance of surviving securely in a law school library as does a state's witness in a Mafia trial. "The first student who gets his hands on an [assigned] book will take it," says one law librarian.

"Law school libraries have horrible times," says Dr. Deanna B. Marcum, president of the Council on Library and Information Resources. "I think it is because law school students are so competitive." By stealing a book, would-be lawyers not only can use it as long as they wish, but also deny its use to others. Apparently attuned to nuances of the law, law students often avoid stealing books in the technical sense. They just hide them in other parts of the library.

"Steal-and-hide" is also a problem at medical and business school libraries. And it remains a problem after professionals get out of school. A state-funded institution, the George Mason University law library in Virginia is open to the public. "A lot of losses come from attorneys," its former director, Phil Berwick, told me before he moved to another hotbed of crime, the Washington University School of Law.

If we need evidence that white-collar crime is as rampant as any other, this is it. Studies show that good students are more inclined to steal books than underachievers.

Number Seven: The Encyclopaedia Britannica

This book is grossly overpriced and unpleasant to buy, as anyone who ever has dealt with its pushy sales force knows. Lots of average people—and criminal middlemen who cater to them—avoid these annoyances and steal encyclopedias, as well as other pricey reference books. *The Encyclopedia of Tropical Fish* (price: seventy-five pounds) disappeared within half an hour of being placed on the shelves of a library in Cardiff, Wales. A standard tactic for obtaining multivolume reference books is to go from library to library picking up volumes until a complete set is assembled.

No book or set of books is too big to steal. A woman once stopped, horror struck, before a New York Public Library guard. Like the not-so-innocent Pope Innocent X, she had been found out, for from under her dress had fallen the eleven-pound, six-plus-inch-thick *Webster's Unabridged Dictionary.* She had been clutching it between her legs.

Number Eight: The Red Pony

When a teacher tells students to read one of the great books, libraries should double the guard. The first thief apprehended at the Lennox Library, a forerunner of the New York Public Library, was a sixteen-year-old boy. In 1897, he filched "a few books to help him in his school work," according to Phyllis Dain's history of the library. The library fined the boy twenty-five dollars, which must have cut a swath through a kid's allowance in those days. Today, youngsters rip off *For Whom the Bell Tolls*, Shakespeare's works, and that long-time teenage favorite, *Catcher in the Rye*. My guess is that *The Red Pony*, with one hundred or so pages of large-type text, is at the top of the list. In my high school days at Marmion Military Academy, it was the shortest book we knew of that qualified as literature.

Number Nine: The Birds of America

This James Audubon book of color plates defies theft. "It probably weighs more than you do," says Dr. Daniel Traister, curator of research services at the University of Pennsylvania. "It stands four or four-and-one-half feet off the ground." Nevertheless, it is one of the most frequently stolen rare volumes. One book bandit injured himself so badly trying to get *The Birds of America* out a window that he bled all over it.

The collectors' fever pushing the auction of Renoir's *Moulin* and van Gogh's *Portrait of Dr. Gachet* to more than seventy-five million dollars each has driven up the prices of rare books, along with the maps and other art inside them. Professional thieves sometimes don't take the whole volume, but snip out the valuable art work. In 1996, bandits broke into a church museum in the small northern Spanish town of Seu de Urgell, overpowered an attendant, smashed a large glass case, and took the most important piece, a religious book dating from the tenth century. A priest running the museum commented that the "worst would be if they sell off the pages and ruin the book." Audubon's book "goes for millions of dollars," Traister says. "It is almost worth more if sold plate-by-plate."

Skyrocketing prices, says Winston Tabb, associate librarian of Congress, are "one of the scariest things that is happening. . . . The value of your collection may triple overnight."

Money, though, is not always the motive, Traister says. Some people steal priceless books "they want to love; they think they can take care of them better than you can." A Spanish monk murdered eight people in the course of his rare book thefts in the 1830s. After being apprehended, Don Vicente showed little remorse. "Every man must die sooner or later, but good books must be conserved."*

Number Ten: The China Lobby in American Politics

Some books are stolen as a public service. Chiang Kai-shek's right-wing supporters did everything possible to keep Ross Koen's 1960s book on the China lobby from polluting thought. Not only did they steal it from libraries, they replaced it with the more favorable volume, *The China Lobby.*† Quite often censorious citizens remove library books that challenge "family values," leaving behind religious tracts.

One useful subranking of book theft would be those books stolen because someone wants them and those stolen because someone doesn't want others to read them. Book puritans are always sneaking into libraries and taking out the books people are trying to steal: sex and the occult, for instance, and the classics, which nobody wants to read but must filch to fulfill a classroom assignment. "Every year I go through this [listing of banned books] and think, good God, this is a Who's Who and a What's What of twentieth-century material," says Judith Krug, director of the American Library Association's Office for Intellectual Freedom.

It is impossible to rank the least stolen books with any certainty. But one type of undesirable book stands out, and that is poetry. The late American poet laureate Joseph Brodsky argued that to improve our citizenry we should put poetry in motel rooms, where it could be stolen along with Bibles and copies of Hilton's autobiography. One of Brodsky's disci-

*For a variation of this public service rationale, there is the case of the head of the National Weather Service in Fairbanks. He admitted taking a collection of late nineteeth- and twentieth-century weather statistics books, which had been housed in an Anchorage facility. This bookish Robin Hood said he planned to keep them at home for a "cooling off period," after which he would put them in the university archives in Fairbanks, where they would be used more often.

†When destroying *The China Lobby*, the publisher apparently overlooked one carton filled with copies of Koen's book. A friend of mine, now retired from publishing, spotted it and, fittingly, stole a copy.

ples, Andrew Carroll, actually has tried to put this idea into action. Carroll, executive director of American Poetry and Literacy, claims to have had some success, but the norm is the hotel executive who asked Carroll, "Who's this Robert Frost guy you work for again?" Carroll should learn from the Roman emperor Nero. Among his most hated civic projects were public poetry contests.

Book Crime and Punishment

Paul Washington, who has worked in security at the New York Public Library for many years, tells of investigators tracking "book crooks." One time, an investigator called on a woman who was painting the inside of her house in the nude. She invited him inside and gave him the overdue books. Mostly, though, efforts to staunch thievery are unamusing and frustrating. Librarians face unpleasant damned-if-you-do, damned-if-you-don't choices.

The ultimate fear of the conscientious librarian comes through in a story told by Sean O'Faolain. The Irish writer returned to a town where he had seen a well-stocked library. Finding it closed, he asked around. "Well, you see how 'twas," a local told him, "people came borrowing books, and borrowing books, until sure in the end we had to close it down."

The best way to safeguard books is not to lend them at all. Unfortunately, this approach defeats the purpose of the library, which is to make it easy for people to read. Similarly, most security measures potentially contribute to the feeling that a library is inhospitable. Librarians must learn to live with risk if they are to facilitate reading. It is a cost of doing business.

Prosecuting people who steal a couple of books or simply don't bother to bring them back after the due date may serve as a deterrent. On the downside, lawyers and the courts are pricey. It is much cheaper to buy a new copy of the purloined book.

Similarly, charging fines for overdue books is self-defeating when a book is overdue more than a couple of weeks. In no time at all, the late charge exceeds the cost of the book in the first place. In 1764, someone checked out *The Complete History of England with the Lives of All the Kings and Queens Thereof,* Volume III, from the Harvard Library. It reappeared in 1997. A two-dollar-a-week late fee would have come to $24,232. Many borrowers aren't willing to come up with a measly $24, even if it means giving up reading.

Amnesties, which let long-term book borrowers return their booty without penalty, help get books returned. They also send the message that if you wait long enough you will suffer no consequences.

By calling attention to book thefts, librarians can put the problem higher on professional crime-fighters' agendas. Unfortunately, news of active crime fighting suggests that books are being stolen, which is bad publicity. Taxpayers might become angry about the management of public libraries. Donors to university and private libraries might stop being generous. (For the same reason, libraries don't tell the public that each year they discard many books that are no longer in demand to make room for books people want to steal.)

As a result of the bull market in rare books, librarians have begun to talk a little more frankly. The late Dr. William A. Moffett became a leading authority on book theft when, as the Oberlin librarian, he apprehended a big-time crook. The culprit was a rare-book dealer, who pillaged libraries around the country using as aliases the names of presidential advisers. Sensitized to the problem of large-scale theft, Moffett held a national conference on the subject.

Jail sentences have become more common. An Arkansas thief, whose specialties included books about outlaws, got a fifteen-year sentence not long ago. Massachusetts passed a law with fines of up to $25,000 and five years jail time for stealing from libraries.

Virtually every library system seems to be searching for ways to improve book security. The Library of Congress hired as its director of security a former army intelligence officer who previously buttressed security for NASA space shuttle launches. The library has put theft-detection tags in especially valuable books, installed security cameras and electronic doors operated by pass cards, uses patrols, and limits the number of researchers who can roam freely about the stacks. The New York Public Library's guards learn verbal judo to retrieve books from malefactors. Checkpoint, a company that installs security devices in convenience stores, has a booming business working with some thirty thousand libraries across the country, according to Emmett Erwin, director of its library group. "Libraries are going to have to be less user-friendly and more security-conscious," says a former campus policeman who helped capture a library thief and decided to become a library security consultant.

Russian humorists Ilya Ilf and Evgeny Petrov once wryly commented on the scarcity of books in their country: "Tell me what you read, and I'll tell you whom you stole it from." Now technology does just that. Libraries can report stolen books on Internet networks. Rare-book dealers can check these to see if they are about to buy a stolen book.

Although no one can blame librarians for trying to protect their books, no one should expect them to have much success either. History is replete with failed efforts to stymie book thieves: chaining books to shelves and desks; threatening book thieves with excommunication, as one papal bull did; suing people for not returning books, as citizens of Renaissance Poland did; exiling thieves to Siberia, as happened in 1891 to Alois Pichler, who took four thousand books from the Imperial Public Library in St. Petersburg; even inserting curses in books, as in: "Whoever steals this Book of Prayer / May he be ripped apart by swine, / His heart be splintered, this I swear, / And his body dragged along the Rhine."

Nothing helps, not even declining literacy. Even the illiterate can appreciate that books make nice decoration, and the next best thing to being literate is to appear to be literate. The New York Public Library's Paul Washington mentions a guy who had two apartments, one to live in and another for his stolen books, which reached to the ceiling even in the bathroom. He didn't have any particular specialty. "He didn't read 'em. He just liked to be around books."

Despite all the new security at the Library of Congress, one of its staffers was recently indicted on twenty-two counts of theft. (And don't forget about members of the House and Senate, and their staffs, who can check books out of the library. What will get them to return the volumes, impeachment?) The sophistication of book thieves increases faster than the sophistication of libraries, says Katherine Leab of *American Book Prices Current*.

The courts have come to recognize that book theft is a natural, if not a legal, act. In 1991, the federal court in Des Moines tried Stephen C. Blumberg for stealing more than twenty thousand rare books worth twenty million dollars from 268 libraries and museums in forty-five states and the District of Columbia, two Canadian provinces, and possibly Europe. ("Possibly" because finding the owners for these books was a formidable task. The Online Computer Library Center with the help of forty volunteers worked five weeks to sort out the books and still could not find the proper homes of all of them.) "This son of mine is an oddball if you ever saw one," Blumberg's wealthy father said. In addition to wearing long underwear and wool overcoats year round, he was a collector of brass doorknobs. When he was having trouble in high school, specialists diagnosed him as schizophrenic, and he was institutionalized. His lawyer in the book caper case didn't take long to decide on an insanity defense. The jury disagreed, thus establishing the legal principle that anyone who has the urge to steal a book must be sane. Only the insane don't want to take a book that does not belong to them.

Mega–book thief Stephen C. Blumberg stole more than twenty thousand rare books worth twenty million dollars from 268 libraries and museums in forty-five states and the District of Columbia, two Canadian provinces, and possibly Europe. The Online Computer Library Center, with the help of these and many others, worked five weeks to sort out the books. They still could not find the proper homes for all of them. OCLC staff members helped prepare an inventory list of recovered stolen and rare books.
Courtesy of OCLC

EIGHT

Dear Mr. Politician: Please Don't Write

—⟨∿⟩—

In which budding presidents are
advised not to build their careers on
the false assumption that politics
lies easily with letters and that the
authorship of a good book will
chisel their visages on Mt.
Rushmore.

—⟨∿⟩—

—◦ν◦—

I can't think of a book that ever elected anybody.
—KEN MCCORMICK, PUBLISHER AND LITERARY
MIDWIFE TO PRESIDENTS

May our nation continue to be a beakon [*sic*] of hope to the world.
—DAN QUAYLE'S 1989 CHRISTMAS CARD

We don't hire presidents for their literary skills.
—RAY PRICE, SPEECH WRITER FOR "AUTHOR"
RICHARD M. NIXON

—◦ν◦—

Dear Political Friend:

I am sorry to hear that you are thinking about writing "a thoughtful, presidential book on some aspect of world affairs." I appreciate why you believe that this is an important brick on the road that you are paving to the White House. But as your friend and political confidant I counsel in the strongest terms possible against dissipating your energy this way. It is a detour at best and, if history is a guide, probably worse—and not only for you. Nothing good for the Republic comes from politicians writing books.

You've raised a number of reasons for writing a book. Please read carefully as I knock down each one.

You say, for starters, that "writing a lucid, trenchant book is a patriotic act in tune with our deepest aspirations."

I agree that our rhetoric, possibly some of our history, supports the view that it is an All-American pursuit to string words together. The Founding Fathers, as Theodore Draper put it, "ransacked the storehouse of ancient and modern history and literature for precedents, heroes, and inspiration." Then they wrote. First came rabble-rousing tracts against the king and Committees of Correspondence to ensure that grievances were widely broadcast. The Declaration of Independence, the Constitution, and the Bill of Rights, which followed, affirmed the sanctity of expression. The Constitution was the first ever to be printed, hence the first distributed widely as books are. We have come to think of our nation as one that lives by words and writing. We do not vote in the streets by force of arms; we cast *written* ballots. We live by codified law, not caprice, and write to our legislator when we are angry. It can be said—in fact, historian Henry Steele Commager did say it—that "It is inconceivable to think of the United States without thinking of books."

But we should not let this perspective of history mesmerize us. Other perspectives tell us much more about our relationship to the written word.

We do not have a corner on writing revolutionaries. Writers are in the front ranks of almost all assaults on existing regimes.* "Men of words,"

*I am not referring to bomb throwers who make no attempt to disguise their ambition with philosophical arguments. My favorite tin-pot revolutionaries come from Bolivia, which changes government the way most people change underwear. In one upheaval, a

Eric Hoffer once noted, do the "preliminary work of undermining existing institutions." Vladimir Lenin took crates of books with him on his Siberian exile in 1897 and wrote *What Is to Be Done?*, the basis for the political system he introduced. Josef Stalin, Mao Zedong, Ho Chi Minh, and Fidel Castro dabbled in poetry. (One wag has suggested a collection of their work could be illustrated by Hitler, who dabbled in painting.)

What these communist revolutionaries wrote, anticommunist revolutionaries subsequently rewrote. Remarkable writing credentials exist among the political leaders who erased the hammer and sickle in Eastern and Central Europe. Václav Havel, a dissident playwright who became president of the Czech Republic, described the phenomenon in a 1992 speech: "Poets, philosophers, singers became members of Parliament, government ministers, or even presidents. The president of Bulgaria is a philosopher, and the vice-president of that country is a poet. In Hungary, the president is a writer and the prime minister a historian."

Some of these recent politician-writers are about as admirable as Stalin. We have had reports that Ratko Mladic, the Bosnian Serb General wanted on two counts of genocide, is writing his memoirs in Belgrade. Radovan Karadzic, the Bosnian Serb political leader also wanted for war crimes, is an amateur poet. Cambodia's Hun Sen writes songs with titles like "In the Shade of the Palm Trees of Krang Yoev Development Center." Just as Henry Steele Commager said, "It is inconceivable to think of the United States without thinking of books," it is inconceivable to think about today's Cambodia without thinking of Hun Sen's songs. That is because the tunes are played on the country's FM radio stations, nearly all of which are controlled by Hun Sen's party.

Our American system, you might argue, distinguished itself by hewing to written documents *after* the revolution was over. This too can be misleading. Establishing written words as the basis for government is not the same thing as establishing writing as the basis for government. Words embedded in sacred documents are static. New words, on the other hand, are dynamite. They explode the status quo. John Adams said, "Let us dare to read, think, speak, and write." But that was before the Republic was

---

a general from a poor farming family became president briefly. When his mother was asked for a comment, she sighed, "If I had known he was going to be president I would have taught him to read and write."

firmly in place. When we Americans say we believe in the Founding Fathers' words, we mean we ought to *follow* the Constitution, not write a new one ourselves. We don't want anyone playing with matches. Remember, the National Archives encases the Declaration of Independence, the Constitution, and the Bill of Rights in oxygen-free containers. It doesn't leave them out for people to edit.

Alexis de Tocqueville, whose views on the United States Americans have long consulted, brought as much insight to his study of France's revolution. He thought France did more than any other nation to blend revolution and literature. "There were none, from the thick treatise to the popular song, which did not contain a little politics." American revolutionaries, he said, "seemed merely to apply what our writers had thought of." He considered this tendency in the French to be a defect. "What is merit in an author," he said, "is often a defect in a statesman, and characteristics which improve a book may be fatal to a revolution."

Once in office and faced with the practical aspects of governing, our Founding Fathers formed reservations about free speech. "Many of the Jeffersonians, most notably Jefferson himself, behaved when in power in ways that belied their fine libertarian sentiments," constitutional historian Leonard Levy observed. Levy concluded that only one of the Framers, James Madison, had a consistently supportive record on the First Amendment. The delegates to the 1887 Constitutional Convention in Philadelphia hired printers to provide copies of various drafts, but the copies were for delegates' eyes only. The printers swore an oath of secrecy. The government showed its gratitude to the printers by delaying payment to them for five years.

Today, we Americans preach to the rest of the world about our cherished freedom of expression. Occasionally, a big legal case gives us the opportunity to reaffirm the First Amendment. But let a parent find *Lady Chatterley's Lover* or *Huckleberry Finn* in the school library, much less actually read it. A lynch mob is likely to form. Or let a radical writer from abroad ask to visit the United States. Government officials likely will deny a visa. We tell our children about the virtues of the government system based on our Constitution, but according to the *New York Times*, more American teenagers can name the Three Stooges than can name the three branches of the Federal Government.

The public absolutely believes in free speech in the abstract and violently opposes it in the specific, especially when the specific relates to a bugaboo du jour. Eighty-nine percent of respondents to a 1980s study believed in "free speech for all no matter what their views might be." Eighty percent agreed that "people who hate our way of life should still have the chance to talk and be heard." But when asked if they would let the American Nazi Party use the local town hall for a public meeting, fewer than one out of five said yes. Ditto for those preaching atheism in a local civic auditorium. Half agreed that "if the majority votes in a referendum to ban the public expression of certain opinions, its will should be followed."

Business leaders, your largest source of campaign funds, talk about the importance of a literate work force; they say the free flow of ideas is crucial to economic democracy. You should echo that. But keep in mind that what they really want are better-educated workers—up to a point. Thoughtful, individual expression worries employers, and many actively discourage it. I recall a squib in the *Washington Post* a few years back. The item reported that the Sparta Corporation, a research company in Laguna Hills, California, fined any employee caught talking to a reporter five thousand dollars.* Difficult as it is to believe, even organizations dedicated to ideas and words try to limit expression. Media companies will tell reporters that they must clear book ideas or place their books with publishing houses owned by the corporation. Some years back, I was interviewed for a job working with foreign affairs grants at the Ford Foundation.

"So, what kinds of projects do you want to fund?" I asked the interviewer.

"We want to promote civil liberties. Human rights is a major thrust of our program."

What about staff members doing a little writing on such issues, I asked. "Is that encouraged?"

"No. I don't want staff members spending time writing, even their own time. The best staffers submerge themselves in the institution and speak through the grants they give."

Little wonder that a 1990 survey of employee attitudes found that the

*In her study of Procter & Gamble, Alecia Swasy reports that the company once videotaped employees to see how they navigated the cafeteria salad bar. No one questioned this, for such observation was typical. Swasy also recounted how staffers were scolded "for not walking fast enough." The employee magazine offered various ways to promote humor in the workplace. Among other things, it suggested, "Pretend something is funny, even when you can't quite feel it."

"workplace is the area where most Americans feel most restricted in our society—and least protected by the Constitution." Which gets us back to modern politicians, the people from whom you want endorsement. In an ethics law passed in 1989, Congress banned federal employees at all levels from earning money for writing articles and speaking. The law did not discriminate between an IRS tax agent writing about how to circumvent the latest tax legislation and an FBI agent writing about gardening. Although the Supreme Court overturned the legislation, Congress did not give up. The House ethics committee voted unanimously to limit lawmakers' book royalties to the $20,400 cap on outside earned annual income and to ban book advances. After debate on that proposed measure, the House voted not to restrict the income that could be earned, but it did prohibit advances. The House ethics committee, however, must approve all book contracts.

What of those legislators who did not agree with such restrictions? Here is one well-honed argument against restrictions by Representative Gerald Solomon: "Members have had books bomb, and they did not make a dime. And given the current public approval rating of Congress, that is not too surprising, really; right? Right? We are not considered to be leading intellectual lights in our society, let us get our egos back down, let alone literary geniuses. I do not see a literary genius in the room."

Meanwhile, government funding for long-term scholarly projects to collect and save the oeuvre of Washington, Jefferson, Adams, Madison, and Franklin has been tenuous. Vocal proponents narrowly staved off major cuts in 1997. Face it, it's easier to glorify the Founding Fathers than to preserve their words.

"It is by the goodness of God," Mark Twain wisely observed, "that in our country we have those three unspeakably precious things: freedom of speech, freedom of conscience, and the prudence never to practice either of them."

> *You quote from a volume you found on your bookshelf,* Facts about the Presidents: A Compilation of Biographic and Historical Information: *"Practically all of the Presidents distinguished themselves as writers."*

The author of this bit of nonsense also believes, no doubt, that President Ronald Reagan only feigned sleep in cabinet meetings, leaving his eyes open just a little to see if any of his appointees talked behind his back.

Here is the truth: Presidential book writing is uneven, at its best, and steadily getting worse. Its history falls into four periods:

The Founding Writers (1789–1829)
The Great Literary Drought (1829–1869)
The Renaissance (1869–1933)
The Age of Smoke and Mirrors (1933–present)

As I've acknowledged, words and books anchored the Founding Fathers, the *Founding Writers* who became the first presidents. Jefferson, who said "I cannot live without books," has been called "the most accomplished rhetorician of his time." Two of the three achievements he wanted listed on his tombstone involved his writing: The Declaration of Independence and the Virginia Statute of Religious Liberty. James Madison gets the same literary respect. Eager to sway public opinion in favor of ratifying the Constitution, Madison along with Alexander Hamilton and John Jay wrote a series of newspaper essays under the pen name Publius. As president, Madison ghosted material for his secretary of state, Robert Smith, not the other way around. As a relatively young man, John Adams blamed his financial problems partly on "having spent an estate in books." His jottings, beginning with his diary as a young man, set in motion a love of writing that rolled through one Adams generation after another, right up to Henry Adams, who lived into the twentieth century.

But while these men loved books, they did not write many. And those they did write were not memorable.

Washington had none to his credit, which is fortunate. He was an awful writer. The Library of America's collection of Washington's writings includes a two-hundred-plus-word letter to someone named Robin that contains only one period. "That Washington was not a scholar is certain," John Adams said. "That he was too illiterate, unlearned, unread for his station and reputation is equally past dispute."*

*Washington, I will admit, was much more creative when writing up his expense account while general of the army. He took no salary and asked only to be reimbursed for out-of-pocket costs. As noted in *George Washington's Expense Account,* edited by Marvin Kitman, the father of our country listed such charges as "Cash paid for cleaning the House

Adams could be warm and interesting in his diary and in private correspondence. (One author put together a book based on the second president's lively, insightful marginalia written in the books in his library.) His
public writing, though, is soporific and, to put it kindly, derivative. His
three-volume *Defence of the Constitutions of Government of the United
States of America* was once described as "a morbid anatomy of a hundred
dead republics." Were Adams's *Discourses on Davila* to appear today, the
press would destroy him the way they did presidential aspirant Senator
Joe Biden, who was found to have lifted large portions of a speech by
British Labor Party leader Neil Kinnock, including personal references to
Kinnock's family history. As one scholar has noted, "Eighteen of its
thirty-two chapters are straight translations from the French version of
E. C. Davila's *Historia delle guerre civili de Francia*, the remaining fourteen
being 'useful reflections' on avarice, emulation, ambition, and fame, all
based upon one chapter in Adam Smith's *Theory of Moral Sentiments*."
Years later one of Adams's grandsons restored the quotation marks in
much of his grandfather's writing.

Some twenty-eight thousand of Jefferson's letters survive, but he kept
no diary, produced a thin autobiography that does not deserve the name,
and wrote one full-length book, *Notes on Virginia*. The latter, which he
published himself in Paris (two hundred copies), held significant scientific
interest at the time and remains a memorable book. But he may well not
have written with publication in mind. In addition, he was not *the* author
of the Declaration of Independence. He borrowed liberally from George
Mason's preliminary draft of Virginia's Declaration of Human Rights, including the immortal "all men are created equal." Others in Philadelphia
at the time helped with rewriting and cutting. By the time the Continental Congress was done, a quarter of the text lay on the floor. Instead of
being grateful for the successful group effort, Jefferson sulked the rest of
his life over the "mutilations."

For all his writing ability, Madison didn't have much ambition to write
a book. Devoting most of his retirement to farming and letter writing, he
dictated "the merest skeleton" of a hurried autobiography at the very end

---

which was provided for my Quarters & had been occupied by the Marblehead Regm . . .
$65" and a visit for Mrs. Washington to his winter quarters, a trip that cost the taxpayers
$27,665.

A letter from George Washington
was a painful experience for both writer and reader

Dear Friend Robin

As its the greatest mark of friendship and esteem absent Friends can shew each other in Writing and often communicating their thoughts to his fellow companions makes me endeavor to signalize myself in acquainting you from time to time and at all times my situation and employments of Life and could Wish you would take half the Pains of contriving me a Letter by an oppertunity as you may be well assured of its meeting with a very welcome reception my Place of Residence is at present at his Lordships where I might was my heart disengag'd pass my time very pleasantly as theres a very agreeable Young Lady Lives in the same house (Colo. George Fairfax's Wife's sister) but as thats only adding Fuel to fire it makes me the more uneasy for by often and unavoidably being in Company with her revives my former Passion for your Low Land Beauty whereas was I to live more retired from yound Women I might in some measure alleviate my sorrows by burying that chast and troublesome Passion in the grave of oblivion or etarnall forgetfulness for as I am very well assured that's the only antidote or remedy that I ever shall be releivd by or only recess than can administer any cure or help to me as I am well convinced was I ever to attempt any thing I should only get a denial which would be only adding grief to uneasiness.

G. Washington

circa 1749-1750

of his life, when rheumatism had crippled his wrists and hands. The Publius newspaper articles became the book-length *Federalist Papers* long after the fact.

John Quincy Adams, who might properly be called a Founding Son, is a transitional figure in this literary history. He pledged long before he was president to "render a service to my country by devoting to [literature] the remainder of my life." He left a pile of books: biography, poetry, translations of German poets, travel writings, a collection of letters of religious instruction to his son, and collections of his orations and lectures. "He took to diary writing early," his son said, "and he took to it bad." Perhaps the son meant that writing took possession of JQA. One wonders, though, if he thought his father a tiresome writer. Adams's enthusiasm for writing and range of interests are admirable, but only a handful of scholars remember what he wrote or care to find out. If you wonder why, consider this nifty bit of prose, which he wrote about James Madison at the request of Congress: "When the imperial despot of Persia surveyed the myriads of his vassals, whom he had assembled for the invasion and conquest of Greece, we are told by the father of profane history [Herodotus], that the monarch's heart at first, distended with pride, but immediately afterwards sunk within him, and turned to tears of anguish at the thought, that within one hundred years from that day, not one of all the countless numbers of his host would remain in the land of the living."

After the Founding Writers comes the *Great Literary Drought*, which began with the election of log-cabin presidents such as Andrew Jackson. Jackson's critics charged that he brought Jacksonian democracy to his prose, treating adverbs and verbs equally. John Quincy Adams refused to attend the ceremony when his alma mater, Harvard, gave an honorary degree to Jackson, "a barbarian who could not write a sentence of grammar and hardly could spell his name." Jackson left a few scraps of paper to posterity, as did John Tyler, Zachary Taylor, Franklin Pierce, and Andrew Johnson. Only slightly better were Martin Van Buren, William Henry Harrison, James Polk, Millard Fillmore, and James Buchanan. Toward the end of his life, Buchanan wrote his defensive *Mr. Buchanan's Administration on the Eve of the Rebellion*. It purported to show that he "never failed, upon all suitable occasions, to warn his countrymen of the approaching danger [of a civil war], and to advise them of the proper means to avert it." Van Buren began to write desultorily a dozen years after his retirement, although without letting the scribbling interfere with other business. He never came close to finishing his memoirs. His turgid study of political parties, edited by others, appeared after his death. Millard Fillmore's only "book," *Early Life of Honorable Millard Fillmore: A Personal Reminiscence,* is fifteen pages long.

The one exception of the period is Abraham Lincoln. He did not write any books. The longest piece of writing in his own handwriting was found in old Illinois courthouse records in 1991, a forty-three-page legal document relating to a railroad deal. Had he lived to retirement, Lincoln possibly could have written our best presidential memoir. "There is now little argument," Gore Vidal has observed, "that Lincoln is one of the great masters of prose in our language." His second inaugural address, Alfred Kazin has said, "is the only one that has ever reflected literary genius." One of his early poems, doggerel making fun of some locals in the southern Indiana of his boyhood, became, in the words of one settler, known "better than the Bible." But, whatever he could have done in writing books, he resisted doing. His real literary genius may live in that self-restraint and his writing nasty anonymous newspaper articles about his opponents.

The *Renaissance* in presidential writing began with Lincoln's general, U. S. Grant. Grant wrote his two-volume memoir of the Civil War during a slow, painful decline to death from cancer. (He finished reviewing page proofs on July 14, 1885, and died nine days later.) The book, Edmund Wilson said, is "the most remarkable work of its kind since the *Commentaries* of Julius Caesar." Mark Twain, his publisher, paid Mrs. Grant $450,000 in royalties.

"When I lived much in cow camps I often carried a volume of Swinburne, as a kind of antiseptic to alkali dust, tepid, muddy water, frying-pan bread, sow-belly bacon, and the too-infrequent washing of sweat-drenched clothing," Theodore Roosevelt wrote in *A Book-Lover's Holiday in the Open. A Book-Lover's Holiday* is one of his thirty-eight books of history, biography, travel, and nature. He also produced scores of articles for popular journals, maintaining the literary output while in the White House. His *Naval War of 1812* remains the definitive work on the subject. For a time in the 1880s, he had a financial investment in G. P. Putnam, which published some of his books. No president has written more, written better, or produced books of greater significance.

Woodrow Wilson did what you might expect of a college professor with political ambitions. He wrote about American politics. He was not a particularly gifted historian, and his writing was florid. Still, he was prodigious. From 1893 through 1902, when he became president of Princeton, he completed nine books, including a five-volume *History of the American People*, as well as thirty-five articles.

Herbert Hoover was a determined writer. He wrote history, biography (including the admirable *The Ordeal of Woodrow Wilson*), and *Fishing for Fun—And to Wash Your Soul*. His *Principles of Mining* became a standard text on the subject. Toward the end of his life, he had four desks in his New York apartment, noted biographer Richard Norton Smith, "one for each book he wrote simultaneously to add to the two dozen already bearing his name."

Good writers don't necessarily become good presidents. Odds are, they will turn out to be like Ulysses S. Grant, one of our worst. Here Grant is finishing his memoirs while dying of cancer of the throat. "The most remarkable work of its kind," said critic Edmund Wilson, "since the *Commentaries* of Julius Caesar."

New York Public Library Picture Collection

Grover Cleveland, Calvin Coolidge, William Howard Taft, and Benjamin Harrison served as presidents during this period. Their work is not as voluminous as other contemporaries; nor did they write classics. They were tolerable writers nonetheless. Harrison's *This Country of Ours*, which appeared in a slightly shorter form in a series of articles for the *Ladies' Home Journal*, is accessible and interesting. Cleveland produced articles for the *Saturday Evening Post* and managed a book about hunting and fishing. Writing was Coolidge's chief source of income after leaving office. The "silent president's" published work included a regular newspaper column, magazine articles, and an autobiography.

The United States was not alone in this renaissance. The pens of our English cousins on 10 Downing Street flew during the period. William Gladstone wrote volumes covering not only contemporary political topics

Theodore Roosevelt, our most energetic presidential writer, is seen here shortly before he mustered out of the Rough Riders. That was in September 1898. By the end of the year, he was New York's governor and well along in writing his memoir of the Spanish-American War.

Photograph of Colonel Roosevelt at Camp Wickoff, Theodore Roosevelt Collection, Harvard College Library

but also the Homeric basis of Christianity.* His arch political enemy, Benjamin Disraeli, wrote his first novel at age twenty-three. His final one appeared when he was sixty-seven, four months before he died. "When I want to read a novel," he said, "I write one." Lord Robert Cecil (the marquis of Salisbury), Arthur Balfour, Herbert Asquith, and Ramsay MacDonald wrote articles and books. Stanley Baldwin "loved language," one commentator has noted. "No other Prime Minister has invested so much time and nervous energy in speeches—particularly in non-political speeches. They won him great reputation: collections of them sold by the thousand."

Even the bad presidential writing in this era was memorable. Warren Harding, H. L. Mencken commented, wrote "the worst English that I have ever encountered. It reminds me of a string of wet sponges; it reminds me of tattered washing on the line; it reminds me of stale bean-soup, of college yells, of dogs barking idiotically though endless nights. It is so bad that a sort of grandeur creeps into it." The grandeur to which Mencken referred may have been Harding's misstatements. Among other things, he inadvertently invented the word *normalcy:* "America's present need is not heroics but healing, not nostrums but normalcy."

Which gets us to the *Age of Smoke and Mirrors,* our age. This may seem to you to be the most productive writing era of all. The last nine presidents alone—Dwight Eisenhower to Bill Clinton—have close to forty books to their names. But one must not judge a book by the credit on its cover. The test is the quality of the words inside and who really wrote them. Here the historical record is bleak. Contemporary presidents are to writing as Russian leaders are to national anthems. (The new one in Russia doesn't have words.)

Franklin Roosevelt and Harry Truman, the first presidents of the Age of Smoke and Mirrors, are also its literary Lewis and Clark. Roosevelt began work on a couple of book ideas while he was ill with polio. He lost interest after only a few pages. He preferred to leave the writing to ghosts, then lie about it when possible. Roosevelt pinned a note to the draft of his first inaugural speech, saying he wrote it. As he hoped, the speech and the

*Gladstone's voracious reading has led to exaggeration akin to that which surrounded John Kennedy, who was often described as a godlike speed reader. Gladstone was supposed to have read 20,000 books. This is 219 books for each of the ninety-one years he lived. Assuming that he read a book a day, from the age of one, he only had weekends free.

note ended up in the Roosevelt Library at Hyde Park, although the truth came out eventually: he had rewritten by hand the words of aide Raymond Moley. Truman, who lived beyond his presidency, might have been expected to relish the opportunity to write his memoirs. He was an avid book reader, for which he received considerable praise. Right up front in his two-volume memoirs, he observed, "The presidency of the United States carries with it a responsibility so personal as to be without parallel. Very few are ever authorized to speak for the President." Even so, he authorized people to speak for him in his book. As he admitted in his acknowledgments, "I have received invaluable aid and suggestions from many people." Tim Seldes, who worked with Truman's publisher, Doubleday, didn't give editing suggestions to the former president; he gave them to Truman's writing surrogates, who brought them to Truman's attention if they had a question.

Dwight Eisenhower, John Kennedy, and Richard Nixon have to their credit some of the better books of our Age of Smoke and Mirrors. But they are not authors in the way we normally regard that job, plowing through information to research a topic and sitting alone in front of blank sheets of paper or a computer screen wondering how to pull thoughts together. They show, above all, that ghostwriters have become as integral to the modern presidency as Air Force One.

"All my life I have been an incorrigible reviser of written material," Eisenhower confessed in *At Ease: Stories I Tell to Friends*—reviser of someone else's material, that is. Just as Ike relied on an enormous staff to help him plot and launch the invasion of Normandy, he relied on a large team to help organize, research, and write his presidential memoirs. When Ike dictated thoughts and recollections, he couldn't abide pacing solitarily in his Gettysburg study talking into a tape recorder. He had to dictate to a real person. "One of the jobs of a guy like me," Sam Vaughan, a Random House editor who worked with Eisenhower, told me once, "was to get [Ike's dictation] past the report stage."

Kennedy's authorship of *Profiles in Courage* is intensely debated. Historian Herbert Parmet has made the strongest case that blue-ribbon historians gave liberal counsel, the Library of Congress staff and others did substantial research, and various people drafted chapters. Nevertheless, Kennedy went on to describe the book as his own work and accepted the 1957 Pulitzer Prize for biography the way a full-fledged author would. One of the real authors, Jules Davids, a Georgetown University professor, received seven hundred dollars cash and no royalties.

Nixon publicly disdained Kennedy's use of ghostwriters. "A public figure when he's running for President shouldn't be just a puppet who echoes his speechmaker. The ideas should be *his*, the opinions *his*, the words *his*." In practice, meanwhile, Nixon worked pretty much the way Kennedy did. He jotted thoughts on yellow tablets and dictated ideas to stenographers. After that, wordsmiths hammered out his prose. He revealed this in an elliptical comment to an interviewer: "Writing a book is very, very hard work. . . . And then I have good people that work with me."

Not that Nixon didn't have the potential to be a real writer. Ken McCormick, the late, venerable editor at Doubleday, liked to recall the collective surprise when, during the writing of *Six Crises*, Nixon said he wanted to write one of the chapters—the one describing the renowned Checkers speech that saved his vice-presidential spot on Eisenhower's 1952 ticket. McCormick and his colleagues were astonished how well Nixon's contribution conformed to the style of the book.

Although the ghosts were still with him, Nixon apparently became more involved in his books after he was forced into retirement. "In editing later drafts," he said, "I would sometimes take a full day to craft a sentence to convey a precise thought or to formulate a memorable line." (Do you, by the way, happen to remember any of these memorable lines? I doubt it.)

Ghostwriters, the Hamburger Helpers of presidential literature, don't guarantee a good book. Doris Kearns and others worked hard to help Lyndon Johnson on *The Vantage Point: Perspective of the Presidency*. But Johnson could never bring himself to concentrate on the book, let alone allow the ghosts to give it any zest. Ford's ghostwriter did not save his *A Time to Heal* from the extraordinary confession: "Throughout my political life, I always believed what I was told." No publisher was interested in buying the paperback rights for the book. A "professional team" of about two dozen people, headed by journalist-writer Robert Lindsey, wrote Ronald Reagan's memoir, *An American Life*. Reagan wasn't much interested in the details, such as remembering anything about his marriage to Jane Wyman. The book landed with a thud, not that Reagan read the reviews—or, for that matter, the book. "I hear it's a terrific book!" he said shortly after it came out. "One of these days I'm going to read it myself."* *Millie's Book,* ostensibly written by Barbara Bush and her dog, sold better. The Bush administration establishes the low-water mark of our era so far. His presidency is to writing what Mike Tyson is to sportsmanship. On his way to the White House, Bush acquired a reputation for writing spirited "thank-you" notes; once in the Oval Office he spoke of the "vision thing." He pilfered dark corners of presidential history for occasional glimmerings of wit. In trouble for saying "read my lips" and raising taxes anyway, he said henceforth we should "read my hips," a phrase that originated with someone else. Muckraker Lincoln Steffens said Theodore Roosevelt, the Rough Riding president, "thought with his hips." *Looking Forward,* the title of Bush's campaign autobiography, written by Vic Gold, was also the name of a book-length collection of magazine articles ghosted for Franklin Roosevelt.

Vice-president Dan Quayle was Jeff to Bush's Mutt. Judging from the acknowledgments in Quayle's memoir, everyone in Washington and Indiana except dangerous Dan had a hand in writing *Standing Firm.* You'll recall that Quayle could not spell "potato," scored well below average on the National Guard communications skills exam, and insightfully observed that the book *Nicholas and Alexandra* "shows how people that are really very weird can get into sensitive positions and have a tremendous impact on history."

Jimmy Carter is the lone modern president who may qualify as a legitimate author. To his credit, he prides himself on writing a dozen books "at home on my trusty word processor." His campaign biography, however, has all the style of a high school term paper; his poetry is not poetic; and memoirs such as *Keeping Faith* and *Living Faith* are cloyingly self-righteous. In the words of one reviewer, Carter is "an excruciatingly trite thinker whose musings on religion and politics have landed him, this time around, on the best-seller list." One exception is his book on fishing. It is almost lyrical, says Leo Ribuffo, a historian working on a study of the Carter presidency.

You will note that I haven't elaborated on Clinton yet. I'm saving his

---

*Reagan was not much for reading anyway. Rather than reading the briefing notes left him by aide James Baker before an economic summit, he watched a television rerun of *The Sound of Music.* William Clark, his national security adviser and no genius himself, showed films to educate Reagan about foreign policy issues.

writing for later. For the moment, I'll merely observe that one of his favorite authors as a boy was John Kennedy.

So, my friend, all presidents are not distinguished writers or, for that matter, writers at all. The big question, however, is not whether presidents write. It is whether it makes any difference, which gets to the next point you raise . . .

"Demonstrating the ability to write well will help me get elected."
Actually, it can do just the opposite.

When I first came to Washington and began to work on Capitol Hill, I encountered the phrase "political judgment." People were always saying this fellow had it, that one didn't. What, I wondered, distinguished political judgment from any other kind of judgment? Over time, I learned. Political judgment was different, a sixth sense about public perceptions and the process of government. I also found that book writing is mostly an exercise in bad political judgment if you want to get into office or stay there.

Here are the lessons about book writing you should repeat over and over to yourself.

Lesson Number One: You don't have time for book writing.

"Writing," as Mark Green pointed out, "requires years of diversion from fund raising and visibility." Green is an authority. He is the author of more than a dozen books and a defeated candidate for the U.S. Senate.

To get elected, you need money, wheelbarrows of it. It is difficult to think of a less effective way to shovel it in than writing a serious book. Instead, you should spend hours on the telephone asking people to donate to your campaign or fly from city to city to attend one-thousand-dollar-a-plate dinners.

You might think your supporters would revel in your book writing, a sign that you are above venal money grubbing. Not so. They regard writing as the equivalent of a long cigarette break by a goof-off employee, who might also take home the company pencils. When Gary Hart was beginning his run for president, he worked with fellow senator William Cohen on a thriller, *The Double Man.* Angry supporters chided Hart for not scouring the land for campaign contributions.

The other part of Green's admonition—the need for visibility—reflects the fact that writers work alone, invisibly, for long stretches. Presidential candidates need to be in front of the public every day, preferably on camera. An author sometimes gets lucky, of course, and lands a couple of minutes on *Good Morning America*. But a long, thoughtful book will not get you any more time on the air than uttering a zippy sentence that fits on a Post-it Note. Al Gore didn't have to write his environmental book to be invited to appear on the *Late Show* with David Letterman, where he captured attention by smashing a government ashtray with a mallet.

"When I entered politics," Peruvian author Mario Vargas Llosa said in 1990, "I thought I would be fighting for values and ideas. In fact, daily politics is pure intrigue, blind and cynical maneuvering. . . . It's dangerous to put imaginative people in power. It's much better to have mediocre politicians." Discount these remarks. Vargas Llosa had just lost his bid for the presidency of his country. As noted by Mark Malloch Brown, an English public relations man who helped him, "Mario, who works with words and pages, did not adequately understand the power of electronic visual images."

> Lesson Number Two: The public thinks that book writing is
> vaguely effete, perhaps even a telltale sign of incompetence.

From kindergarten on, teachers tell Johnny and Jane that writing is a sign of intellectual accomplishment. Not surprisingly, then, voting adults believe that presidents, who hold the supreme office in the land, should be able to reach the pinnacle of writing, a book. But this belief coexists with a sense that book writers have no calluses on their hands and that a way with words betrays deep-seated fecklessness when it comes to fixing a leaky faucet or running a government.

This schizophrenia predates the United States. When King James I took up his pen, Isaac D'Israeli observed, his Cavaliers let out a cry. They did not like the idea of a king writing books, carrying on war "by the pen instead of the pike, and spending his passion on paper instead of powder."

"Read men," Patrick Henry warned, "not books." In his insightful (and ghosted) comments at the turn of the century, political boss George Washington Plunkett praised Tammany Hall leaders as "plain American citizens, of the people and near to the people [with] all the education they need to whip the dudes who part their name in the middle and to run the City Government. We've got bookworms, too, in the organization. But we don't make them district leaders. We keep them for ornaments on parade days."

Writing from the heart also has the problem of seeming too emotional. "If supposedly crying in the rain can eliminate a candidate as good as Ed Muskie . . . what would showing emotion and waxing poetic do to a candidate on the way up?" said Sam Vaughan, the Random House editor.

Lesson Number Three: Writing a book is like painting a large target on your chest to help your opponent sight in better.

"Behold, my desire is that . . . mine adversary had written a book," Job observed in the Old Testament. That venerable man of many tribulations knew a fundamental political truth. A sturdy book is a lethal weapon in the hands of a political opponent. This is especially so in our ad hominem political culture where adversaries pick up anything they find lying about to bludgeon you, especially if bludgeoning helps avoid serious debate.

If any job in the land requires the ability to write powerfully, it is being a justice on the Supreme Court. Yet woe be unto the nominee who has written as much as Robert Bork did. His extensive writings, some of them speculating tentatively on complicated legal issues, were Exhibit A in the case that prevailed against his stepping up to the bench. His fate, Bork warned in a subsequent book, would dissuade presidents from nominating anyone who had written much. That, in turn, would eliminate some of the best people. "People who have thought much about the role proper to judges," he said, "are likely . . . to have written or spoken on the subject." Clarence Thomas won Senate confirmation because he had written little and, as he argued, hadn't thought very much about legal issues. To dodge questions about abortion laws, he made the fantastic statement that he had never discussed the case of *Roe v Wade*.

James Bryce, the English viscount and student of the United States, explained why accomplished men are not chosen president. By achieving much before seeking office, say by writing great books, eminent men and women "make more enemies, and give those enemies more assailable points, than obscure men do." Clinton campaign strategist James Carville advises against writing anything. Never write a letter, he says, and never throw one away.

Some have said that Al Gore's *Earth in the Balance: Ecology and the Human Spirit* is "the most graphic analysis of the world's environmental condition and the most advanced plan for economic solutions that has ever been written by an American politician." Maybe so. But instead of telling Bush to write something worthwhile in reply, the Bush-Quayle campaign team snidely commented that "Gore should have spent less of the taxpayers' time and money on his own book and a little bit more time on legislation." In the next election, Bob Dole tried to score cheap rhetorical points on Clinton's wife's book, *It Takes a Village*, by saying it "takes a family." When Upton Sinclair ran for governor of California for the third time, his adversaries quoted anti-marriage remarks in one of his books. The problem was that the book was a novel, and Sinclair had written the quoted words for a fictional character. He had been married twenty years.

What your opponent doesn't figure out, the press will. In his slim, ghostwritten book, *United We Stand: How We Can Take Back Our Country*, Ross Perot said federal officials should fly on commercial airlines. To be precise, he said that "They should go out to the airport, get in line, lose their baggage, eat a bad meal, and stay in touch with how normal people live." The press gleefully reported that Perot always flew in a private jet.

And don't try to defend words with words. Dan Quayle did himself no favors devoting an entire chapter of his vice-presidential memoir, *Standing Firm*, to why he had not recognized the proper spelling of *potato* during a classroom photo-op. ("No one ever actually asked me to spell *potato* that afternoon," he insisted. "If they had, I imagine I'd have gotten it right, though I wouldn't swear to it. I'm not the world's greatest speller.") This was reminiscent of West Virginia senator William Scott holding a press conference to deny that he was "the dumbest congressman of them all," as had been suggested by *New Times*, a liberal magazine that did not circulate widely in his conservative state.

Spiro Agnew, if you think back on it, fell into the same trap. He had been accused of accepting $147,500 in kickbacks from Maryland state contractors when he was Baltimore county executive, governor, and vice-president. In a memoir after he was forced to resign as vice-president, *Go Quietly . . . or Else: His Own Story of the Events Leading to His Resignation* (dedicated to Frank Sinatra), he said that he had done nothing wrong. Contractors had given him campaign contributions. Because Agnew quoted conversations with his attorney, a judge ruled that the lawyer-client privilege no longer applied. The attorney testified that Agnew admitted statehouse bribery to him. Agnew ended up paying the state of Maryland $248,735 in restitution. No doubt he would have liked to take back the comment in his prologue, "I am also grateful to my lawyers . . . for their recollections and assistance."

Just in case it is not obvious to you, there is a corollary to my point that book writing makes you a big target on the campaign trail. Books also make you a big target in office—and it doesn't make any difference what you write in the book. The Senate censured one of its members, David Durenberger, for financial misconduct in connection with a book-promotion deal and reimbursement for housing expenses in Minnesota. But the most noticeable victims have been speakers of the House, whom you will recall are second in line to the presidency.

Speaker Jim Wright stumbled over his *Reflections of a Public Man.* Charges surfaced that a former staffer, paid with congressional funds, edited the book; that campaign funds paid for publication; that the Fertilizer Institute bought copies in bulk to circumvent House rules on honoraria; and that Wright's royalties were 55 percent, an astronomical amount for an author. None of this technically violated House ethics rules at the time, but Newt Gingrich generated enough hysteria to force Wright's resignation.

Having loosed the hounds, Gingrich found them on his own heels as a result of *his* books. While he was attacking Wright, it was learned that wealthy supporters paid Gingrich $13,000 to write a novel he never delivered. Then there was a 1984 partnership deal that funded his book *Window of Opportunity.* This arrangement included $105,000 to promote the book and $11,500 to his wife to manage the partnership. Gingrich weathered the controversy and became speaker himself. Brimming with literary self-confidence, he then landed a $4.5- million book advance with HarperCollins. All of this was before Congress outlawed book advances. But in signing the contract, he ignored the advice of the House ethics committee. It was concerned that an outsized advance would give media titan Rupert Murdoch, who owned HarperCollins, a special line into the speaker's office. With all the press attention, Gingrich had to return the advance and pay for his book tour himself.

Few may have read *To Renew America,* which is just as well considering that it is the most half-baked book ever written by a senior politician. But many were aware of his ethical problems with the book and the more damaging charges over the tax-exempt fund related to his televised course at Kennesaw State College. While Gingrich's book shenanigans did not lead to his removal from the speakership in 1999, they showed why he did not deserve his colleagues' support. He should have remembered that he was elected speaker (not writer) of the House.

"The times are such that one should think carefully before writing books," a Jesuit priest said during the Spanish Inquisition. We live in such a time. Whenever your mind turns to the idea of writing as a way to secure yourself a place in office, think of that remark as well as the example set by Abdala Bucaram. When president of Ecuador, he was given to reciting original poetry in public. After the coup, the Ecuadoran Congress passed a law preventing him from holding the office ever again. The specific wording bans leaders who have been sacked for "mental incapacity."

You remind me that "every presidential candidate has a campaign book."

I agree. But you must follow several rules that boil down to this: Your campaign book should have the physical heft of a book but, apart from that, shouldn't have any of the properties one would expect to find in one. For guidance, I suggest you look to Bill Clinton's *Between Hope and History: Meeting America's Challenges for the 21st Century,* published during his reelection campaign.

First, Clinton didn't take an advance for the book and declined royalties. This allowed the publisher to sell it for a lower price, $16.95, which gave the president a fine populist appearance.

Second, the book was similar to party platforms these days. It did not say anything. It was a pastiche of three dozen old speeches, originally written by others, and then cobbled together into a book by a team consisting of political consultant William Nordurft and two White House aides.

"A book offers a medium for a serious, fully articulated statement of philosophy, a purpose," a *New York Times* review concluded, ". . . What Mr. Clinton offers instead is not a sound bite but a word bite, an easy-to-read, effortlessly digested porridge of previous statements, some feel-good homilies here, a snap argument for a new initiative there, platitudes all over the place." This, however, was not a problem for the president. His opponent wasn't writing anything better. Besides, who reads the book review section? Most people are watching television, which gets to the third point I want to make.

Clinton dexterously straddled American schizoid feelings about book writing. In the final days before publication, his handlers put out the word that the vacationing president was sweating over the final draft. At the same time, Clinton got in a little golf, the slow-moving presidential sport that gives press photographers a chance to snap action shots. Nor did Clinton neglect fund raising. Before the book's publication, his staff staged a big birthday bash at Radio City Music Hall, which was beamed by satellite to eighty other fund-raising parties across the country. He expected that would net between eight and ten million dollars in campaign contributions.

Sixty-five years ago, journalist Westbrook Pegler named Babe Ruth and other athletic stars with ghostwriters the "sweating literati." Aspiring presidents should fabricate the same image, striving to be a blur while nodding occasionally toward books just to show they feel comfortable with weighty thoughts. Rather than writing, they should promote literacy campaigns that give them opportunities to appear in front of TV cameras with a couple of towheaded youngsters and read *The Little Engine That Could.**

*Presidential literacy campaigns seem to have begun with FDR, who adopted the World War II slogan "Books Are Weapons." Jimmy Carter's plan challenged one hundred thousand college students to help youngsters learn to read. Carter never explained where this many literate college kids could be found. Bush's wife promoted literacy, as has Hillary Clinton with her Prescription for Reading Initiative, which recommends placing books for children in doctors' offices. Bill Clinton's literacy program calls for one million reading mentors to achieve the result of every fourth grader reading at or above the basic level.

While it is fine to make heartfelt speeches and hold press conferences about the importance of literacy, it is not a good idea to think creatively about improving writing. Teddy Roosevelt tried to reform American spelling, which saddled citizens with archaic words such as "through" and "comptroller." As a start, he directed the government printers to use simplified spelling. The Supreme Court and Congress refused to use the reforms; the press ridiculed Roosevelt. Eventually, he gave up.

Clinton has done a much wiser thing in this regard. He launched a Plain Language Initiative, which required everyday words in government documents and use of the active voice. But he did not take it seriously. The press release announcing the initiative noted in the passive voice that the program "was developed by an interagency group of plain language enthusiasts."

George Bush was a bona fide member of the "sweating literati" (a trait he may have picked up playing baseball at Yale). He called himself the education president and signed the National Literacy Act, which among other things funded family literacy shows on television. Asked what he was doing during one of his Maine summer vacations, he replied, "I'll play a good deal of golf here, a good deal of tennis, a good deal of horseshoes, a good deal of fishing, a good deal of running—and some reading. I have to throw that in for the intellectuals out there."

I realize that you do not want "merely to be in office." You want to be a great president. It could be that getting elected requires one set of skills, and achieving greatness another, including the ability to write books. It could be, as you argue, "that writing a book will limber me up to score a knock out as president."

It could be . . . but it won't.

Arthur Schlesinger Jr. is responsible for what is probably the best-known contemporary ranking of presidents. Done in 1996, on the eve of Clinton's second term, it repeated similar studies conducted by his father in 1948 and 1962. Schlesinger invited thirty-two experts, mostly fellow academics, to rank presidents (excluding William Henry Harrison and James Garfield, who died shortly after taking office) as great, near great, average, below average, and failure. As is almost always the case, three presidents came out on top: George Washington, Abraham Lincoln, and Franklin Roosevelt. Likewise, the list was not surprising in showing Franklin Pierce, James Buchanan, Andrew Johnson, Ulysses Grant, Warren Harding, Herbert Hoover, and Richard Nixon as failures.

Where does writing fit into this scorecard? It doesn't. The group of presidents rated the worst had two of the best writers, Grant and Hoover, and one of the most illiterate, Harding. Only one of the three great presidents could be considered literary, Lincoln. Washington, on the other hand, is on par with Harding for literary prowess. Still, Washington was a great president, and Harding was not.

Social scientists have searched for ways to predict outstanding presidential leadership, administrative prowess, and historical greatness. None of their efforts to cram life into neat little formulas have done for presidential forecasting what $E=mc^2$ did for physics. Still their work is revealing. Rarely have they bothered to consider book writing a worthwhile indicator, probably because they realize it isn't. When they have bothered to consider book writing, the conclusion is that they have wasted their time.

Here is one of their formulas to determine greatness: Greatness = 1.24 + .17 x (the number of years the president served in office) + .26 x (the number of years the country was at war during his or her presidential service) - 1.7 x (1 if the administration had a cabinet-level scandal and 0 if it did not) + .89 x (1 if the president is assassinated in office and 0 if not) + .82 x (1 if the president is a war hero and 0 if not).

When factoring in the number of books a president wrote before assuming office, the author of this formula found that "presidential authorship does not affect in any substantial degree the direction, magnitude, or significance of the effects of the [original] five variables."

If wading through this formula is too troublesome, think of the lesson of Alexander the Great. In the words of one student of military leadership, "we have no word-for-word record of anything that he said or of anything that he wrote. He left no code of laws, no theory of war, no philosophy of kingship. He certainly kept no diary." Alexander was great because he was fabulously successful at war and conquest, he endured a variety of war wounds, he died while still on the march (he may have been assassinated), and he had no apparent compunction about imprisoning his court historian, a nephew of Aristotle, who dared to suggest that he really wasn't a god.

Napoleon did not leave written instructions of his most brutal orders. Winston Churchill, who won the Nobel Prize for literature, did not maintain his diary during World War II, when he was prime minister; he wanted to dodge his mistakes.

Contrast this with the case of Richard Nixon. His electronic diary, those damning White House tapes, ensured that he passed infamously into history. "I brought myself down," Nixon said later of the 3,700 hours of tapes. "I gave them a sword. And they stuck it in." After Nixon resigned from office, his lawyers did their best to keep his tapes and documents from the public. Inevitably, however, they failed. Beginning in 1996, 3,700 hours worth of taping became available in book form, thereby giving Nixon haters plenty of reading in the years to come. Roughly the same fate befell Oregon Senator Bob Packwood. Each morning for twenty-five years, he made notes of the previous day's events, which included warm memories of pawing women staffers. The diary helped unseat him. In the

Great Presidential Book Writers ≠ Great Presidents

If you want your face carved on Mount Rushmore, don't waste time writing books, as the chart below shows. It is adapted from the 1996 Arthur Schlesinger Jr, poll ranking presidents. To see how those presidents ranked as writers, look for ✒ in front of their names. Those with two ✒ were prolific book authors or had at least one great book to their credit. Those with a literary bent but no books are marked with one ✒. Teddy Roosevelt, our greatest presidential writer, and George Washington, one of our worst, are both on Rushmore. So, what is the crucial factor in greatness? As other polls show, untidiness around the office is as good a characteristic as any.

GREAT
Washington, ✒Lincoln, F. Roosevelt

NEAR GREAT
✒Jefferson, Jackson, Polk, ✒✒T. Roosevelt,
✒✒Wilson, Truman

AVERAGE (high)
✒J. Adams, Monroe, ✒✒Cleveland, McKinley,
Eisenhower, Kennedy, L. Johnson

AVERAGE (low)
✒Madison, ✒✒J. Q. Adams, Van Buren, Hayes,
Arthur, B. Harrison,
✒✒Taft, Ford, ✒✒Carter, Reagan, Bush, Clinton

BELOW AVERAGE
Tyler, Taylor, Fillmore, Coolidge

FAILURE
Pierce, Buchanan, A. Johnson, ✒✒Grant, Harding,
✒✒Hoover, Nixon

Not included are short-termers William Henry Harrison and James Garfield, who died soon after taking office. Neither is remembered as a remarkable writer, although Garfield was able to write Latin with one hand and Greek with the other.

Mount Rushmore edited: Grant, Hoover, Taft, and Carter

sixteenth century, the great kept diaries as a way to establish their virtue. Today, daily record-keeping does just the opposite. Those records are a paper trail to establish your guilt.

Also keep in mind that the traits of great writers are not the traits of visionary presidents. Writing is an exercise in micromanagement, sweating over each word the way Calvin Coolidge did in writing presidential addresses. Such exacting work, he observed in his autobiography, "requires the most laborious and extended research and study, and the most careful and painstaking thought. Each word has to be weighed." Because of this attitude, Coolidge never came close to being on Mount Rushmore. When sculptor Gutzon Borglum chiseled away at the Black Hills of South Dakota, he proposed to etch an uplifting historical essay by Coolidge in bronze at the site. Coolidge wrote the little passage but, taking himself too seriously, resisted Borglum's editing. Remember your visit to Mount Rushmore recently? Coolidge is nowhere near the presidential monument.

Contrast Coolidge with George Washington. During the war for independence, the general had at least thirty-two private secretaries, in batches of four or five, writing for him. As president, he continued to let others write for him. Madison wrote the first draft of Washington's great Farewell Address. Washington deleted a few paragraphs, scrawled some unorganized thoughts, and shipped it all to Alexander Hamilton with instructions that he could edit it or "throw the whole into a different form." Hamilton chose the latter, and Washington spoke the immortal words handed to him.

One sign that a president is not a big picture person is a White House full of speech writers disgruntled because the boss won't let them be prose ventriloquists. "If Carter had the time," complained James Fallows, one of his speech writers and now a well-known journalist, "he'd prefer to have no speech writers and just write everything himself, as he did his own inaugural address." After leaving his post, Fallows revealed that Carter—a below-average president and above-average presidential writer—personally decided who could play on the White House tennis court.

Václav Havel has spoken passionately about the value of writers becoming politicians. "A writer with an aversion to politics is like a scientist studying the holes in the ozone, while ignoring the fact that his boss is inventing chlorofluorocarbons." But an admiring comment from one of Havel's fans inadvertently shows that a writing mentality has led the Czech president to lavish "meticulous care . . . on everything from the design of new uniforms for the Castle guard to the formulation of two new constitutions."

Our country, with its global responsibilities, demands presidents who can manage unmanageable staffs. When it comes to book writing, Saudi Prince Khalid is a more worthy model than Carter or Havel. Angry that General Norman Schwarzkopf had written a blockbuster book (with a six-million-dollar advance) in which he cast himself as the hero of Desert Storm, the prince wanted a glorifying book of his own. He gave himself an advance via the usual rake-off from military arms purchases and hired a ghostwriter whom I know. The ghost submitted each chapter to Khalid, as well as to a council assembled by the prince. The council included a mullah, a lawyer, and a retired Egyptian general who had been a military adviser to the prince during the war. "They would argue for hours about one sentence," said the ghostwriter.

A president who writes his or her own words is less likely to modify them than is a leader who uses words supplied by others. And killing your own literary offspring is essential if you plan to get anything done in the give-and-take of politics and rise to the status of a real leader. Remember how effectively Ronald Reagan distanced himself from his handlers? The most dramatic case was when Larry Speakes, his former press secretary, revealed that he had manufactured quotes for the Great Communicator and didn't bother to show them to the president beforehand. People were outraged at Speakes. Speakes lost his cushy job at Merrill Lynch Pierce Fenner and Smith as a result. As for Reagan, he said that he hadn't noticed that Speakes was putting words in his mouth. Some might have thought Reagan's lack of attention to his job was worse than Speakes quote-mongering, but no one brought that up. Whatever his failings, Warren Harding wisely complained that he did not always comprehend the speeches drafted by his ghostwriters.

Woodrow Wilson's intellectual weight and arrogance, as historian James McGregor Burns once suggested, made him "stubborn, fixed, inflexible." The sort of person who could write himself into a corner, Wilson did not negotiate constructively when he tried to create the League of Nations. Franklin Roosevelt, in contrast, did not have the single-mindedness of a writer. What he relished was the deal making of politics. When Roosevelt's war was over, his quest for a United Nations was realized. Wilson was a near-great president, which isn't bad. Roosevelt was a great one, which is better.

Walter Lippmann decried ghostwriting, even for speeches: "The truth is that anyone who knows what he is doing can say what he is doing, and anyone who knows what he thinks can say what he thinks. Those who cannot speak for themselves are, with very rare exceptions, not very sure of what they are doing and of what they mean. The sooner they are found out the better." This is naïve. Ghostwriters do for your thoughts what those Secret Service agents do for your body. They protect you, especially from history.*

Just as writing time is limited during a campaign, it is scarce while in

---

*As yet another example, George Wallace late in his life wanted to improve his standing in history. No blemish was more obvious than his 1963 inauguration speech as governor of Alabama in which he said, "Segregation now! Segregation tomorrow! Segregation forever!" To clean his record years after the fact, he told journalist Carl Rowan, "I did not write those words about segregation now, tomorrow, and forever. I saw them in the speech

office. "The blacksmith, when the allotted hours of work are over, banks his fire, lays aside his leather apron, washes his grimy hands and goes home. And he gets a taste of unsmoked morning air before he resumes his work," Benjamin Harrison noted nearly a century ago in *This Country of Ours*. "There is only a door—one that is never locked—between the president's office and what are not very accurately called his private apartments."

The job is more demanding now. "There is little time for leaders to reflect," Henry Kissinger wrote in *The White House Years*. "They are locked in an endless battle in which the urgent constantly gains on the important." What's more, they are expected to do in office what they did on the campaign trail, stay in clear public view. Solitude for writing is out of the question.

In his study of presidential character, James David Barber looked for clues to predict how well presidents will perform in office. Paradoxically, writing presidents did not fare especially well at communicating with the public. Hoover's discomfort with the public and public speaking was the flip side to his pleasurable solitude while writing a book or drafting and redrafting a speech. In the words of one of his supporters, Hoover did not "have the least appreciation of the poetry, the music, and the drama of politics." Clinton does, and he has the wit to stay away from writing when he tries to organize his thoughts. "He has so much intellectual energy that he has to siphon some of it off in order to be able to think," former White House adviser Dick Morris observed of Clinton's penchant for solitaire. The game satisfies "a kind of need to bring order out of chaos and entropy."

"Politics is not an intellectual process, although that can be brought to the surface," says Richard E. Neustadt, an expert on the presidency. "But it is a human process." He is coauthor of *Thinking in Time: The Uses of History for Decision Makers*, a book about political decision making. Drawing from that book, he can't think of a single occasion when a president's writing accomplishments helped him make the right decision in a crisis.

---

written for me and planned to skip over them. But the wind-chill factor was five below zero when I gave that speech. I started reading just to get it over and read those words without thinking." For similar reasons, Jefferson would have been better off if he had not written his *Notes on the State of Virginia*. While he acknowledged that blacks were superior to whites in some endeavors (music), he noted as well that "they are dull, tasteless, and anomalous." These observations have not helped his reputation.

My favorite equation for predicting greatness includes these factors: IQ, years in office, achievement, drive, tidiness, achievement motive, height, attractiveness, and something called the Zeitgeist factor, which relates to the nature of the times during which the president serves (national crises are better than calm periods when it comes to demonstrating presidential greatness). This is my favorite because the only thing you have control over is tidiness—and being tidy in this formula is supposed to be a minus, not a plus. Otherwise greatness is up to the fates. So, if you get elected, you might as well sit back, enjoy the experience, and let the White House staff pick up after you.

> *You say that "book writing never gets any easier and that seeking authorship after you're out of politics is like learning to slide after you are in the baseball hall of fame."*

This is partly true. Once you are done with politics you have every reason to produce scores of books, although I frankly don't see much reason for you to aspire to create great literature.

Book writing is your opportunity to redefine your record the way you want history to see it. It can't have escaped your attention that the most besmirched modern president, Richard Nixon, created a high-powered literary machine. Once he was pushed out of the White House, books came out under his name, as well as under the names of henchmen who showed no previous inclination to write more than a simple enemies list. Among these authors were Spiro Agnew, Chuck Colson, Maurice Stans, Jeb Stuart Magruder, G. Gordon Liddy, James McCord, John Ehrlichman, H. R. Haldeman, and John Dean. Both Dean's and Magruder's wives got a book out of Watergate, and Watergate helped revive the writing career of E. Howard Hunt, one of the conspirators. Nixon also helped launch writing careers for Samuel Dash, chief counsel to the Senate Watergate Committee, and Fred Thompson, the minority counsel.

Not all of this was redemptive literature, nor did it do much good in Nixon's case. But it helped pay court costs, which provides a second rationale for writing. You should view a book as the strongest asset in your White House retirement package. Publishers happily throw millions of dollars at former presidents. By some estimates, Simon & Schuster lost five million dollars on its deal with Ronald Reagan for his memoirs and a book of speeches. When publishers give you big bucks, your book is only one of the things they are buying. They are also buying the right to say at cocktail parties, "Did I tell you what President Reagan said to me yesterday?" Irving "Swifty" Lazar conjured a two-million-dollar advance for Nixon's memoirs in 1974. "Warner Books was a paperback house with no cachet whatsoever," Lazar recalled in his own memoirs, "and here was some potentially great publicity for the house."

While I do not want you to do any work at all on your memoirs while you still reside in the White House, you certainly can sell them while you are there. As publisher Michael Korda has noted, this allows you to meet with your prospective publisher "in the full majesty of the Oval Office or in his private quarters at the White House." Who is going to haggle over adding a few hundred thousand dollars to the advance when they are seated in the inner sanctum?

By the way, those publishers don't expect you to write your book. (For that matter, they don't expect *your* ghostwriters to write *their* books. George Stephanopoulos employed someone else to do what he called his "honest book" on his Washington experiences.) Everyone's time is better spent doing Bob Dole–type gigs such as *Saturday Night Live* and television commercials for Viagra, which have higher standards than publishers and don't accept stand-ins. Bush may not be articulate, but Atlantic Richfield Company paid him one hundred thousand dollars for moving his lips at the ribbon-cutting ceremony for a natural gas project in China. Quayle claimed he had the last laugh on the *potato* spelling incident when he made a cameo appearance in a television commercial for Lay's potato chips, which aired during a Super Bowl half time.

Besides, you'll also need time to build your presidential library. This relatively recent invention provides yet another way to glorify yourself, provided you understand, as Nixon did, that it has nothing to do with books. When inaugurated in 1990, Nixon's library had no books other than his, and they were on sale in the gift shop.

Sincerely,
Your Adviser

P.S. Just in case you missed the point in this letter, remember that Clinton's troubles over Monica Lewinsky began with onetime White House staffer Linda Tripp's book idea, gathered momentum when literary agent Lucianne Goldberg got involved, and became a big problem when

Ken Starr hired a professional author to write his report to Congress. I am not suggesting that there is any way to stop this sort of problem. Jacqueline Kennedy required all White House domestic employees to sign an agreement that they would not write about their White House experiences. The First Lady's secretary, Lillian Parks, who was responsible for getting the pledges, did not sign one herself and later wrote *My Boss*. You'll have to live with literary infidelity from staffers. But let that be yet another reminder to beware of books.

P.P.S. Monica reminds me of something else: be careful, too, about drawing lessons from other countries, especially France. François Mitterrand, the two-term French president, was a prolific book writer. "I observe— and I write," he said. "I like the written word." He also said his dream was "to die with a book in my hand." But the French are just the opposite of Americans. We honor politicians for being faithful to their wives and unfaithful to literature. At his funeral, Mitterrand's mistress stood shoulder to shoulder with his wife. Mitterrand, by the way, treasured Casanova's *Memoirs*, something no sane American president would admit if they remembered all the trouble Jimmy Carter got into when he innocently admitted in a *Playboy* interview that he had "looked on a lot of women with lust. . . . I have committed adultery in my heart many times."

NINE

The Universal Library

—⟲⟳—

In which conversations with staff at
the world's greatest library reveal that the
ancient ambition of gathering everything
in one place is no longer a dream, but a
nightmare; and in which it is shown
that this nightmare may be
good for librarians.

—⟲⟳—

—⟋⟋⟋—

Littera scripta manet. [The written word endures.]
—Inscribed on the domed ceiling of the
Librarian's Room, the office used by the
librarian of Congress from 1897 to 1980

The future of this institution lies in more and more qualitative
selection, more and more emphasis on the word "important."
—James H. Billington, Librarian of Congress

—⟋⟋⟋—

The tourmobile that takes out-of-towners to Capitol Hill drives by the magnificent Jefferson Building, behind the Capitol. "You are looking at the oldest part of the Library of Congress," the guide says.

"Didn't I hear the library had two copies of every book?" asks a passenger. "No, one copy of every book since 1800."

Across the street on the fourth floor of the newer Madison Building, Lolita Silva stands at her post at the sluice of knowledge. Before her lies a sea of books and other items that have streamed to the library-run Copyright Office. As demanded by copyright law, the books arrive in pairs. Silva dons an apron and reviews them methodically, quickly, confidently. She inserts a yellow slip into *From the Browder File: 22 Essays on the African American Experience,* published by the Institute of Karmic Guidance. The slip tells clerks who come behind her to keep both books for the library's permanent collection. She decides not to keep the related cassette. *Pacing Yourself: Steps to Save Energy* gets a blue check on its flyleaf, a signal to hold only one copy for the library. A loose-leaf, how-to book for aspiring soap opera actors gets a red X; that signifies she is rejecting both books.

So it goes, pile after pile, year after year. She keeps two copies of home repair books, but not answer guides to student workbooks; two copies of pop-up kids' books, like the one she encounters on King Arthur, but not coloring books. She doesn't keep calendars, but does save one copy of *Longarm and the Hatchet Woman* and other mass market paperbacks. Occasionally, she pauses to thumb through a volume. She holds up a self-published children's book for me to see. The illustrations inside are primitive. She is not keeping either copy. "It's not too hot," she sighs. She has rules, but they are general. She will keep a community-published cookbook with local recipes, but not a city hospital league cookbook with generic dishes—although she did keep one done by the Washington Redskins' wives. "If you're in doubt," she says, "someone else might want it."

When a pair of books spill into oblivion, one copy is given away, exchanged, or, if no one wants it, destroyed. The other is shunted off to a copyright holding facility in Landover, Maryland. It stays there for five years, the time in which a copyright infringement case is most likely to arise.* After that, it goes back to the library, where it suffers the fate of the first book. Should someone someday decide that the book was worth keeping, the library won't have a copy. Maybe no one will.

The Library of Congress, says James H. Billington, the thirteenth head of the institution in its two-hundred-year history, is "the largest and most diverse collection of recorded knowledge ever assembled on earth." The mission is to stay at that pinnacle, "to sustain and preserve a universal collection of knowledge and creativity for future generations." The key word here is *universal*, a term that does not mean what it might at first suggest.

The great Alexandrian Library in ancient Egypt could aspire to obtain one copy of every book floating in the universe of knowledge. Although that goal could never be reached, getting as much as possible of everything was a useful guiding principle. At least until recently. In the Information Age *everything* is too much. Hence, Billington's Library of Congress, the modern equivalent of its Alexandrian ancestor, seeks a different universality, a comprehensiveness which "aspires to have something of everything and to have the most important things of everything." Billington argues that "the future of this institution lies in more and more qualitative selection, more and more emphasis on the word 'important.'"

Silva is aptly called a *selection* officer, not an acquisition officer. The distinction is important to Billington's vision of the library's mission. Before the library created that position in 1944, the common practice was to keep two copies of every book. The job in the last half of the twentieth century has been to weed.

The Library of Congress estimates that it receives about 22,000 items a day. This number by itself does not signify much. The Gutenberg Bible, one letter in Walt Whitman's papers (which the library holds), and one reel of microfilm containing as much as a month's worth of the *Wichita Eagle* each count as a single "item" in the Library of Congress's total collection of 115,505,659 items as of 1998. But it means a great deal when compared to the number of items that the library keeps on an average day: 7,000, or less than one-third of the total.

---

*An unpublished work submitted for copyright must be retained for the entire time it is protected under the law. Because of the Sonny Bono Copyright Term Extension Act of 1998, this term has been extended. For pre-1978 works, the time period is now ninety-five years from the time the copyright was originally acquired. This means the library's bulging holding facilities will swell even more.

No one is better prepared to make these life-or-death decisions than Silva, who loves books. Born in Latvia, she came to the United States after World War II. She studied literature at New York University and earned a master of library science degree from Columbia. She can "manage," as she puts it, twenty-eight Western languages, among them Russian, Danish, German, Spanish, and Romanian. She has been studying Greek for her own edification. "Some you manage less," she says modestly, "some you manage more."

While I watch Silva work on the piles of books, a clerk wearing a Harley Davidson headband comes over. He tells her that a Stephen King novel is gone. "Someone put the bite on it," he says.

"A lot of books around here get misplaced for a while," she tells me. Workers will sometimes take a book. She doesn't call it stealing. It's borrowing. Besides, she says, she knows what various people are interested in reading and will go ask if they have the book.

The Uncertain Rise of the Library of Congress

The Library of Congress houses the largest Chinese, Japanese, and Russian collections outside those countries, as well as the largest collection in the Western Hemisphere of incunabula, as books printed before 1500 are called. The library believes "its collections of maps, atlases, newspapers, music, motion pictures, photographs, and microforms are probably the largest in the world." While it defers to the National Library of Medicine and the National Agricultural Library, it nevertheless collects items from those fields. It also has the largest historical collection of U.S. telephone directories in the world, as well as the largest collection of posters, the largest collection of comic books, and the world's most extensive newspaper collection. Woven into this extraordinary collection, presided over by a staff of four thousand, are the recordings of American Indian tribal chants, the original manuscript of Aaron Copland's *Appalachian Spring,* an original copy of the Magna Carta, one of the world's three perfect copies of the Gutenberg Bible, and—typical of the library's quirky collecting habits— five Stradivari violins and a box containing the contents of Abraham Lincoln's pockets the night he was assassinated at Ford's Theater.

This magnificence is not what Congress had in mind in the beginning. Congress was not certain it wanted a library at all, let alone a library that was good. As early as 1790, legislators discussed buying a few books "nec-essary for the use of the legislative and executive departments." Not until the spring of 1800 did they take action. The initial collection consisted of 740 books and three maps, the number of items that Lolita Silva might consider for the collection in a typical day. Critics had opposed the library because, they argued, the senators and representatives already knew every-thing that they needed to know. True or not, the library was not one of the perks that legislators most cherished. In 1911, only 93 out of a total of 490 solons used the library.

The Library of Congress overcame this indifference, partly through the leadership of a few enterprising librarians, partly through good luck. The first break for the library came in an unlikely manner. During the War of 1812, the British army burned the Capitol, where the library was then housed. Thomas Jefferson, retired to Monticello and financially hard pressed, offered to sell his prized collection of books to Congress.* The legislators were not wildly enthusiastic. The measure to authorize the purchase passed in the House by a ten-vote margin, and then Congress only agreed to pay $23,950, about half the books' auction value. Never-theless, the 6,487 volumes from Jefferson more than doubled the library's previous holdings. More important, as the library likes to point out, the Jeffersonian concept of collecting knowledge broadly became "the ratio-nale for the comprehensive collecting policies of today's Library of Congress."

Another fire, caused by a faulty chimney flue in 1852, destroyed about two-thirds of the collection, including many of Jefferson's books. Con-gress appropriated money to bring the library holdings back to its former level, about fifty-five thousand books, but that was it. The Harvard and Yale libraries, the Boston Public Library, the Boston Athenaeum, and the Astor Library were larger than the Library of Congress by the mid-1850s, and the Library Company of Philadelphia was as large. During that time, the federal library striving for national prominence was the Smithsonian Institution. Charles Coffin Jewett, the Smithsonian librarian, might well have succeeded, except that his boss, Joseph Henry, wanted the Smith-

---

*Billington says Jefferson had to choose between selling his wine collection and his book collection, both of which were superior. I asked the library staff to find out where Billington got this bit of lore, but they could not locate it. *Jefferson and Wine,* however, does report that "no president ever assembled a finer or more diverse cellar."

sonian staff to concentrate on the creation of knowledge—research and writing—not the storage of it. Increasingly irritated over Jewett's relentless and distracting agenda, Henry fired him in 1854. A few years later, Henry transferred the Smithsonian's 40,000 books to the Library of Congress.

Ainsworth Rand Spofford, appointed librarian of Congress by President Lincoln, solidified these gains. As librarians for many centuries had realized, government power used wisely builds great libraries. The Ordonnance de Montpellier of 1537, one of the earliest deposit laws, decreed that one copy of all books printed in France or imported into the country be offered to the library at Blois. When Spofford assumed office in 1865, he successfully lobbied for a new copyright law that transferred oversight responsibility from the Patent Office to the Library of Congress and required that the library receive two copies of every United States book, pamphlet, map, print, photograph, and piece of music. A subsequent law, passed in 1891, broadened coverage to include foreign works for which an author wished United States copyright protection. (Even later, copies were required if a foreign publisher wanted to distribute in the United States.) In 1897, Spofford's last year as librarian, the library moved out of the Capitol into the Renaissance-style Thomas Jefferson Building, replete with Greek columns, statuary, paintings, and a 195-foot-high gilded dome. The Library of Congress now had the largest, most comprehensive collection in the land.

Even so, the Library of Congress was not the official national library and still isn't. That has been a de facto role. Librarians of Congress have always understood that the Congress was the chief client. Accordingly, early in the century, the library created what is today called the Congressional Research Service. The service's 750-person staff still helps legislators and their aides with research and prepares background papers. Congress remains the stated "first priority" in the library's current strategic plan.

The Information Glut

"Universal in Scope; National in Service" was the slogan coined by Herbert Putnam, one of Spofford's successors. But it's doubtful he foresaw what the universe would come to look like. In 1901, when Putnam ran the library, it had 1 million books. By the end of the century, it contained more than 18 million books.

The commercialization of thought, beginning with mass-produced books in the middle of the nineteenth century, accounts for much of this increase. The Library of Congress registered 5,600 works in 1870 and 558,645 in 1998. Not only has the number of new books published each year increased, so has the number of periodicals. Three decades ago, *Ulrich's International Periodicals Directory* listed 70,000 serials; it more than doubled to 156,000 by 1998.

As books and magazines have multiplied, so have new media. First came photographs, then movies, then videocassettes. Phonograph records have given way to CDs and DVDs. The printed page, in many instances, has yielded to the computer screen. Often the quickest way to look up a word or topic in a dictionary or encyclopedia is to turn on the computer.

The result is an information explosion. Newspapers now typically publish their ink-on-paper product *and* an electronic version accessible through the World Wide Web. The provider of a database can publish a new edition daily or hourly. People with an urge to write don't have to worry anymore about pleasing an editor or publisher who tells them to stick to the point. "On the Net," writes linguistics professor Gregory Nunberg, "there is no strong material or economic incentive to rule out prolixity or to winnow redundant postings."

"It's so easy to self-publish a book that looks professional," Silva comments. Besides this, knowing how to make intelligent marks on a piece of paper has become less important. Songwriters previously had to score music to get a copyright. Now they can sing the words onto a cassette recording. "One thing you learn quickly in our office," says Richard Anderson of the copyright staff, "is that just about everyone in America is a songwriter."

Like a giant intellectual trawler, the library casts different nets to collect all this material. The Copyright Office snags printed matter and virtually anything else that qualifies under the broad definition of "original works of authorship." Copyright specialists have grappled with a twelve-thousand-pound birdbath, board games, and T-shirts with pictures of somebody's girl friend. "I saw the Pet Rock come in," Silva recalls.

The library automatically receives copies of many United States government documents and surplus publications from federal agencies. Some fifteen thousand exchange agreements aid in collecting pamphlets, catalogs, and other specialized material from such institutions as the Lenin State Library in Russia and the Wisconsin State Historical Society. The library also receives donations of materials from institutions ranging from the American Red Cross to Harvard University.

The Library of Congress enjoys a great advantage over other libraries in that it obtains all copyrighted material for free. The average cost of a book purchased by research libraries jumped from $28.65 to $46.42 during the ten-year period ending in 1997, according to a study of the 122-member Association of Research Libraries (ARL). Periodical subscriptions increased from $88.81 to $238.69. *Comparative Biochemistry and Physiology* runs $8,835 a year; the *Journal of Comparative Neurology* $13,900. The relatively small group of scholars doing research in such narrowly focused scientific and medical fields cannot function without access to these journals, and the commercial publishers who own the journals happily charge high fees for them. Strapped to meet rising prices, research libraries spend more money to buy less. The ARL study found that serial expenditures doubled, while overall purchases declined 6 percent; book purchases declined 14 percent.

Though free acquisition through the Copyright Office gives the Library of Congress an advantage, still its quest for universal acquisition comes with a high price tag. The library must purchase books to fill gaps in the collection and to acquire items that would not be sent otherwise. In developed countries, the library relies largely on dealers with whom it has placed standing orders. The library plays a more active role in developing regions of the world where central institutions are less efficient. It runs regional acquisitions offices in Rio de Janeiro, Cairo, New Delhi, Karachi, Jakarta, and Nairobi. The staff made a special buying trip to Hong Kong in 1998 to collect campaign documents, buttons, and other paraphernalia related to the first election after the British handed over the government to China. About the same time, a mission visited warring regions in former Yugoslavia. The trip was urgent, says Nancy Davenport, director for acquisitions; the fighting threatened the existence of records and documents that showed what life was like during this period.

Acquisition is one problem; processing items into the collection is another. From time to time, serious backlogs of unprocessed material occur. This is not surprising. It takes considerable time to process a collection of papers. Former Massachusetts Senator Edward Brooke's personal papers arrived in 1978 and were not fully available to the public until 1991. The NAACP's legal files and heaps of original scripts submitted to the Copyright Office over the years by both known and unknown authors have had to wait their turn. Arrearages, as the library calls unprocessed materials, currently come to twenty million items. This is a considerable improvement over a decade ago, when the number of unprocessed materials was twice as high. A General Accounting Office study at the time concluded that the library was unable "to effectively account for and control its collection." But arrearages still constitute a problem. An item in arrearage is an item that cannot be used, and twenty million items is about one-sixth of the entire collection.

Finding room for everything is yet another problem. One theme that runs constantly through the history of the library is space, or lack of it. The first Library of Congress was tucked inside the Capitol itself. Illustrations from this period show books piled in a library room. The photo

The first Library of Congress was tucked inside the Capitol itself. Turn-of-the-century illustrations dramatize Spofford's warning to Congress that he would soon preside over the "greatest chaos in America." What the librarian of Congress did not foresee is that there would never be enough space.

"Scene in the Old Congressional Library," W. Bengough, 1897, Library of Congress dramatized Spofford's warning to Congress that he would soon preside over the "greatest chaos in America." After the Jefferson Building came two more buildings, in 1939 and 1980, and still the library doesn't have enough room. "It's always a matter of space," Silva says.

Always in the background is the question of whether the library should be collecting more, not less. "I have a colleague who can argue that a matchbook could be collected," says Bill Schenck, who helps set the collections policy. The challenge is not simply to decide what is worthwhile now, but what people will consider worthwhile later. Historians in the nineteenth century didn't pay attention to popular culture. Today, they study pulp romances for insights into everyday life. Movies depicting urban crime were considered lowbrow when they appeared in the 1940s and 1950s; today they are valued as *film noir*. "You can't imagine anything that people might not want to know about," says Winston Tabb, who as associate librarian for library services is one of Billington's chief lieutenants.

These two strands—the desire for universality, the lack of space—create a Gordian knot for the library. Billington tries to cut through it with his standard response about the library aspiring "to have something of everything and to have the most important things of everything." But as good as this sounds, it leaves considerable room for judgment. Does the library need the paper version of the *Boston Globe and* the electronic version, even if they are only slightly different? (The answer, for the time being, is yes.) When confronted with a compact disk, Lolita Silva does not have time to listen to it. She makes her decision to keep it or not by reading the accompanying instruction manual. The library has a good collection of early advertisements. How much of the new Internet commerce should it try to capture? Library officials admit that they have missed much of it up to this point.

The problems are magnified at the international level. The library wants to collect at least one newspaper from each country. But even that is not practical with the many small countries in the South Pacific. With increased globalization, more countries are producing literature about each other. Established collection mechanisms ensure that the library acquires French scholarship on France, but who is responsible for collecting French scholarship on Japan, the French or the Japanese dealers on whom the library relies? With easier self-publishing, people can write in local dialects that are not generally available.

A three-inch-thick book of directives tells library staff what to keep and what to throw away. "Our policy statements are under continuous review for what we are going to take and not going to take," Davenport says. At its most profound level, the library is asking, What is a publication and what does it mean to have it?

As part of this inquiry, the Copyright Office has launched an experiment called the Copyright Office Electronic Registration, Recordation & Deposit System (CORDS). CORDS permits an author to file a copyright application over the Internet. The test is being done with unpublished works created in a digital format. If successful, says Peter Vankevich, a senior staff member with the Copyright Office, it may be used later with works published on paper, which would be saved in the library electronically. As another tentative step in this direction, the library signed an agreement in 1999 with UMI Dissertation Services, a Bell & Howell company. Dissertations, digitally deposited for copyright purposes, will be available though UMI's Web site, not through the library itself.

A recent change in management structure has spread responsibility for implementation of the library acquisition policies to many more staffers. Lolita Silva, who previously reviewed books and materials from many countries, concentrates now on United States copyright material. Selection officers work in each of the regional divisions. The challenge is to ensure that everyone applies the rules the same way. The need for training is all the more important because many of the veterans, like Silva, who joined the library in 1966, will soon be eligible for retirement.

Saving the Past

While Silva manages the flow of new information into the library, Tom Albro, four floors below, stands in front of a workbench laden with tools book crafters have used for centuries. With obvious pride, he shows a volume he is working on at the moment: a 1763 copy of Algernon Sydney's *On Government.* The book belonged to Thomas Jefferson. Albro took the book apart, washed and treated each page, and rebound it in red leather. He is about to letter the cover and make a special box for the book. The complete job will take ninety-five hours. Albro hopes the book will last for two hundred to three hundred years.

Albro likens his preservation work to that of ancient craftsmen. No button-down shirt and tie for him. He wears blue jeans and a light sweater, its sleeves jammed up to his elbows. Classical music plays in the background. With obvious relish, he tells me not to talk to his staff. It would interrupt the rhythm of their work. Restoring rare material "reflects on our society," Albro says. "It's not just Milli Vanilli and lip-syncing. This is dead honest."

Albro and the score of professional book restorers with whom he works in the Conservation Division are yet another dimension of universality. It is not enough to obtain one of everything worth collecting. The Library of Congress has to keep one of everything intact and make it available to scholars. The library has enough ancient manuscripts, maps, and posters to keep Albro and his colleagues busy for eternity. But those items that come under Albro's loving care are only a part of the problem. In recent years, the library has encountered a cruel irony embedded in mass literacy.

When reading was an elite activity, publishers handstitched books and used high-quality paper that lasted for centuries. When a large reading public materialized in the mid-1800s, publishers sought to reduce costs for mass-produced books by using cheaper binding techniques. "In the rage for cheapness we have sacrificed everything for slop," *Publishers Weekly* lamented in 1884, "and a dainty bit of bookmaking is like a jewel in the swine's snout." Not only did books wear out more quickly, they also self-destructed. Paper mills switched from making rag-content paper to making paper entirely from wood pulp to meet increased demand. Wood-fiber paper, treated with acid-producing chemicals, eventually turns brown and brittle. The first edition of the *Congressional Record*, the published proceedings of the House and Senate, is printed on such paper.

Commonly cited studies estimate that 80 percent of the books in U.S. research collections are printed on acidic paper and 30 percent—or 80 million volumes—are embrittled. The Library of Congress has made estimates of its own collection. One reckons that seventy thousand of its volumes annually move from the "weak" to the "brittle" category and roughly 25 percent cannot withstand normal handling. In another attempt to understand the problem, the staff took a close look at the 2,000 books requested from readers on one day at the Jefferson Building. Of these, 54 were considered brittle but serviceable, that is to say okay to use with care. They could not, however, withstand the wear and tear of being put in a photocopy machine. Another 26 volumes were too brittle to leave in use.

Taking embrittled books out of circulation to protect them, as is the practice, is nearly the same thing as destroying them. A book has no intellectual value if someone cannot read it.

Books are not the only endangered species dwelling in libraries. The
Library of Congress has one hundred thousand posters, 25 to 50 percent
of which need preservation, says Doris A. Hamburg, head of the paper
conservation section. She estimated that in 1999 the library will mend or
conserve only eight or so and make protective folders for fifty to one hundred larger posters that otherwise could not be available to scholars.

Motion pictures, stored in row after row of metal canisters, self-
destruct, too. Cellulose nitrate film, used for almost all movies produced
before 1950, is highly flammable and, if not stored properly, eventually
deteriorates to a brown powder. Some 80 percent of all silent films have
been lost forever; half of all pre-1950 films are gone as well. The library,
the nation's largest motion picture preservation archives, has limited options for saving films, including conservation, cold storage, and copying.
The costs of copying start at ten thousand dollars for black-and-white,
forty thousand dollars for color.

Book and paper preservation offers several approaches, the most laborious and costly of which is Tom Albro's method of rebuilding Jefferson's
book. Standing next to his broad workbench, one of Albro's colleagues
calculates that some twenty-four hours of surgery are necessary to save a
crumbling six-foot-high, nineteenth-century British poster of a beefeater
guard.

The most cost-effective solution to the problem of embrittlement is for
publishers to print new books on acid-free paper, a practice that is becoming more common. When books are already too brittle to be saved, the library can microfilm them. This was done in 1998 with 15 thousand to 20
thousand volumes, says Irene Schubert, chief of the Preservations
Reformatting Division. That comes to a little less than four million pages.
In this time-consuming process, material must be selected, examined to
ensure it is all present, and cataloged. Each page must be prepared for
filming. "It's not just Xeroxing," one staffer comments. The library sends
one-third of its microfilming to outside companies. A commercial vendor
supplies microfilm versions of the *Congressional Record.*

Even at this rate, the staff cannot keep pace with the need for microfilming. Just how far behind, however, is difficult to estimate, Schubert

says. Staffers working in various parts of the collection are always on the look-out for troubled books. But the library does not examine each book requested daily in the Jefferson Reading Room. If they had a use-driven program to find and fix books, she says, the library would need to increase its $1.8–million microfilm budget by 50 percent.

Meanwhile, to prevent disintegration of old books and manuscripts that haven't yet crumbled, the library has tried various alchemy. It developed and patented a deacidification process, which involved gassing endangered books with diethyl zinc (DEZ). Unfortunately, the test facility outside Washington exploded when, as the *Wall Street Journal* put it, "a library contractor pulled the wrong switch and discovered that DEZ reacts violently with water." The library next hired a private company to perfect the process in a Texas pilot plant. The contractor solved the problem of explosions only to create a new one. The odor of treated books sickened readers. This, too, was solved, but by then the company had closed the plant because it could not foresee enough demand.

The current procedure, developed by an entrepreneur near Pittsburgh, involves dipping books in a solution of perfluoroalkane. The chemical neutralizes the acid. The library says the treatment extends the shelf life of books by three hundred years. The treatment, however, is expensive, about fifteen dollars a book, including labor and transportation. That cost may decrease if enough libraries around the country use the Pittsburgh facility, says Winston Tabb. Alternatively, there is the possibility that the lone company involved in the process will stop offering the service if more libraries don't become involved.

In 1990, the library's goal was to deacidify one million books a year for the next twenty years. As of the end of 1998, Tabb says that the library has only deacidified 120,000 books. He hesitates when asked how many more books now need treatment. "I can't really answer that question."

Faced with unrealistic costs, the library is rethinking what it means to save books. One strategy is to lower the temperature and use other storage techniques that slow deterioration. The new Fort Meade storage facility will have improved climate control. Another strategy is to save materials in other forms, possibly using computer technology. But this way may lead to worse problems.

"If the book had been invented after the laptop," wrote technology guru Neil Gershenfeld, "it would be hailed as a great breakthrough." The traditional book has been around so long because it works so well. And because it has been around so long, we know what to expect from it. We know, for instance, how long a book is likely to survive physically. Electronic technology is not time-tested. No one is certain what potentially lethal genes lie in CDs and other new information mediums. Optical disks, a relatively new vehicle for displaying words and pictures, probably won't last as long as a book printed on acidic paper. By some estimates, an optical disk's life span may be fifteen to twenty years.

The problem inherent in new technology is not confined to its limited physical life. One of the fears pervading the library is that rapid technological progress will bring equally rapid technological obsolescence. What happens, librarians ask, if CDs go the way of phonograph records? In that case, only one or two manufacturers may continue to make CD players and charge a premium for them—or, worse, everyone may get out of the CD business. Or new software may overtake today's software to such an extent that the old version becomes unreadable on contemporary hardware.

Many worry, too, that reading a book on a computer screen diminishes the experience for the scholar. Anyone who has leafed through old magazines in a library realizes that the physical feel of that old *Saturday Evening Post* and the advertisements, among other things, provide context to the article that one is studying. Computer guru Bill Gates says that when he reads long documents, such as books, he prefers reading words on paper to reading on a computer screen.

"We are constantly making decisions about how far we go when we save something," says Mark Roosa, chief of the Conservation Division. "Every decision is a decision to reacquire it." One of his strategies is to involve curators from various parts of the library collection in deciding what deserves the most immediate attention, and what must languish. "We'll never do it all," Roosa says.

Everything, Albro adds, "is going to capitulate in the end."

Champagne into Six-packs

"The chief task of a librarian is to get people to read," says the level-headed heroine in Sinclair Lewis's *Main Street.*

"You feel so?" replies a Gopher Prairie matron. "My feeling, Mrs.

Kennicott, and I am merely quoting the librarians of a very large college, is that the first duty of the *conscientious* librarian is to preserve the books." For most of our history, the Gopher Prairie matron has prevailed. The watchword has been hoarding, not diffusion.

Remember how small Jefferson's library was, only 6,487 volumes; yet it was considered one of the best in the country. Before Gutenberg, only one library in the Western Christian world held more than 2,000 books. Early librarians, such as those at the famous library in ancient Alexandria, were called "keepers of the scrolls," not lenders of scrolls. Ptolemy classified the manufacturing techniques for papyrus the way nations today classify information about making nuclear weapons, as a national secret. Later the Benedictines, among the most dedicated copyists in the Middle Ages, required each monastery to have one book per monk. Once that goal was reached, collections grew slowly. What is often considered history's first copyright dispute is also a story about hoarding. An Irish monk secretly copied a fine book against the wishes of its owner in the sixth century. When discovered, the monk had to relinquish his copy to the owner of the original. Lorenzo de Medici's librarian was horrified that the printing press would "put a hundred evil volumes into a thousand clumsy hands and madmen will be loosed upon the world."

Sir Thomas Bodley, founder of the Oxford library named after him, thought librarians should be celibate and did not want idlers mixing with students, "pestering the room with their gazing and babbling." On the day the library opened in 1602, he was delighted that "all proceeded orderly, and with such silence!" This was a time when librarians still chained books to desks and shelves, a practice that would continue for some time. The idea of lending books through free public libraries did not materialize in the United States until the middle of the nineteenth century and did not take flight until Andrew Carnegie subsidized library building. In 1896, just before Carnegie's major donations began, the United States had 971 public libraries. He added 1,679.*

As expected of a library that sees itself as the ultimate collector, the Library of Congress has thought chiefly in the preservation terms that

---

*Carnegie, always the shrewd businessman, mostly built the library buildings and left it to the local taxpayers to pay for the books in them. A study years later showed that in the few towns in which he provided endowments, the library endowments did not grow and the townspeople were not in the habit of providing extra support.

Gopher Prairie matrons would appreciate. Only a small group of people can check out its books, chiefly members of Congress and their staffs, who can request that books be sent to their offices. Spofford, the great nineteenth-century librarian of Congress, extended the hours of service in 1865 to keep the library open every weekday all year long. In 1869, he advocated evening hours, but Congress did not approve this until 1898, nearly thirty years later. Still later, the library participated in interlibrary loan programs. As an alternative to open check-out, the library has offered other services, for instance, providing cataloging information for use by other libraries, a measure that helped ensure standardization.

Unfortunately, these services are not highly visible to the average taxpayer. Few write to their legislator requesting Congress raise the library's appropriation so that it can put out more cataloging information.

Eager to gain favor with the public, Billington has displayed the attitude of Mrs. Kennicott. His battle cry is "to get the champagne out of the bottle and into the six-packs." John Y. Cole, the director of the library's Center for the Book and a frank propagandist, calls this "a universal service mission."

Cole's Center for the Book is an emblem of this service mission. Created in 1977, it aims to promote reading and interest in books. It now has well over thirty affiliated state centers.

One of the headiest projects created under Billington is the National Digital Library Program (NDLP). The computer-based scheme has created an Internet-accessed lending library that will never have an overdue book. Without ever going into the Library of Congress, a patron with a computer at home, office, or school can read four of Walt Whitman's early notebooks, see Mathew Brady's Civil War Photographs, and listen to World War I recordings of speeches by American leaders. Its goal is to have 5 million of the library's 115 million items online by the library's bicentennial year in 2000.

The digital library's virtue is the potential to excite the average reader, especially school children. "We want to hook young people's interest in a way that will take them back into books," says Laura Campbell, the NDLP director. Youngsters learn how to use primary sources for research purposes. With a little luck, those youngsters will also talk over the dinner table about what they are learning from the Library of Congress, which in turn may motivate mothers and fathers, who vote, to write supportive letters to their legislators. The library has a special fellowship program that brings fifty teachers to Washington for a week of training each summer. When they go home, Campbell says, they spread the word.

In this time of scarce government resources and escalating costs to keep up with the information explosion, such lobbying becomes more important. The congressional appropriation increased at a modest annual rate of 2.5 percent from 1994 to 1999, when it was $391 million. "In terms of the absolute dollar amount the Library of Congress has done well, but in relation to the creation of new knowledge and multiple formats of new knowledge its funding has not kept pace," says Duane Webster, executive director of the Association of Research Libraries. To contain costs, the library shrank staff from 4,700 in 1994 to about 4,250 in 1999. It is as if the Information Age is riding to the future in a speedboat, and the Library of Congress is trying to keep up in a dinghy. The library needs a national constituency, Cole says: "A bargain for the taxpayers. That's our line."

The library also has become more skilled at creating a universe of donors. Billington established an official fund raising office in 1988 and in 1990 created the James Madison Council, a private-sector support body of business executives and entrepreneurs. The current digitalization project will cost $60 million. Only $15 million of that is coming from Congress, the rest from the likes of David Packard and John Kluge (who gave $5 million or more each) as well as American Express, AT&T, Occidental Petroleum, and others (each of which gave at least $1 million). By 1999, Billington had raised $98 million in private money for a variety of library activities.

The library wrings considerable public relations out of its carefully preserved materials. With a conspiratorial air, Albro ushers me, as he has so many journalists before, to a bench laden with boxes containing some of the library's most sacred relics: James Madison's Princeton dissertation and the contents of Lincoln's pockets on the night he was assassinated, which include a Confederate five-dollar bill and eyeglasses tied with string. I half expect him to tell me to genuflect. Lolita Silva is also a star attraction for journalists. Her genius has made her a regular stop for visiting reporters who want to know about the library.

An $81-million renovation program eliminated the old card catalog files that once spilled out of the reading room in the Thomas Jefferson

Building. Researchers may plug their personal computers into desk sockets. The library has erased decades of grime from the now gleaming columns and sumptuous art work. The newly brightened spaces are used more often than in the past to display portions of the collection in special exhibitions. "We are part a museum now," Cole says of the tendency to show off its holdings and staff.

The library has planned an elaborate bicentennial agenda, replete with new publications about itself (*The Library of Congress: Two Hundred Years*), a commemorative coin and stamp, symposia, and more exhibitions. The centerpiece for the bicentennial is supposed to be the reconstituted collection that Thomas Jefferson sold to the library. The library is hoping private donors will help replace some of the volumes that were destroyed in the fire of 1852. Dallas Cowboy owner Jerry Jones and his wife, Gene, kicked off the fund drive in 1999 with a $1-million gift. To provide a photo opportunity, Billington's staff arranged for the couple to present the first book purchased with their gift, *Hermes or a Philosophical Inquiry Concerning Universal Grammar*, 2nd edition, 1765 (London), by James

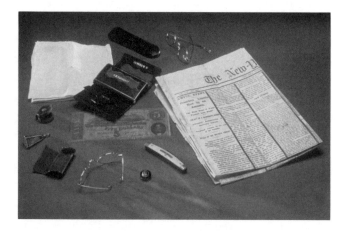

"Lincoln's pockets," as the Library of Congress reverently calls the stuff that Lincoln had with him the evening he was assassinated, have nothing to do with books. But the library is desperate to make itself interesting, for that may help generate badly needed financial support. Staffers happily usher journalists into the presence of Lincoln's pockets and provide photos such as this one.

Library of Congress

Harris. These books let us see Jefferson's "mind at work," Billington said on the occasion, although he did not elaborate on what Harris's book might tell us, and the generous couple admitted that they did not go in much for reading (a point the library's bulletin politely did not report).

"It's in the air," says one senior staffer of the increasing emphasis on public relations at the library. Individual divisions try to raise money for their preferred conservation and collection projects. The library trotted out Tara Holland, Miss America 1997, to brighten the Center for the Book's press conference announcing a national reading promotion program for 1997–2000. When the Chicago Cubs' Sammy Sosa and the St. Louis Cardinals' Mark McGwire had their home-run derby in the summer of 1998, the National Digital Library staff moved quickly to put part of its baseball card collection online. "This is our juiciest stuff," Campbell says.

Despite all these efforts, not everyone is persuaded the library is more universal in service than before. Increased security has restricted access to library stacks. Interlibrary loans, the library says, are "still an important part of the LC mission, as the LC is the 'library of last resort.'" Critics, however, say that the library is not particularly helpful in this regard. In 1997, the National Library of Medicine provided interlibrary loans amounting to 406,846 books and the University of Minnesota (the number one university lender) lent 264,092. The Library of Congress lent only 22,408 books, which was on a par with Oklahoma State University.

In the 1940s, the library began compiling the *National Union Catalog*, which identified the holdings in more than 1,100 North American libraries. It is no longer updated because of online records. Many librarians say that the library has become much less important to universal book cataloging. The Online Computer Library Center (OCLC) in Dublin, Ohio, provides "dirtier" bibliographic data (meaning that it is compiling from many sources, some of which may be inaccurate), but it is also more comprehensive than the Library of Congress.

Some fear that the National Digital Library and similar high-profile activities divert resources from traditional collection activities inside the library. A $3.5-million donation from AT&T was used to digitize the Alexander Graham Bell and Samuel F. B. Morse Collections, something telephone people no doubt care about passionately. But should Bell and Morse be one of the library's top digital priorities?

Heavy-duty fund raising by the library also may hurt fund raising by other research libraries around the country that have relied on private contributions to stay healthy. As librarians at other institutions see it, the Library of Congress is unfairly situated to court donors, who relish having wine and cheese with political leaders more than they do with university presidents. What's more, as private donors step up, Congress may feel free to cut its appropriation.

Strike up a conversation about the Library of Congress with a professional librarian at a research library somewhere in the country and bitterness is likely to surface. The Library of Congress is not our national library, rival librarians say. We do not have a national library. They criticize Billington for pursuing a self-appointed universal mission. His *National Digital Library* seems to many a sneaky way to get the word *national* somewhere in the library's name.

A better approach, critics say, would be for the Library of Congress to make the ultimate concession to universality and share its mission. In this scenario, different specialized research libraries would be responsible for mastering narrow areas. Linked to a network, they would form a universal whole.

The idea of a national library is outmoded, says Brian Lang, chief executive of the British Library. Future libraries "may not actually contain any publications at all. The librarian in this scenario will not be someone who acquires books and cares for a collection, but rather a person who helps a researcher to identify where a particular piece of information is located and arranges access to it." In this context, the ultimate library is not the one with the most items. It is the one with the best card catalog accessible over the Internet. It may also be one with lavish private financing. Lang shocked many people when he announced in 1998 that he was proposing to charge users of the British Library a hefty three hundred pounds annually. "Pessimistic about extracting more money from the public purse," said the *Times Literary Supplement*, "Mr. Lang came up with the idea of going commercial."

A network of libraries, pooling these resources, offers economies of scale. It also offers special risks. Each information center must maintain the quality of its collection. Many of the best special library collections are in universities, and university trustees are typically uneasy about the costs of running libraries. Local taxpayers are not likely to be enthusiastic about maintaining a special collection to be used largely by experts from around the country. There is also the question of oversight. Who will decide if each library is doing its job and, if not, who should do it instead?

Professional librarians traditionally have disliked having their future shaped by people like Billington, who is a historian, not a librarian. Yet nonlibrarians are likely to become more involved in modern library activities. Campbell, not a librarian by training, came from the private sector. She was an officer with Arthur Young & Company and vice-president of QueTel Corporation. Her current job, she says, is to be a rainmaker, not a scholar. Her staff members, who number just over one hundred, are mostly new hires.

No formal decision has been made to continue the National Digital Library beyond 2001. Campbell obviously is prepared to make the case for what she sees as a success. She pulls out a "brag list" (on her list, the *New York Times*'s online *CyberTimes* is quoted as saying that the Library of Congress Web site is "remarkable"). We have this list "for obvious reasons," she says, "to let people know that what we are doing is getting national recognition."

The digital library, she says, has stimulated others in the library to put more online. Staffers throughout the library have come for advice on putting their collections into this digital form.

"If you can get support," Cole says of this new brand of universality, "you can do good things."

A Fate Worse than Fire

The first ancient books on clay tablets did not have titles. A reader or librarian identified them by the first few lines of the text. Medieval catalogs, which came along later, listed books in descending order of holiness, that is, starting with the Bible and working down to secular literature. Books on saints' lives appeared in calendar order, an approach that facilitated finding the proper book to read from on the saint's feast day. For centuries, librarians shelved a book based on its size or in the order it had arrived at the library. Even shelving, furniture we take for granted, came gradually. Librarians tucked clay tablets in reed baskets and placed them in the temple storeroom; they stored papyrus rolls in wooden trunks and pots. Not until the late thirteenth century did books come out of the chests and into desk-bookcases.*

One aspect of the written work, however, remained fairly constant from the fourth century onward: the basic book format of binding pages between stiff covers. No doubt the decisions about which papyrus rolls to convert and which to ignore caused angst among librarians. But once that work was done, the basic book form was settled and would remain settled for nearly 1,500 years. For all the innovations brought by Gutenberg, he did not alter the basic book form. King Charlemagne's copy of *The City of God* by St. Augustine and a copy of *Jane Fonda's Workout Book* look fundamentally alike. Twenty years ago, almost no one thought that a book would look any other way than it did. Even today, before we put our paperback book on the nightstand and turn out the light, we do not ponder how three thousand years ago we would have had to coil a forty-meter papyrus roll.

But change is now coming fast. We sometimes do look up from the computer screen to recall how we once did *all* of our reading on paper— or to recall that last week's software program didn't do nearly as much as the one blinking away at the moment. Every aspect of the book and the printed word that we once took for granted is on the table for discussion. That includes libraries.

The debates among librarians are intense, hopeful, and often frantic. It may be possible, as an IBM executive has suggested, to someday store all of the Library of Congress's books on a penny-sized disk. "If all existing texts, manuscript or printed, were digitalized," book scholar Roger Chartier says, "then the universal availability of the written inheritance would become possible." But no one is certain how that will happen.

"Most envision a future with universal access, by student and faculty, to information in all possible media via a single, multifunction workstation," observed Brian L. Hawkins, Brown University's vice-president for aca-

---

*Similarly, the internal parts of books as we know them developed slowly too. When monks worked in dank scriptoria, they ran words together without punctuation. Consecutively numbered pages, tables of contents, and indexes were not regular features until the sixteenth century, when printing technology put a higher premium on standardization and readers wanted to navigate more easily among the many books that had become available.

demic planning and administration. But no one has *"any plan or vision on how we might achieve this dream and get from here to there!"*

Many traditionalists worry that our love affair with computers will destroy books. "There has never yet been a technology invented to solve a problem which did not itself become part of the problem," said Daniel Boorstin. Boorstin, Billington's predecessor, is a historian who devoted part of his career to decrying the "graphic revolution" that has glorified making copies rather than pondering the original.

No one perusing the National Digital Library fails to notice it is long on pictures and short on books. According to the library's public relations department, it had only 388 complete books online in early 1999. Among these "books," *Legislative Wrongs to Labor* has sixteen pages and *The Land of Gold* three hundred. Scholars may peruse Whitman's notebooks or "click" through George Washington's papers. They can get ideas from viewing Brady's photographs. But the potential for original research through the digital library is limited.

Just how much the digital library can add to its offerings is uncertain. Besides the technological hurdles, there is the matter of copyright. Living authors who own the copyright to their books can block the creation of electronic versions and may well want to for the obvious reason that it will make it much easier for people to get the books without paying. Contrary to the library's propaganda, its digital library may not whet young people's appetites for knowledge, encouraging them to roam through real books. "We have found that once you automate your library," says Duane Webster of the Association of Research Libraries, "students only use what is automated."

How can we know where technology will take us? In 1999, Borders Group invested in a high-tech company whose equipment will allow Borders to print quality paperbacks in its bookstores. Customers will have immediate access to out-of-print classics. A spokesperson at rival Barnes & Noble tells us that traditionally printed books about computers "are its top sellers." We have reports that our computer-driven society is using more paper, not less. United States consumption jumped from sixteen million tons for printing and writing in 1980 to twenty-five million ten years later. Alternatively, we read news reports that a nonprofit company, Project Gutenberg, is digitizing *Paradise Lost* and more than one thousand other public domain works that can be read on a portable electronic gizmo called Rocket eBook, which in 1998 cost five hundred dollars. Literary critics tell us that poetry has no future. The computer, they say, goes for speed, not depth. For evidence, look at the way we casually treat grammar and punctuation when writing an e-mail—something we are less inclined to do when writing on a piece of paper.

Librarians will not decide whether or not publishers stop printing books on paper. They will decide what published materials, in whatever form, survive. That responsibility is unnerving. Talking on the telephone or being interviewed in his office, with its magnificent view of the Jefferson Building's dome in twilight, Billington makes statements that weave like a sail ship tacking in a choppy sea.

- "Selectivity doesn't mean we are going to become less universal, if you see what I mean. The library must justify its existence, it must collect everything that is important."

- "I think the most important thing is that we do not exclude any category."

- "I constantly worry about this question of playing God with the human memory. There is nothing more important than keeping the variety, the richness, the unrealized possibilities of the past and the present, alive for the future."

One of the signal events told in the history of books is the burning of the entire Alexandrian Library in 48 B.C. The story, however, is wrong. Only part of the library was lost to fire. The real culprit in Alexandria was far worse than flames and offers a stronger lesson. At some point, Alexandrians simply stopped caring about their books. A legend, possibly no more accurate that the myth of the all-destructive fire, has it that citizens burned books to keep themselves warm.

The need for concerted attention to protecting books has not changed since that time. But the way in which it must be done has. A surfeit of undifferentiated information is as useless as books burned to ashes. Someone has to choose, and librarians are better prepared for the task than anyone else. For several centuries, they have suffered from lack of status. Casanova spent thirteen unhappy years as a librarian to Count Joseph Charles de Waldenstein, seigneur of the Castle of Dux. He was bored and, as he saw it, constantly insulted. Among other things, he complained about having to eat with other heavy-lifters in the servants' dining hall. To get even, he wrote his famous memoirs. In the future, librarians will sit at the table with royalty. Anthony Smith anticipated this elevated status for them twenty years ago in a book about information technology. The librarian, he observed, "now becomes a kind of author."

Meanwhile, back in the Library of Congress Madison Building, I am starting to leave Lolita Silva's work area and peer into a cart filled with books destined for the permanent collection. Inside is an IBM manual, a book I would have expected Silva to reject. What about this, I ask? She looks at it. Apparently an absent-minded staff flipped it into the wrong cart, she says. Unfazed, Silva puts the manual in its proper place, the "out" cart.

APPENDIX A

Book Promotion: The Business
Established by the Author of Our Nature

—⟨⟨⟨⟩⟩⟩—

In which it is shown that this book
has an appendix.

—⟨∂∂⟩—

Nothing gives such weight and dignity to a book as an Appendix.
—HERODOTUS*

—⟨∂∂⟩—

*According to Mark Twain in *A Tramp Abroad.*

P.T. Barnum attracted people to his American Museum in New York by sponsoring a beauty contest for "the handsomest women in America" (he posted the daguerreotypes in a Gallery of Beauty), stringing a line of Old Glories across Broadway to celebrate the Fourth of July, and planting stories in local newspapers to warm interest for his exhibit of the mermaid from Feejee (the mermaid seems to have been the concoction of a Japanese fisherman who united the upper half of a monkey with the lower half of a fish). "I printed whole columns in the papers, setting forth the wonders of my establishment," he said.

In *The Life of P. T. Barnum, Written by Himself*, Barnum revealed his promotional tricks. Then, to get even more readers, he put the book in the public domain so that it could be reprinted endlessly by others, which would bring him more attention. "This is a trading world," he wrote, "and men, women, and children, who cannot live on gravity alone, need something to satisfy their gayer, lighter moods and hours, and he who ministers to this want is in a business established by the Author of our nature."

The spirit of the Great Showman lives today. At a recent American Booksellers Association, Turner Publishers drew attention to *Level Four: Virus Hunters of the C.D.C.*, a book about Centers for Disease Control, by handing out ball-point pens shaped like hypodermic needles. Crown, another publishing house, threw a party for Judith Krantz's *Till We Meet Again* in an airplane hangar.

Like circuses, books depend on salesmanship. Apart from school assignments, most book reading is voluntary. While people must buy bread, they choose—or are persuasively nudged—to buy books. This is why the grocery store places magazines and romance novels at the check-out counter next to the candy. While you are killing time in line waiting to pay for bread, the store management hopes that on impulse you will decide you want to know why Cher doesn't want to have Billy Graham's baby, or that you will spot an entwined couple on the cover of a romance novel and throw it in your shopping cart.

Also like circuses, books are largely for entertainment. As such, they lend themselves to all the hype and advertising gimmicks that go with promoting hyphenated mermaids from Feejee.

It has always been so. As soon as books went on the market, book marketing began. Most contemporary sales ploys are old ideas in new book jackets.

Here are examples:

Then, Mason Locke Weems was an employee of Matthew Carey, a publisher whom Benjamin Franklin had encouraged in the business. To hustle his own biography of a cherry-tree-chopping George Washington, as well as books by other authors that Carey published, Parson Weems traveled (and wrote while on the road) "regardless of blizzards, mosquitoes, flood and fatigue," as Van Wyck Brooks noted. Weems sold books until his death in 1825.

Now, authors complain about book tours, but most hit the road if the publisher is willing to pay—and if they have any sense. Some writers, says veteran publisher Clarkson Potter, "think self-promotion is demeaning. . . . Unfortunately, authors that feel this way are wrong. You do have to sell yourself."

Then, Herman Melville's story in the *The Confidence-Man* began with this sentence: "At sunrise on a first of April, there appeared, suddenly as Manco Capac at the Lake Titicaca, a man in cream-colors, at the waterside in the city of St. Louis." Realizing the publicity that comes with clever timing, he had the book published on All Fool's Day, April 1.

Now, increasingly cagey writers find other ways to use the calendar to their advantage. The flip side of paying attention to dates in order to garner good publicity is doing so to avoid bad publicity. John O'Hara supposedly told his publisher to set the publication dates for his books on Thanksgiving. That was a day that the *New York Times's* daily reviewer, Orville Prescott, did not appear. Prescott did not like O'Hara's books. At the same time, writers look for opportunities to do anniversary literature, for instance cranking out millennium books. By the end of 1998, *Books in Print* listed roughly seventy-five books under the subject of the millennium. In mid-1999, Mary Morouse, merchandising vice-president at Amazon.com, told *Publishers Weekly* that "We have a Millennium Store." And there were six months to go before the fireworks.

Then, just before the turn of the century, a publisher let it be known that there was a hundred-dollar bill in one of its books stacked up in a department store. The store sold every copy the first day.

In the meantime, Thomas Chastain wrote a mystery with eight unresolved murders, and Bill Adler, a book packager who dreamed up marketing schemes, came up with this promotional scheme. "There's a $10,000 reward for solving the crime," said a banner on the cover of *Who Killed the Robins Family?* "It could be yours!" Four married couples in Denver won. The book made the *New York Times* best-seller list. Adler, who put up the reward money, shared credit with Chastain (as creator) and evenly split the royalties with him.

Now, in connection with Olivia Goldsmith's *The Bestseller,* a book about the vagaries of authorship, HarperCollins promised a contract to an unpublished author with the best "one-page synopsis and thirty pages from your completed original novel." The offer drew seven thousand submissions. The winner was Dalia Rabinovich's *Flora's Suitcase,* which appeared in 1998.

Then, flaunting all her talents, French novelist Colette burst naked from a cake.

Now, ex–rock critic Elizabeth Wurtzel appears in the buff on the cover of her book *Bitch: In Praise of Difficult Women.*

Way back then, playwright Richard Sheridan wrote *The Critic,* in which his character Puff relates the latest book-hyping tricks. In one of these ploys, a critic is supposed to feign outrage and note that a work is "too warmly coloured for female delicacy." Puff says, "Here you see the two strongest inducements are held forth;—First, that nobody ought to read it;—secondly, that everybody buys it."

Now, Madonna's oversized picture book, *Sex,* is sold in a silver Mylar bag overprinted with "Warning! Adults Only!" This disclaimer had the forbidden-fruit effect of making people want to look inside all the more.

Then, in the 1920s, dignified Alfred Knopf used sandwich boards to advertise books.

Now, Danielle Steel uses her Web site (http://www.daniellesteel.com) to tell you about her upcoming marriage, show you photos of her pets and antique cars, and relate fascinating details about her doings with the kids (they like her French toast and scrambled eggs).

Then, careful about readership loyalty, Louisa May Alcott, of *Little Women* fame, wrote delightful books for children under her real name and *Pauline's Passion and Punishment, Skeleton in the Closet,* and other books on transvestism, dope, and feminism under the pseudonym A. M. Barnard.

Now, Stephen King gives a convoluted explanation for writing novels under the name Richard Bachman, but ultimately admits that his publisher thought he was "overpublishing the market." A prolific writer, King can easily saturate the market. He wrote *The Running Man* in seventy-two hours. Bachman died in 1985 of "cancer of the pseudonym," but Bachman's *The Regulators* appeared posthumously as a "lost work."

Then, in the mid–nineteenth century, Abbé Jacques-Paul Migne published an average of one religious book every ten days for thirty years and owned at least ten newspapers, including one that eventually became today's *Le Monde.* Eager to promote his *Bibliothèque universelle du clergé,* he appears to have written book blurbs and put them in the mouths of others. "Excellent books at a modest price," says the archbishop of Paris.*

Now, Russell Baker of the *New York Times* says that Herbert Mitgang, also of the *New York Times,* has written a book that is peachy. "I romped right through [*The Montauk Fault*]. . . . It's like reading next week's newspaper." After reading Baker's *So This Is Depravity,* Mitgang returns the favor with an equally nice quote. Baker, he says, is "the best since Mark Twain, H. L. Mencken and S. J. Perelman."

Then, writing anonymously was a good way to get a gossipy buzz started in nineteenth-century London's literary circles. Alexander Pope was among the wiliest at such sleight of hand. To get around the convention that one did not publish one's own letters, Pope contrived to have his private correspondence published without it appearing he was involved. Afterward, he cried foul (although he was receiving royalties). He also said that the

---

*As befitted a man who came from a family in the dry goods business, the good abbé also sold organs, stations of the cross, and religious paintings and statues. He trafficked in illegal masses. His printing plant had a bank in it.

unauthorized versions were not accurate and, honorable man that he said he was, that he felt obliged to publish an authorized version, in which he added previously unpublished letters. Other Pope tricks included accepting money to suppress his writings and then publishing them anyway. The author, says a student of his handiwork, was "one of the most thoroughgoing hypocrites that English literature has ever known."

Now, journalist Joe Klein writes *Primary Colors* as "Anonymous" and, when asked by close friends, repeatedly and vehemently denies his authorship. This generates wild speculation about the book's patrimony (which generates reader interest and sales). "I wanted the book to be reviewed, not the author," he argues, acknowledging in a casual aside that "I realize I've been the commercial beneficiary of all this." When he finally admits that he lied (which generates even more publicity), he says he will continue to write under "Anonymous" (which means he now gets credit for books he does not write). Were Pope alive, he would kick himself in the rear, saying "Why didn't I think of that?"

Still, there are differences between then and now. One might say these differences are a matter of degree, but only if one appreciates that the degree is large.

Then, marketing was a new idea, mostly tried by the naturally clever and disdained by the majority of publishers who considered most advertising bad form. "The copywriter who described *Leaves of Grass* as 'a daisy—and don't you forget it,' was fired," book historian John Tebbel noted. "Authors frequently complain that their books do not sell," said a *New York Times* editorial in 1885, "and they do not seem to understand the reason of this unpleasant state of things. The reason is plain. Publishers have no real conception of the art of advertising. . . . They are content to let books sell 'on their merits,' as they express it." The term book *blurb* does not seem to have come into use until the 1920s.

Now, so many publishers are heavily into marketing that the rest, however conservative they may be, fear being elbowed off the shelves if they don't make a spectacle of themselves, too. Publishing has become a big, competitive business, and all those involved today are more focused than ever on moving products off the line and into consumers' hands.

APPENDIX B

Self-Publishing: The American Dream

—◦◦◦—

In which it is shown that this book
is even weightier because it has
two appendices.

———❦———

Self-publishing is a perfect example of the American dream.
—Marilyn and Tom Ross

———❦———

Missionaries for self-publishing, Marilyn and Tom Ross sniff self-righteously at authors who pay a vanity press to publish their books. This, they say, is a craven way to "feed the ego." Nevertheless self-publishing and vanity publishing have much in common. Both often involve paying others to do the printing and promotion. Both offer equal amounts of what a vanity publisher in the 1950s called "immortality." And both search for polite terms to describe the process. Vanity publishing calls itself *subsidy* publishing; self-publishers like to be thought of as *independent* publishers. A big difference is that a vanity press can conceivably turn you down. If a self-publisher ever has rejected his or her own book, no one has reported the fact. Another big difference is that in self-publishing you stand to make more money, one of the surest routes to self-righteousness and attainment of the American Dream.

Just how many people want to cash in on that dream is hard to say. But the number is large and growing. R. R. Bowker is responsible for International Standard Book Numbers (ISBN) in the United States. Between 1968 and 1978, it assigned 9,863 publisher prefixes, says Don Riseborough who runs R. R. Bowker's ISBN agency. By 1998, twenty years later, it had assigned 112,445. Some large publishers have more than one prefix, for instance to handle different imprints, but many are tiny operations that are in business only for a short time. Riseborough says that 8,100 new publishers appeared in 1998 alone, with about 95 percent of them being like Joe Black, the fellow who publishes his own books and no one else's. And this still does not account for all publishers. ISBN numbers are only needed if a publisher sells in a bookstore. Many self-publishers never go near a bookstore. These small publishers often don't bother to list their wares in *Books in Print* either. Nevertheless, a whopping 62,000 United States publishers had registered titles in *Books in Print* in 1998. "I had three e-mails today," said Riseborough of inquiries from self-publishers interested in securing ISBN numbers. And it was only three in the afternoon.*

Today's self-publishers differ from self-publishers in Franklin's time. Franklin knew the printing business; they do not. Instead, they turn to people such as the Rosses. The Rosses run a company called About

---

*Riseborough also offered his Internet address for other self-publishers who want to register their books. It is www.isbn.org/.

Books, Incorporated, "a writing, publishing and marketing consulting service." They also started SPAN, the 1,100-member Small Publishers Association of North America, which holds an annual conference. Advertisers in their newsletter, *Span Connection*, include people who design book jackets, printers, book display firms, book distributors, book publishing software retailers, publicists, copyright specialists, editors—everything you need to publish your book yourself without doing the work.

These consultants are not bashful about marketing. "Contrary to what Mama always said," advise the Rosses in *The Complete Guide to Self-Publishing*, "you must become a braggart." Another self-publishing adviser, Jerrold Jenkins, certainly agrees. He is coauthor (he puts the names of coauthors—professional writers—in small type) of *Inside the Best Sellers* and *Publish to Win: Smart Strategies to Sell More Books*. Always looking for a chance to promote his product, Jenkins said he would send me a copy of his latest book because I had just said in our telephone conversation that he had created a "mini-empire" in the world of how-to self-publishing. I would mention he had a mini-empire in this book, Jenkins explained, which would be good for him.

In addition to making back-of-the room sales after speeches, self-publishers can hit the road creatively. Gregory J. P. Godek, author and self-publisher of *1001 Ways to Be Romantic*, decorated a recreational vehicle with a mural of a couple embracing and drove it to trade conferences, where he was known to hand out long-stemmed roses to promote the book. Mark Victor Hansen, co–inspirational speaker and coauthor of *Chicken Soup for the Soul*, calls this "by-pass marketing." Readers can find his inspirational "chicken soup" stories in bakeries and nail salons.

The Rosses and Jenkins frequently mention Mark Twain and a few other author-publishers. The message is that these venerable authors made money publishing books and so can you. This, however, is ahistorical. First, Twain published other authors' work as well as his own. Second, he went broke doing it. "The billows of hell have been rolling over me," Twain said shortly before declaring the bankruptcy of his publishing business, a step designed to avoid business distractions and concentrate, instead, on writing. Besides, many famous self-publishers, for instance Horace Walpole, printed their own books to avoid any semblance of commercialism.

Judging from *Independent Publisher*, one of the magazines in Jenkins's "mini-empire" (there, I said it again), all self-published books are good. In one month, taken at random, the magazine reviewed 117 books. Each review was an endorsement. In conversation, however, Jenkins acknowledges, somewhat circuitously, that it is not common for people to come up with original information worthy of books. In the clearer words of Marilyn Ross, "Some of these books should never be published."

Nevertheless, on occasion a traditional trade publisher will discover a successfully self-published book and reprint it. This minimizes the trade publisher's risk. The Rosses, for instance, published their *Complete Guide to Self-Publishing;* now Writers Digest Books publishes it.

Paul Richards Evans's *The Christmas Box* has become the Horatio Alger story of self-publishing. A Mormon advertising executive, Evans wrote the book for his children. Friends liked it. He sent it to publishers,

Apostles for self-publishing point to Mark Twain as an example of how one can publish one's own books and still be a good author. They forget to mention that Twain published other people's books, too, and went broke. "The billows of hell have been rolling over me," Twain said shortly before declaring bankruptcy, a step designed to avoid business distractions and concentrate, instead, on writing. Twain, incidentally, would no doubt argue that every appendix should have a photo.

Photograph of Mark Twain/Samuel Clemens. Still Pictures Branch of the National Archives at College Park

who didn't. Taking matters into his own hands, he published eight thousand copies of the eighty-seven-page tale and had them distributed to Utah bookstores. When these sold out, he printed more. When the paperback book made best-seller lists, Simon & Schuster paid a reported $4.2 million to add the book to their list. One plus seemed to be that this was a book that could be sold year after year; another was that Evans would remain an aggressive self-promoter. He keeps names and addresses of readers who have corresponded with him; they get postcards when he writes new books, which Simon & Schuster now also publishes.

Which just goes to show that in the end the best thing that can happen to a self-publisher is that they get out of the publishing business—and stick to self-promotion.

APPENDIX C

Four Bad Mistakes about Editing Errors

—⁓—

In which it is certain that a doctor
can take out an appendix by mistake,
but a writer can never put one in
by mistake.

—⁓—

—⟨∿∿⟩—

I object to publishers: the one service they have done me
is to teach me to do without them. They combine commercial rascality
with artistic touchiness and pettishness, without being
either good business men or fine judges of literature.
All that is necessary in the production of a book
is an author and a bookseller, without the intermediate parasite.
—George Bernard Shaw

Errors, like straws, upon the surface flow;
He who would search for pearls must dive below.
—John Dryden, "All for Love"

—⟨∿∿⟩—

When my first book arrived fresh from the printer, my wife, young son, and I drove to the publisher to pick up a copy. In the final stages of editing, I had been careful to check and double-check the page proofs, called galleys, for errors. I had sent them to my eagle-eyed mother. Now, on the way home from the publisher, I sat in the back seat of the car and cracked open the book somewhere in the middle to savor the fruits of all my labor. The first sentence I read had a misspelling. I think that I read no further. I know for certain that when I arrived home in the middle of the afternoon, I went straight to bed and fell into that deep sleep reserved for those who are in denial.

That experience and similar ones since give credence to the faith that some believers put in bibliomancy, opening the Good Book at random, feeling certain that the lord will reveal words of wisdom to guide them. If there is only one editing mistake in a 1,100-page book, some celestial law guarantees that the author will turn to it immediately. "The moment when the finished book or, better yet, a tightly packed carton of finished books arrives on my doorstep is the moment of truth, of culmination," John Updike wrote; "its bliss lasts as much as five minutes, until the first typographical error or production flaw is noticed."

As time has passed and I have written other books, it has become clear to me that book errors, like divine wisdom, are not always what they seem at first. They reveal themselves to us gradually and all the more fully if we ponder them. I am not saying that we should welcome book errors. We should shun them. But shunning them effectively requires us to know more about them. That is the point of this appendix, to crack open book mistakes to look for the pearls.

Big Mistake Number One: Bad book editing is a recent problem.

"Once upon a time writers wrote and editors edited," Jacob Weisberg said in a 1991 article that generated much nodding of heads. "Today most writers still write, but most editors don't do much editing if they can help it." Haphazard editing, insouciant fact checking, slipshod book design, and errant promotional copy are common authors' complaints.

The biggest publishing houses, critics say, relentlessly look for ways to increase profits. In the 1990s, the number of New York publishing professionals, most of them editors, declined by 16 percent, reported the *New York Times*'s Doreen Carvajal. "At the same time," she observed, "the number of books published in the United States has surged." Even the editors left behind are not focused on improving writers' prose, critics add. "Truth to tell, few publishers are much interested in exercising those [editorial] powers these days," said *Washington Post* critic Jonathan Yardley; "they think of editors as experts in acquisition rather than correction and revision."

True as these observations may be, however, a quick look at history tells us that lousy editing is the norm. Consider the complaint that bottom-line oriented publishers rush books into print. Few books today go through the publishing process as quickly as did *Jane Eyre*. Charlotte Brontë sent it to the publisher on August 24, 1847. It appeared in print on October 16 that same year. George Eliot sent *Silas Marner* on March 10, 1861; it came back to the author as a bound book on March 25. All of this was before the advent of high-speed technology that allows printers to work from computer disks, rather than setting type by hand, as was done in Brontë's day. The only advantage to computer technology may be that it is more difficult to decide who is at fault when an error occurs.

Moreover, few books today have the number of blunders found in *The Anatomy of the Mass*, written by a monk in the sixteenth century. Only 172 pages long, it had so many mistakes that the author included a fifteen-page list of errata. He blamed the mistakes on the devil, who supposedly objected to the publication of the book. Worse still was Timothy Dexter's early-nineteenth-century philosophical autobiography, *A Pickle for the Knowing Ones*. It did not contain a single punctuation mark. The spelling was erratic. Moved to correct these lapses, Dexter added the following page to later editions:

fourder mister printer the Nowing ones complane of my book the fust edition had no stops I put in A nuf here and they may peper and solt it as they please

, ,
, ,
, ,
; ;
: :
. . . .
. . . . ! . . . .
. . . . ! ! ! ! ! ! ! ! ! ! ! ! ! ! ! ! . . . .
. . . . ! ! ! ! ! ! ! ! ! ! ! . . . .
. . . . ! . . . .
, ,
. . . . ? ? ? ? ? ? ? ? ? ? ? ? ? ? ? ? . . . .

Editing seems worse today possibly because of the comparison with a brief time earlier in this century when it was relatively good. That, significantly, was a time when publishers took editing responsibility away from writers. Even so, it is a mistake for us to glorify the time when editors supposedly wielded their pens with great force, as Weisberg did in the *New Republic* when he said we want more people like legendary editor Maxwell Perkins. Charles Scribner, Jr., Perkins' boss, recalled that "the editor was totally useless when it came to copyediting or correcting a text. Such details meant very little to him. Consequently, the early editions of books like F. Scott Fitzgerald's novel *The Great Gatsby* were textually corrupt to a nauseating degree."

Big Mistake Number Two: Most errors are the fault of sloppy editing.

Errors can creep into a book at any number of stages. The editor can introduce mistakes at the beginning of the process when fiddling with the manuscript. It can happen when the printed book goes to the bindery, as was the case with a book titled *Ignorance*: It was accidentally bound in the cover of another book, *Knowledge*.

But the biggest perpetrators of errors are authors. One of the most common ways they introduce errors in their books is by rewriting galleys. Publishing houses try to curtail this with contract provisions that require the author to pay for printer's changes that exceed 10 percent of the original cost of the composition. This does not stop many writers from scrib-

bling all over galleys. When they are new at the business, they don't realize how quickly those overcharges mount up. When they are name writers, they don't care because they have leverage over publishers. In a long-
term publishing contract he negotiated, George Bernard Shaw said "you
may charge me for all corrections over and above 95% of the total cost of
production." This was a horrifying thought in view of Shaw's enthusiasm
for introducing all variety of printing idiosyncrasies.

Some writers openly resist editors. Thomas Harris, author of *The
Silence of the Lambs*, won't give interviews, won't do book signing, and
takes no editorial suggestions. The hero in Georges Simenon's *L'Evadé*
started out with the name Jean-Pierre and ended up as Jean-Paul. Instead
of recognizing that he had a weakness for details, Simenon fought every
attempt to change a comma. In an effort to handcuff his longtime editor,
he once gave her a photocopy of his manuscript. She was free to mark it
up as she saw fit. He would transcribe the recommended changes to his
original as *he* saw fit. Farther back in time, Pope Sixtus V imposed firmer
restraints with worse results. To ensure no one would mess with his new
version of the Bible, he prefixed a warning that any printer who altered
the work when reprinting it would be excommunicated. Unfortunately,
the first edition with that notice was riddled with errors.

In yet another example why writers are as guilty as anyone of editorial
offenses, consider the author who was signed to write bicycle touring
books. The writer promised to have the routes checked by other bicyclists.
He didn't do the checking, but said he did, which was too bad. The author
was dyslexic and had mixed up all the directions.

Big Mistake Number Three: Editing errors make books worse.

Okay, let's agree that some printing errors are deadly. For instance Penn
and Teller's *How to Play With Your Food* should not have given readers the
tools for the old sugar-packet-that-does-not-open trick. The sugar pack-
ets did open and, too bad about this, they did not have sugar in them.
They had a silica gel dyed with cobalt chloride, which was later described
as a potential health hazard if ingested. A book called *Great Cakes* similarly made the unfortunate mistake of telling readers that lilies-of-the-
valley are edible and good for garnishing a cake. Lilies-of-the-valley are
poisonous if eaten.

But other mistakes can improve books. Edgar Snow submitted his manuscript for his classic book on the Chinese Communists with the title *Red Star in China*. When his agent referred to it as *Red Star Over China*, he had the perfect title. William Burroughs sent a manuscript to his friend Allen Ginsberg, who read parts of it to another friend, Jack Kerouac. Burroughs had sloppy handwriting. When Ginsberg misread the phrase *naked lust* as *naked lunch*, Kerouac realized that they had the ideal title. Burroughs subsequently came up with a rationale for *Naked Lunch*: "The title means exactly what the words say: NAKED lunch—a frozen moment when everyone sees what is on the end of every fork." *

Keep in mind, too, that errors in good books raise their value. A 1926 first edition of *The Sun Also Rises* with "stopped" spelled with three p's is worth eight thousand dollars.

Big Mistake Number Four: People notice if books are full of errors.

Which came first, bad editing or bad reading? One sign that our culture is flagging may be that many editors don't care much about producing a quality text. Another sign is that no one is objecting. A book called *The Literature of Possibility* by Hazel Barnes went through at least four reprintings with the spelling "Possiblity" emblazoned on the cover. "Never a single comment from our customers," said Debra Turner, an assistant director and production manager at the University of Nebraska Press, which published the book; "and these are folks who regularly call to tell us such things as: a cover painting shows cavalry uniforms which are five years out of style for the book's subject." There are readers out there who, as a Denver bookstore owner discovered, march into the store and demand *Bury the Head That Wounded Me*.

James Feather, a friend who had been managing director at Basil Blackwell, a British publishing house, once did a book on social psychology. Eleven lines of type were garbled in the final printed version. The author did not complain. After a time, Feather asked him to read the offending passage. He did and, looking up, said, "It's alright, isn't it?"

---

*Burroughs had a habit of turning mistakes to his advantage. Like the drunken day he suggested to his wife, Joan, "It's about time for our William Tell act." She put a glass on her head. He shot and missed the glass. He later commented that "I am forced to the appalling conclusion that I would never have become a writer but for Joan's death."

Notes on Sources

—⁓—

In which it is shown that the author has
enthusiastically and systematically lifted
ideas from other authors.

—⟨∽⟩—

The safest general characterization of the European philosophical
tradition is that it consists of a series of footnotes to Plato.
—Alfred North Whitehead

—⟨∽⟩—

When it comes to scholarship, this book has nothing to hide. Everything in it is true—even the stuff I made up about there being ten books that are most often stolen. I have not provided an explicit citation for each fact, quotation, etc. Nor have I listed every person who was interviewed. I've sought instead to provide a scholarly backdrop of sources used without making readers hurdle all those little footnote numbers that clutter sentences in many heavyweight books. Readers should think of the endnotes in this book as directional, not definitive. They point to interesting sources, some of which I did not draw from, and underscore the richness of the literature on literature, including the fact that books and authors are in the news all the time. The endnotes also have provided me with an opportunity to introduce observations that do not fit conveniently into the essays themselves. Finally, this book has endnotes because a book without endnotes is like a car without hubcaps. It looks—and is—cheap.

Notes to Introduction

As suggested in the introduction, the study of the history of books is a relatively new field. Among the few who considered the subject before it became popular is Isaac D'Israeli, the father of the British prime minister. His *Curiosities of Literature* (1833), *The Calamities and Quarrels of Authors* (1859), and *Amenities of Literature* (1863) remain worth reading. Robert Darnton, who as much as anyone has created the modern field of book history, has written *The Business of Enlightenment: A Publishing History of the Encyclopédie, 1775–1800* (1979), *The Literary Underground of the Old Regime* (1982), *The Great Cat Massacre and Other Episodes in French Cultural History* (1984), and *The Kiss of Lamourette: Reflections in Cultural History* (1990). An essay on the writing of book history is found in Robert A. Gross, "Communications Revolutions: Writing a History of the Book for an Electronic Age," *Rare Books & Manuscripts* (13:1, 1998). Also useful in this regard are Karen J. Winkler, "In Electronic Age, Scholars Are Drawn to Study of Print," the *Chronicle of Higher Education*, July 14, 1993, and Cathy N. Davidson, editor, *Reading in America* (1989).

Holbrook Jackson, *The Anatomy of Bibliomania* (1979), provides anecdotes used in the introduction and elsewhere in the book. Jack McLaughlin, *Jefferson and Monticello: The Biography of a Builder* (1988), tells how the great man arranged his books. Charles Darwin's reading habits are described in Richard Lee Marks, *Three Men of the Beagle* (1991). Rosenbach is described in Robert Wernick, "The Bookseller Who Couldn't Stand to Sell His Books," *Smithsonian,* April 1992. John Updike writes about our inherent interest in authors' lives in "One Cheer for Literary Biography," the *New York Review of Books,* February 4, 1999. The story on Brian Hunt and the London Library is from Paul Levy, *Wall Street Journal,* June 7, 1991. For an example of using an author's library to learn about his thoughts, see Robert McCrum, *New Yorker,* April 11, 1994; the article deals with Graham Greene's library. Book clubs are discussed in Robert Dahlin, "This '90s Group Activity Is All the Rage," *Publishers Weekly,* November 18, 1996; book festivals are discussed in the *Economist,* February 20, 1999; the marketing of Slates is discussed in Dana Canedy, *New York Times,* October 9, 1996. Walter Benjamin wrote about "Unpacking My Library: A Tale about Book Collecting," in his book *Illuminations* ([1968] 1977), translated by Harry Zohn and edited by Hannah Arendt.

On books as furniture, I used Dora Thornton, *The Scholar in His Study: Ownership and E perience in Renaissance Italy* (1997); Jane Guthrie, "The Decorative Value of Books," *Good Housekeeping,* January 1925; Rita Reif, *New York Times,* February 15, 1998; and Mel Gussow, *New York Times,* February 23, 1998. The story on Dallas Cowboys owner Jerry Jones and his spouse, Gene, was by Linton Weeks, *Washington Post,* April 15, 1999. In fairness to Jones, it should be noted that the first Declarations and Resolves of the Continental Congress (1774) said colonists were entitled to "life, liberty and property." Jefferson altered this to "life, liberty and the pursuit of happiness." I leave it to the reader to decide if Jones knows too much history or too little.

On our mostly sad state of literacy, I used William Celis, III, *New York Times,* September 9, 1993; Pat H. Broeske, *New York Times,* June 21, 1992; Carl F. Kaestle, editor, *Literacy in the United States: Readers and Reading Since 1880* (1991); Nicholas Zill and Marianne Winglee, *Who Reads Literature? The Future of the United States as a Nation of Readers* (1990); a report from the Organization for Economic Cooperation and Development, *Literacy, Economy and Society* (1995); Irvin S. Kirsch, *et al., Adult Literacy in America,* published by the U.S. Department of Education

(September 1993), which is also used in chapter one; and a Pew Center poll released on April 20, 1998.

Anyone who is interested in the books-as-news items cited in the introduction may read three journalists' *New York Times* articles: Michael Kimmelman, January 9, 1998; Michael Finger, February 26, 1993; and Julia Preston, March 10, 1999, as well as a short news item on *Slate,* March 30, 1999. Carlin Romano's comments appeared in "Extra! Extra! The Sad Story of Books as News," *Media Studies Journal* (Summer 1992). For her study, Anita Chang looked in the November 3, 1998, *USA Today* and the October 28, 1998, *Wall Street Journal.* We picked these two newspapers because they happened to be lying around the office.

Casanova gets and deserves continuing attention. Among the books about him are an affectionate essay by Lydia Flem, *Casanova: The Man Who Really Loved Women* (1997 translation by Catherine Temerson) and a more staid biographical summary by J. Rives Childs, *Casanova: A New Perspective* (1988). Best of all are Casanova's twelve-volume memoirs, *History of My Life,* translated by Willard R. Trask and published in paperback by Johns Hopkins University Press (1997).

Many authors write about their love affairs with writing and reading. While I find many of these books tedious and self-glorifying, their existence is remarkable. Someone is reading them, after all, or they wouldn't be published. As such, they reaffirm that lovers of literature are never sated. Below are some—and only some—books that have appeared recently by better known writers: Anna Quindlen, *How Reading Changed My Life* (1998); Anne Fadiman, *Ex Libris: Confessions of a Common Reader* (1998); Denis Donoghue, *The Practice of Reading* (1998); David Denby, *Great Books: My Adventures with Homer, Rousseau, Woolf, and Other Indestructible Writers of the Western World* (1996); Richard Rhodes, *How to Write* (1995); David Lodge, *The Practice of Writing* (1997); Doris Grumbach, *Life in a Day* (1996). The very best book of this genre is Alberto Manguel, *A History of Reading* (1996). I borrow from Manguel on several occasions in this book, for he is amusing on a wide range of book topics.

Notes to Chapter One

Pope, Swift, and other satirists used *Grub Street* to describe—and de-ride—the commercialization of letters. Samuel Johnson made the term famous in his *Dictionary:* "Originally the name of a street in Moorfields in London, much inhabited by writers of small histories, dictionaries, and temporary poems; whence any mean production is called grubstreet." While the connotation is negative, Johnson himself started on Grub Street and romanticized it in the *Life of Richard Savage* (1744). (Of Savage, Johnson characteristically reports, "Thus dissipated was his Life, and thus casual his Subsistence; yet did not the Distraction of his Views hinder him from Reflection, nor the Uncertainty of his Condition depress his Gaiety.") In more recent times, Grub Street has signified the hard life of any writer, including the writer who aspires to quality literature rather than merely the "mean production" of hack work. Moorfields became Milton Street in 1830. Some say it was named after a local builder of that name; others attribute the name to the distinctly non-hack writer John Milton, who resided in the vicinity of Moorfields during 1661 to 1662 and, as this chapter points out, lived by means other than writing.

Grub Street's history is described in Ronald Weber's *Hired Pens: Professional Writers in America's Golden Age of Print* (1997); Pat Rogers's ponderous and confusing *Grub Street: Studies in a Subculture* (1972); Michael Foot's *The Pen & the Sword: A Year in the Life of Jonathan Swift* (1962); and Philip Pinkus's *Grub St. Stripped Bare: The Scandalous Lives & Pornographic Works of the Original Grub St. Writers* (1968). *New Grub Street,* by George Gissing, appeared in 1891 and is available in a 1993 edition. Read it; it's good.

Especially useful history on writing in the United States is found in William Charvat, *The Profession of Authorship in America, 1800–1870: The Papers of William Charvat,* edited by Matthew J. Bruccoli (1968); also Charvat's *Literary Publishing in America, 1790–1850* (1993). Additional historical background in this chapter came from Daniel Pool, *Dickens' Fur Coat and Charlotte's Unanswered Letters: The Rows and Romances of England's Great Victorian Novelists* (1997); William G. Rowland, *Literature and the Marketplace: Romantic Writers and Their Audiences in Great Britain and the United States* (1996); and Lucien Febvre and Henri-Jean Martin, *The Coming of the Book: The Impact of Printing, 1450–1800* (1976).

Two useful social histories of recent vintage include sections on books: Lisa Jardine, *Worldly Goods: A New History of the Renaissance* (1996); and John Brewer, *The Pleasures of the Imagination: English Culture in the Eighteenth Century* (1997). Roger D. Masters provides valuable insights on genius and writing in his marvelous book *Fortune Is a River: Leonardo da Vinci and Niccolò Machiavelli's Magnificent Dream to Change the Course of Florentine History* (1998).

For short biographical information on writers, I relied on Louis Kronenberger, editor, *Brief Lives: A Biographical Companion to the Arts* ([1971] 1991), from which I took the quotation on Robert Greene. Louis D. Rubin, Jr., "Occupations of Famous Writers," *A Writer's Companion* (1995), provided useful leads on hyphenated writers. Among the most useful biographies were Donald R. Howard, *Chaucer: His Life, His Works, His World* (1987); Mary Giffin, *Studies on Chaucer and His Audience* (1956); Park Honan, *Shakespeare: A Life* (1998); Joseph Sobran, *Alias Shakespeare: Solving the Greatest Literary Mystery of All Time* (1997); S. Schoenbaum, *Shakespeare and Others* (1985); William Riley Parker, revised by Gordon Campbell, *Milton: A Biography* (1996, vol. 1); Jonathan Keates, *Stendhal* (1997); Richard West, *Daniel Defoe: The Life and Strange Surprising Adventures* (1998); David Laskin, *A Common Life: Four Generations of American Literary Friendship and Influence* (1994); Jay Parini, *John Steinbeck: A Biography* (1994); Constance Webb, *Richard Wright: A Biography* (1968); Jeffrey Meyers, *Scott Fitzgerald: A Biography* (1994); James Longenbach, *Wallace Stevens: The Plain Sense of Things* (1991); George S. Lensing, *Wallace Stevens: A Poet's Growth* (1986); Charles Chaplin, *My Autobiography* (1964); Pierre Assóuline, *Simenon* ([1992] 1997).

On the difficulties of writing for a living, see Ian Hamilton, "How much?" *London Review of Books,* June 18, 1998; Valentine Cunningham, "Unto him (or her) that hath," *Times Literary Supplement,* September 11, 1998; Ralph Blumenthal, *New York Times,* March 12, 1997; Cynthia Crossen, *Wall Street Journal,* January 10, 1997; Ken Auletta, "The Impossible Business," *New Yorker;* Daniel Menaker, "Unsolicited, Unloved MSS.," *New York Times Book Review,* March 1, 1981; John Greenya, "Washington Writers: Fortunes and Missed Fortunes," *Washington Post Book World,* January 4, 1981; Melissa Ludtke Lincoln, "The Free-lance Life," *Columbia Journalism Review,* September/October

1981, which includes information gathered by the American Society of Journalists and Authors; John F. Baker, "Literary Lions Now & Then," *Publishers Weekly*, June 5, 1995; Paul William Kingston and Jonathan R. Cole, *The Wages of Writing: Per Word, Per Piece, or Perhaps* (1986); Oscar G. Brockett with Franklin J. Hildy, *History of the Theatre* (1999), which explains how playwrights made a living; and Lewis A. Coser, Charles Kadushin, and Walker W. Powell, *Books: The Culture and Commerce of Publishing* (1982), which also proved helpful for other chapters in this book. Wilcox's tax tribulations are chronicled in James B. Stewart, "Moby Dick in Manhattan," *New Yorker*, June 27/July 4, 1994. Virginia Woolf writes beautifully on women and writing in *A Room of One's Own* ([1929] 1989). The one writing occupation not discussed in the chapter is homelessness. Lee Stringer, author of *Grand Central Winter: Stories from the Street* (1997), is our best-known author in that line of work, which in a sense is a full-time writing job.

For discussion of the surfeit of books, see Jonathan Karp, a senior editor at Random House; he gives his views in "Conglomerates—A Good Thing for Books," *Media Studies Journal*, Spring/Summer 1996.

Anyone interested in how Thomas Lynch, the undertaker, views his trade may read his essay "The Undertaking," *London Review of Books*, December 22, 1994. The postal historian quoted in the chapter is Richard R. John, and his book is *Spreading the News: The American Postal System from Franklin to Morse* (1995). Hawthorne talked about his experience in the Customs House in an essay that served as an "Introductory to 'The Scarlet Letter.'" I did not use Mukul Pandya's article on today's corporate poets (*New York Times*, November 27, 1994), but it is worthwhile for anyone interested in the subject. I did use the following sources to describe ways to write on the boss's time:

On church writings, William Manchester, *A World Lit Only by Fire: The Medieval Mind and the Renaissance, Portrait of an Age* (1992); Richard Marius, *Martin Luther: The Christian between God and Death* (1999); Damian Thompson, *Daily Telegraph*, July 15, 1994; Victoria Combe, *Daily Telegraph*, October 2, 1997; Joe Wakelee-Lynch, "16 Religious Houses Combine . . . ," *Publishers Weekly*, May 16, 1994; Carol McGraw, *Orange County Register*, January 3, 1995; Donald Barr, *New York Times*, June 17, 1984. In *The Hunchback of Notre Dame*, Victor Hugo has an interesting chapter on books undermining the church's authority as well as the significance of its grand cathedrals. One of Hugo's characters points with one hand to a book printed with movable type and with another to Notre Dame: "'Just so,' replied Claude, who was still standing, apparently lost in thought, with his forefinger on the folio from the famous printing-press at Nuremberg. Then he added the mysterious words: 'Alas! alas! small things overmaster the great; a tooth destroys the whole body; the Nile-rat kills the crocodile, the swordfish the whale, and the book will kill the church!'"

On the law, John Grisham, *New York Times Book Review,* October 18, 1992; Mel Gussow, *New York Times,* March 31, 1997; Jo Thomas, *New York Times,* February 11, 1998; Frank McLynn, *Robert Louis Stevenson: A Biography* (1993); and Carol Gelderman, *Louis Auchincloss: A Writer's Life* (1993).

On "serving a sentence," there is H. Bruce Franklin, *Prison Writing in 20th-Century America* (1998), and Bell Gale Chevigny, editor, *Doing Time: 25 Years of Prison Writing* (1999). Blake is quoted in Martha Grace Duncan, *Romantic Outlaws, Beloved Prisons: The Unconscious Meanings of Crime and Punishment* (1996). Wodehouse's imprisonment is told in Malcolm Muggeridge, "Wodehouse in Distress," a chapter in *Homage to P. G. Wodehouse* (1966). The fate of Pramoedya Ananta Toer is related in "An Angry Old Man," the *Economist,* July 18, 1998, and Barbara Crossette, *New York Times,* April 26, 1999. There has been quite an outpouring of material on the marquis de Sade lately. Here are some of the materials I used: Francine du Plessix Gray, *At Home with the Marquis de Sade: A Life* (1998); Laurence L. Bongie, *Sade: A Biographical Essay* (1998); Richard Seaver, translator, *Marquis de Sade: Letters from Prison* (1999); Neil Schaeffer, *The Marquis de Sade: A Life* (1999); and a review of books on Sade by Robert Darnton, "The Real Marquis," *New York Review of Books,* January 14, 1999. The details on the Bastille are from Simon Schama, *Citizens: A Chronicle of the French Revolution* (1989). Norman Podhoretz wrote about Mailer and his fear of asylums, *Ex-Friends: Falling Out with Allen Ginsberg, Lionel & Diana Trilling, Lillian Hellman, Hannah Arendt, and Norman Mailer* (1999). The Son of Sam law is discussed in Ellen Alderman, "Sammy Meets Son of Sam," *Columbia Journalism Review,* March/April 1998. Dr. Minor's story is told by Simon Winchester in *The Professor and the Madman* (1998).

On academic writing and publishing, I read Jonathan Yardley,

Washington Post, January 16, 1989, and March 6, 1989; James Shapiro, *Chronicle of Higher Education,* August 7, 1997. The difficulty of being an original scholar in an academic setting is discussed in Janny Scott, *New York Times,* May 8, 1999.

The author-movie connection is discussed by Jeff Giles and Ray Sawhill, *Newsweek,* December 9, 1996.

Writer-industrialists are discussed in Bruce Watson, "Tom Swift, Nancy Drew, and Pals All Had the Same Dad," *Smithsonian Magazine,* October 1991; Milton Nieuwsma, *Chicago Tribune,* December 27, 1988; Matt Moffett, *Wall Street Journal,* February 5, 1996; the Asimov *Washington Post* obituary, April 7, 1992; Molly O'Neill, *New York Times,* November 5, 1997; Ian Hamilton, *Writers in Hollywood, 1915–1951* (1990); Siegfried Unseld, *The Author and His Publisher: Lectures Delivered in Mainz and Austin* (1980). The Elmer Davis lecture was published as "Some Aspects of the Economics of Authorship" by the New York Public Library in 1940. The statistics on the Writers Guild of America, West were reported in the *New York Times,* March 3, 1997. The reviewer of *Centennial* was James R. Frakes, *New York Times Book Review,* September 8, 1974.

The observation that Gutenberg was the first printer to go broke comes from Leo Bogart, *Commercial Culture: The Media System and the Public Interest* (1995); Bogart got the idea from John P. Feather and David McKitterick, *The History of Books and Libraries: Two Views* (Library of Congress, 1986). Daniel J. Boorstin writes about Gutenberg in *The Discoverers* (1983).

The chapter makes the point that Shakespeare was a good business-man. Other authors, it should be noted, have shown an entrepreneurial touch as well. Voltaire made a fortune through investing and lending. It would gall Henry Thoreau to be put in the same category, but he didn't only get by sponging off of Ralph Waldo Emerson and surveying. He perfected a graphite process used in the family pencil business and enjoyed the profits. Tom Clancy has purchased a quarter interest in the Baltimore Orioles.

While this chapter makes the case that writers are often better off if they do not feel financial pressure to write, I admit that some authors are so liberated that they produce nothing. An interesting example of this is Joseph Mitchell. A newspaper reporter who joined the *New Yorker* in

1938, Mitchell was known for his elegant profiles of people and places, some of which were republished in books. He was so good at what he did that for the last thirty years of his career he wrote nothing to speak of. According to the *New York Times*'s affectionate obituary of Mitchell in 1966, the common feeling among those who worked with Mitchell was that he was a perfectionist and "raising his standards all the time. The janitor would find reams of copy in his wastepaper basket." Mark Singer wrote an endearing profile of Joseph Mitchell, "Joe Mitchell's Secret," *New Yorker*, February 22–March 1, 1999.

Finally, Howard Gardner's book *Creating Minds: An Anatomy of Creativity Seen through the Lives of Freud, Einstein, Picasso, Stravinsky, Eliot, Graham, and Gandhi* (1993), which brings up the rear of this chapter, is provocative and worth reading.

Notes to Chapter Two

Franklin is our greatest writing entrepreneur. It is hard to resist putting all the examples of his ardor for the written word in the chapter. Not in the chapter, but worthy of it, is the fact that lexicographer Noah Webster dedicated a treatise about the English language to Franklin. Franklin, like many writers, was a postmaster several times. Among his inventions was the Dead Letter Office, and his likeness appeared on the first U.S. postage stamp issued in 1847. As a young man he wrote this epitaph for his own amusement:

The Body of
B. Franklin, Printer
(Like the Cover of an Old Book
Its Contents torn Out
And Stript of its Lettering and Gilding)
Lies Here, Food for Worms.
But the Work shall not be Lost;
For it will (as he Believ'd) Appear once More
In a New and More Elegant Edition
Revised and Corrected
By the Author

Of the many biographies of Franklin, one of the best is still Carl Van Doren's *Benjamin Franklin* (1938), and, of course, Franklin's autobiography. Supporting my argument about Franklin's marketing instincts is an interesting chapter on Franklin in R. Jackson Wilson, *American Writers and the Literary Marketplace, from Benjamin Franklin to Emily Dickinson* (1989).

I happily stumbled on Lester Wunderman's *Being Direct: How I Learned to Make Advertising Pay* (1997). Other discussions of book marketing are found in Earl Shorris, *A Nation of Salesman: The Tyranny of the Market and the Subversion of Culture* (1994); Clarkson N. Potter, *Who Does What and Why in Book Publishing* (1990); Charles A. Madison, *Book Publishing in America* (1996); Helmut Lehmann-Haupt, *The Book in America: A History of the Making and Selling of Books in the United States* (1951); and John Tebbel's four-volume *A History of Book Publishing in the United States* (1972, 1975, 1978, 1981), which was also used in Appendix A.

For background on big book businesses, I used Ted Solotaroff, "The Literary-Industrial Complex," *New Republic,* June 6, 1987; Leo Bogart's previously cited *Commercial Culture: The Media System and the Public Interest;* Lorne Manly, "Is He Crazy?" *Brill's Content,* October 1998; R. W. Apple, "The Gold Rush on Publishers' Row," *Saturday Review,* October 6, 1960; and John Mutter's *Publishers Weekly* articles "More than Half Now Buy Their Books in Chains—'PW' Survey," May 12, 1997, and "One Size Doesn't Fit All," January 6, 1997; Daisy Maryles, "They're the Tops!" *Publishers Weekly,* January 4, 1999; and Karen August, "A Common Thread," *Publishers Weekly,* September 14, 1998. The management consultant who says "the new model is marketing" is Peter Kreisky, senior vice-president at Mercer Management Consulting; his quotation appeared in the *Economist,* March 28, 1998.

Scherman and his Book-of-the-Month Club are discussed in Janice A. Radway's *A Feeling for Books: The Book-of-the-Month Club, Literary Taste, and Middle-Class Desire* (1997). Doreen Carvajal reports on the growing influence of marketing at BOMC in *New York Times,* April 1, 1996.

For background on celebrity books, I used Judy Quinn, "Celebrity Book Roulette," *Publishers Weekly,* August 4, 1997; Lawrence K. Grossman, "TV News: The Great Celebrity Chase," *Columbia Journalism Review,* July/August 1998; James B. Stewart, "Best-Seller," *New Yorker,*

September 8, 1997; Sarah Lyall, *New York Times,* September 23, 1993; Thomas Whiteside, *The Blockbuster Complex: Conglomerates, Show Business, and Book Publishing* (1981); Michael Korda, "Wasn't She Great?" *New Yorker,* August 14, 1995; Barbara Seaman, *Lovely Me: The Life of Jacqueline Susann* (1987); Michael Maren, "How to Manufacture a Best Seller," *New York Times Magazine,* March 1, 1998; Daisy Maryles, "Behind the Bestsellers," *Publishers Weekly,* October 12, 1998; Mel Gussow, *New York Times,* October 29, 1998; "Simpson Trial & Trivia," *U.S. News & World Report,* October 16, 1995; Kyle Pope, *Wall Street Journal,* January 25, 1999; David Firestone, *New York Times,* January 10, 1999.

Background on the burgeoning industry of consultants is drawn from a report from the Kennedy Research Group, a portion of which was reprinted on its Web page (dated January 7, 1998); the Fuqua Consulting Club homepage (a handout dated October 1, 1995); Doreen Carvajal, *New York Times,* April 28, 1996, and July 3, 1998; and Timothy D. Schellhardt, Elizabeth MacDonald, and Raju Narissetti, *Wall Street Journal,* October 20, 1998.

Anyone wanting to boost his or her spirits should forget about paying to see a depression clinic consultant; they should read the unintentionally hilarious *The Yearbook of Experts, Authorities, & Spokespersons,* published by Broadcast Interview Source in Washington, D.C. Here consultants specialize in maladies you never dreamed possible. Some are mentioned in the text, but there are many more howlers: Donald Dossey, Ph.D., from the Phobia Institute, specializes in holiday superstition and phobias. Jack M. Springer, executive director of the Cremation Association of North America, also will be glad to talk to you. "Cremation," as he says, "It's a Hot Topic!" Alan Caruba, "the nation's guru of boredom," will talk about you-know-what. Phyllis Kruckenberg, executive vice-president of Jeunique International Corporation will lay bare "the hidden dangers of wrong size bras." Among the questions she suggests you ask is "Why will wearing a non-supportive bra today cause the need for a face lift tomorrow?"

For histories of self-help books, see Judy Hilkey, *Character Is Capital: Success Manuals and Manhood in Gilded Age America* (1977), and James D. Hart, *The Popular Book: A History of America's Literary Taste* ([1950] 1961). As Hart notes, Americans have always been suckers for self-help books. By the end of the last century, an estimated three million people had read *Pushing to the Front* and other books by Orison Swett Marden and subscribed to Marden's magazine, *Success*. But self-help books can be found buried deep in history. For a delightful romp through a book about self-help books for long-ago Latins, read Rudolph M. Bell, *How to Do It: Guides to Good Living for Renaissance Italians* (1999).

On books promoting products and vice versa, I used William L. Hamilton, *New York Times*, October 8, 1998; James Hirsch, *Wall Street Journal*, March 6, 1997; and Larry Tye, *The Father of Spin: Edward L. Bernays & the Birth of Public Relations* (1998). Bernays's own comments on promoting books can be found in his autobiography, *Biography of an Idea: Memoirs of Public Relations Counsel Edward L. Bernays* (1965).

When they first appeared, movies and television seemed a threat to books. Ultimately, as this chapter shows, they have been a friend (unless, of course, you are concerned about the decline in reading). One of the first publishers to realize the value of television was Doubleday. In the 1930s, it published Westerns featuring a character named Hopalong Cassidy. With great foresight, the publisher retained television rights, although no commercial television existed at the time. When Hoppy rode onto TV, Doubleday cashed in.

For more on books and movies: G. Bruce Knecht, *Wall Street Journal*, March 3, 1996; Mary B. W. Tabor, *New York Times*, February 6, 1995; Bernard Weinraub, *New York Times*, October 27, 1997; Marco R. della Cava, *USA Today*, May 10, 1996; and Patti Thorn, *Rocky Mountain News*, February 22, 1998; Helen Gurley Brown, *The Writer's Rules: The Power of Positive Prose—How to Create It and Get It Published* (1998); Robert S. Boynton, "The Hollywood Way," *New Yorker*, March 30, 1998; Paul Nathan, "'Ah, but You Should Have Read the Book'" *Publishers Weekly*, Special Anniversary Issue, July 1997; Jacquelyn Mitchard, "Seeing Your Book on the Big Screen," *Newsweek*, March 1, 1999.

Sources of various anecdotes and quotations used in the chapter are found as follows: On almanacs, James M. Wells, *American Printing: The Search for Self-Sufficiency* (1985). On pricing policy, Edwin McDowell, *New York Times*, October 19, 1990. On the marketing of Tom Clancy, Jeff Zaleski, "The Hunt for Tom Clancy," *Publishers Weekly*, July 13, 1998. On Bertelsmann, Doreen Carvajal, *New York Times*, May 28, 1999. On Edgar Rice Burroughs, John Taliaferro, *Tarzan Forever: The Life of Edgar Rice*

Burroughs (1999). On preacher Jakes, Lisa Miller, *Wall Street Journal,* August 21, 1998. And on Pat Robertson's Bible blitz, Sally Beatty, *Wall Street Journal,* April 1, 1999. On Hitchens's biography of Mother Teresa and other marketing efforts using reverse psychology, Doreen Carvajal, *New York Times,* October 13, 1997; Karen Angel, "Modern Library Helps Bookstores Promote 'the List,'" *Publishers Weekly,* September 14, 1998. On advance book tours, Gayle Feldman, *New York Times,* April 6, 1998; Judith Rosen, *Publishers Weekly,* November 16, 1998; and Ralph Vigoda's funny "Buy Our Book!!!" *American Journalism Review,* October 1998. Olivia Goldsmith's statement is in Geraldine Fabrikant's article, *New York Times,* October 27, 1996. The story on William Elliott Hazelgrove is in Pam Belluck, *New York Times,* November 25, 1997. On Joan Collins's book trial, see Jan Hoffman, *New York Times,* February 13 and 14, 1996.

T. E. Lawrence's capers are described in Joel C. Hodson, *Lawrence of Arabia and American Culture: The Making of a Transatlantic Legend* (1995); John E. Mack, *The Prince of Our Disorder: The Life of T. E. Lawrence* (1976); and in the *New York Times,* February 16, 1926, March 9, 1927, and March 16, 1929. Here and elsewhere in the book, I have made good use of Michael Holroyd's condensed biography *Bernard Shaw* (1998).

For other examples of authors *appearing* not to care about money, the interested reader may look at Steven Fink, *Prophet in the Marketplace: Thoreau's Development as a Professional Writer* (1992); Stacy Schiff, "The Genius and Mrs. Genius," *New Yorker,* February 10, 1997; Susan Ferraro, "Novels You Can Sink Your Teeth Into," *New York Times Magazine,* October 14, 1990; Laura Lippman, *Baltimore Sun,* August 5, 1998; and Meg Cox, *Wall Street Journal,* August 2, 1990.

Of course, some authors can be authentically fey about money. Shortly after he had his first successful book, *Hecate County,* Edmund Wilson paid for his divorce and that of his new bride's. He forgot to save any money for taxes. "I knew that the profits from the book were to some extent subject to income tax," he said, "but I thought that this obligation could always be attended to later." This story is related in Edward de Grazia, *Girls Lean Back Everywhere: The Law of Obscenity and the Assault on Genius* (1992).

A good friend of mine, John Boehnert, once ordered one of Popeil's Ginsu Knives; in case he wants to order Ron Popeil's book, the title is *The Salesman of the Century: Inventing, Marketing, and Selling on TV: How I*

Did It and How You Can Too! (1995). And a final word about another particularly bad book mentioned in the chapter, *101 Ways to Promote Yourself*
(1997) by Visibility Marketing™ expert Raleigh Pinskey. Pinskey advises
people who are stymied in writing their own books to turn to Tom and
Marilyn Ross, who are mentioned at length in Appendix B. After I poked
fun at Pinskey's book and his advice in one of my public radio commentaries, Marilyn Ross thanked me for the publicity and later asked if I
would endorse the coming book she and her husband were writing.

Notes to Chapter Three

No topic is easier to research than one about terrible book acknowledgments and dedications. Survey a row of books on any shelf and, presto, the
results are the same: introductory pages full of inane words. All you have
to do is write them down. The few worthwhile dedications are most often
found in the obvious places, the books of worthwhile writers, although
even the greatest writers are mostly silly in the front matter.

In addition to rummaging through bookshelves, I came across the
good and bad in Adrian Room's *Tuttle Dictionary of Dedications* ([1990]
1992). Some also were suggested by people who had read a shorter essay I
wrote for the *New York Times Book Review*. In particular, I appreciated
comments from John Maass, Richard Nixon (no, not *that* Nixon), Gilbert
Field, Charles Sullivan, William Moran, Chester Hartman, Durrett
Wagner, Jean Portell, Victoria L. Getis, and John Corbett. The fact that
dedicated book lovers collect favorite dedications and acknowledgments
should be a warning to authors: Pay as much attention to the beginning of
the book as to the rest of it.

The Richard H. Rovere article is found in "Author's Acknowl-
edgments," *American Scholar*, 33, Winter 1964. Epstein's comment is in
The Middle of My Tether: Familiar Essays (1983). The 1609 history of fal-
coneering is in Edmund Gosse, "Elizabethan Dedications of Books,"
Harper's Monthly, July 1902. Thackeray's statement is in his essay
"Prefaces and Dedications," *Living Age*, April 1859. The Loveday,
Philips, and Degge dedications are from J. Sydney Boot, "Some Curious
Dedications," *The Gentleman's Magazine*, June 1907. *Writing for Love or
Money*, edited by Norman Cousins, was first published in 1949.

For related reading, there is Paul Theroux's spoof on acknowledgments in the *New Yorker,* September 24, 1979; a short essay in the *Economist,* "Gratitude That Grates," September 7, 1996; John Gross, "The Fine Art of Dedicating," *New York Times Book Review,* April 29, 1984; Fran R. Schumer, "Lovers, Enemies, and Other Dedicatees," *New York Times Book Review,* September 28, 1986; "To Irma, Who Will Know Why," [anonymous], *Christian Century,* January 25, 1961; Brander Matthews, "The True Theory of the Preface," *Pen and Ink* (1888); and Henry B. Wheatley, *The Dedication of Books to Patron and Friend: A Chapter in Literary History* ([1887] 1968).

The Vidal review of Calder's book was in the *New York Review of Books,* February 1, 1990. Isaac D'Israeli's pricing system is noted in his "A Mendicant Author," *The Calamities and Quarrels of Authors,* cited earlier. The history of the dedication to *Rights of Man* is found in John Keane, *Tom Paine: A Political Life* (1995). The story behind e. e. cummings's dedication in *No Thanks* is in Richard S. Kennedy, *Dreams in the Mirror: A Biography of e. e. cummings* (1980). Stephen Potter's *Some Notes on Lifemanship: With a Summary of Recent Researches in Gamesmanship* (1950) is funny across a wide range of subjects, many literary. Any reviewer looking for hints on putting down authors (or anyone else for that matter) may consult it profitably.

And a final note on Mark Twain. As noted in the essay, he is the best of all at front-of-the-book musing. It is not practical, alas, to provide a definitive list of all his funny and poignant openings. There are too many of them. But several examples are worth mentioning in closing.

From the preface to *The Gilded Age*:

> Our quotations are set in a vast number of tongues; this is done for the reason that very few foreign nations among whom the book will circulate can read in any language but their own, whereas we do not write for a particular class or sect or nation, but to take in the whole world.

From *The American Claimant and Other Stories and Sketches*:

THE WEATHER IN THIS BOOK

> No weather will be found in this book. This is an attempt to pull a book through without weather. It being the first attempt of the kind in fictitious literature, it may prove a failure, but it seemed worth the while of some daredevil person to try it, and the author was in just the mood. . . .

Notes to Chapter Four

With the small amount of previously published advice on book etiquette, this chapter should be considered the equivalent of Henry Morton Stanley becoming the first European to travel the length of the Congo River. That I quote the comments of many friends in the course of this journey shows how virgin this terrain is. My friends know less about the subject than I do, but only a fool explores terra incognita alone.

The only etiquette book on communication is Judith Martin, *Miss Manners' Basic Training: Communication* (1997). As noted, it says nothing about books. The few comments she does make on the subject are in other of her books.

On book parties, see Joanne Kaufman, "The Face on the Back of the Book," *New York Times Book Review,* June 25, 1989; Martin Arnold, *New York Times,* January 22, 1998; Michael Wines, *New York Times,* November 18, 1996; Martha Brannigan and James R. Hagerty, *Wall Street Journal,* June 15, 1998. Sarah Booth Conroy wrote two articles on book parties, *Washington Post,* May 12 and May 19, 1991.

On autographing, readers will especially enjoy the Coolidge story related in Howard B. Gotlieb, "Autographing Party," *Bostonia,* Summer 1997. Betty Eppes got that rare interview with Salinger, "What I Did Last Summer," *Paris Review* (Summer 1981). On photographs, see Dick Teresi, "Haul Out the Old Clichés: It's Time to Shoot an Author Photo," *New York Times Book Review,* December 12, 1993. For a sample of Wilson's curmudgeonly attitude, see his "The Literary Worker's Polonius," *Atlantic Monthly,* June 1935. Dickens's "The Begging Letter Writer," is in Michael Slater, editor, *Dickens' Journalism: The Amusements of the People and Other Papers: Reports, Essays, and Reviews, 1834–51,* vol. 2 (1996).

On handling escorts, would-be authors should read Amy Gamerman, *Wall Street Journal,* February 9, 1993; "Author! Author!" *Economist,* March 8, 1997; Richard B. Woodward, "Authors Behaving Badly," *Village Voice,* November 26, 1996. The friend of mine who spotted Clavell up to his tricks is David Wigg.

On ghostwriting, see Joe Queenan, "Working Woman," *New York Times Book Review,* January 5, 1997; "Love's Labor Erased," *Economist,* October 6, 1990; Jack Hitt, "The Writer Is Dead. But His Ghost Is

Thriving," *New York Times Magazine,* May 25, 1997; Alberto Manguel, "If You Sell My Book, I'll Sell Yours," *New York Times,* January 13, 1998; Susan Faludi, *Wall Street Journal,* September 5, 1990. On ghostwriting book blurbs, as some suspected Goodwin did, see David Streitfeld, *Washington Post,* May 17, 1991; Streitfeld and Kim Masters, *Washington Post,* April 16 and April 18, 1991. The review of Goodwin's book was by John Katzenbach, *Washington Post,* June 1, 1992. *Kiki's Memoirs* has been republished (1996).

Notes to Chapter Five

One of the easiest books to "write" is a compilation of literary anecdotes. These seem to sell quite well and are easy to do because they require no cohesive narrative. Typically, these books have a few choice tales about authors' troubles with negative reviews. As an example, there is *The Oxford Book of Literary Anecdotes* ([1975] 1987) edited by James Sutherland, as well as *The Writer's Quotation Book: A Literary Companion* ([1980] 1997) and *Fighting Words: Writers Lambast Other Writers—from Aristotle to Anne Rice* (1994), both edited by James Charlton; *Writing Changes Everything: The 627 Best Things Anyone Ever Said About Writing* (1997), edited by Deborah Brodie. As noted in the beginning of this essay, two books are devoted exclusively to the subject of crummy reviews, Bill Henderson's *Rotten Reviews* (1986) and *Rotten Reviews II* (1987). André Bernard edited *Rotten Rejections* (1990); it has an introduction by Henderson. For details on Engels's reviews of Marx, see *Frederick Engels on Capital: Synopsis, Reviews, and Supplementary Material* (1974), compiled by the Communist Party of the Soviet Union.

The thoughtful essay by Elizabeth Hardwick, "The Decline of Book Reviewing," appeared in *Harper's Magazine,* October 1959. Other essays from which this chapter draws include: T. S. Eliot, "The Perfect Critic" and "The Imperfect Critics," *The Sacred Wood: Essays on Poetry and Criticism* (1960); Lewis A. Coser, Charles Kadushin, Walter W. Powell, "Book Reviewers," a chapter in *Books: The Culture and Commerce of Publishing* (1982); Matthew Arnold, *The Works of Matthew Arnold* (1903); Oscar Wilde, "The Artist as Critic," in Richard Ellmann, editor, *The Artist as Critic: Critical Writings of Oscar Wilde* (1969); Frank Swinnerton, *The Reviewing and Criticism of Books* (1939); James Truslow Adams,

"Reviewing in America," *Saturday Review of Literature*, February 7, 1931; T. S. Eliot, *The Sacred Wood: Essays on Poetry and Criticism* (1983) and *Selected Essays* (1950); George Orwell, "Confessions of a Book Reviewer," *New Republic*, August 5, 1946; H. L. Mencken's "Criticism of Criticism of Criticism," *Prejudices: First Series* (1919) (thanks to Knopf, it is a nicely designed book, too); John Gross, "The 'Literary Supplement' Comes of Age: A History, of Sorts, of the Book Review," *New York Times Book Review*, October 6, 1996; Jay Parini, "The Disappearing Art of Reviewing Books," *Chronicle of Higher Education*, July 25, 1999; William H. Pritchard, "Nasty Reviews: Easy to Give, Hard to Take," *New York Times Book Review*, May 7, 1989; Alan Wolfe, "The Solemn Responsibilities of Book Reviewing," *Chronicle of Higher Education*, April 24, 1998; Steve Weinberg, "The Unruly World of Book Reviews," *Columbia Journalism Review*, March/April 1990; Richard Rosen, "Bullcrit," *New York*, February 6, 1989; and Leo Bogart, "The Culture Beat: A Look at the Numbers," *Gannett Center Journal*, Winter 1990. Two especially helpful articles appeared in the summer 1992 issue of the *Media Studies Journal*: Gerald Howard, "The Cultural Ecology of Book Reviewing," and Carlin Romano's "Extra! Extra! The Sad Story of Books as News." Howard is the publisher who called around to see if reviewers wanted to be "critical agents of natural selection in our cultural evolution."

"Experts," mostly journalists and journalism school types, have written textbooks on reviewing. I mention these not because they are worthwhile guides. Like many this-is-how-to-do-it writing texts, these books ponderously state what ought to be obvious. As an example, John E. Drewry, who was dean of the University of Georgia's Henry W. Grady School of Journalism and president of the American Association of Teachers of Journalism, had this to say in *Writing Book Reviews* (1945): "Reviewers should remember that sometimes there is a little story—worth a sentence or more—in the origin of the title of a book." He devoted an entire chapter to this weighty subject. Two similar books appeared in the 1920s: Wayne Gard's *Book Reviewing* (1928) and Llewellyn Jones, *How to Criticize Books* (1926). Mr. Gard is described on the title page as director of courses in journalism at Grinnell College; Mr. Jones was literary editor of the *Chicago Evening Post*. Other how-to stuff is found in Evelyn Oppenheimer, *Book Reviewing for an Audience: A Practical Guide in Technique for Lecture and Broadcast* (1962), William Zinsser, *On Writing*

Well (1994), and Sylvia E. Kamerman, editor, *Book Reviewing: A Guide to Writing Book Reviews for Newspapers, Magazines, Radio, and Television* (1978). Background on the history of book reviews in newspapers is found in Elmer Davis, *History of the New York Times, 1891–1921* (1921); Gay Talese, *The Kingdom and the Power* (1969); Gerald W. Johnson, *An Honorable Titan: A Biographical Study of Adolph S. Ochs* (1946); Richard F. Shepard, *The Paper's Papers: A Reporter's Journey through the Archives of the New York Times* (1996); Richard Kluger, *The Paper: The Life and Death of the New York Herald Tribune* (1986); Steven Cuozzo, *It's Alive! How America's Oldest Newspaper Cheated Death and Why It Matters* (1996). A few short remarks are found in Frank Luther Mott, *American Journalism* (1947). Fuller's life is told in Arthur Brown, *Margaret Fuller* (1964) and Carlos Baker, *Emerson among the Eccentrics: A Group Portrait* (1996). Of particular interest was a University of Missouri doctoral dissertation by Floris L. McDonald, "Book Reviewing in the American Newspaper" (1936). Michael Wolff (*New York*, October 12, 1998) writes approvingly of the *New York Times Book Review;* James Wood (*New York Observer,* November 30, 1998) writes disapprovingly. A collection of the *New York Times's* reviews are found in Charles McGrath, editor, *Books of the Century: A Hundred Years of Authors, Ideas, and Literature* (1998).

Edmund Wilson's review of a terrible book can be found in the collection of his work, *Classics and Commercials: A Literary Chronicle of the Forties* (1950); the essay is called "Ambushing a Best-Seller." Poe's comments are found in "About Critics and Criticism." He also wrote on "Sarah Margaret Fuller." Those essays are published in *Edgar Allan Poe: Essays and Reviews* (1984). The James T. Farrell quotation is from "Will the Commercialization of Publishing Destroy Good Writing? Some Observations on the Future of Books," *The Fate of Writing in America* (1946).

J. Edgar Hoover's book reviewing is discussed in Natalie Robins, *Alien Ink: The FBI's War on Freedom of Expression* (1992). Creative book reviewing activities by Borges and Eco are in James Woodall, *Borges: A Life* (1996), and Umberto Eco, *Misreadings* (1993). Paul Lukas tells of his book reviewing exploits in *Inconspicuous Consumption: An Obsessive Look at the Stuff We Take for Granted, from the Everyday to the Obscure* (1997).

For background on Lord Byron, see Muriel J. Mellown, "Francis

Jeffrey, Lord Byron, and *English Bards and Scotch Reviewers*," *Studies in Scottish Literature*, E. G. Ross Roy, editor, vol. 14 (1981); Joanne Shattock, *Politics and Reviewers: The Edinburgh and the Quarterly in the Early Victorian Age* (1989); and Benita Eisler, *Byron—Child of Passion, Fool of Fame* (1999). For background on Oprah Winfrey, see Bridget Kinsella, "The Oprah Effect," *Publishers Weekly*, January 20, 1997; and Gayle Feldman, "Making Book on Oprah," *New York Times Book Review*, February 2, 1997; "Testifying to the Power of Books," *Biblio*, January 1998. Many of Brian Lamb's interviews are found in *Booknotes: America's Finest Authors on Reading, Writing, and the Power of Ideas* (1997) and *Booknotes Life Stories: Notable Biographers on the People Who Shaped America* (1999). On Don Imus, see Ken Auletta, "The Don," *New Yorker*, May 25, 1999; Martin Arnold, "Making Books," *New York Times*, October 1, 1998; and Ted Rose, "The I-Man Giveth," *Content*, December 1998/January 1999. Amazon.com is discussed in Doreen Carvajal, *New York Times*, February 2, 1999, and March 2, 1999; Peter de Jonge, *New York Times Sunday Magazine*, March 14, 1999; Rachel Lehmann-Haupt, "On-line Book Reviews: Know What You're Reading," *Content*, October 1998.

Norman Mailer's response to John Simon's review of *Harlot's Ghost*, plus the rejoinders by Simon and book editor Rebecca Sinkler, are simultaneously entertaining and instructive. They are entertaining in the way Byron's personal attacks were; instructive because they reveal much about the difficulty of assigning books for review. This exchange appeared in the *New York Times Book Review* on November 17, 1991. The *Times* review, by the way, was not the only negative one: The *New Yorker* review called *Harlot's Ghost* "not only the most unsatisfying book Mailer has ever written, it is also the most undistinguished."

On best sellers, see two books: Frank Luther Mott, *Golden Multitudes: The Story of Best Sellers in the United States* (1947); Daniel J. Boorstin, *The Image: A Guide to Pseudo-Events in America* (1972). The *Business Week* exposé was by Willy Stern, "Did Dirty Tricks Create a Best-Seller?" August 7, 1995, and "The Unmasking of a Best-Seller: Chapter 2," August 14, 1995. David Stout, *New York Times*, July 27, 1995, also wrote about the incident. Several other articles were also useful: Ron Suskind, *Wall Street Journal*, August 20, 1998; I. Jeanne Dugan, "Battle of the Best-Seller Lists," *Business Week*, December 15, 1997; Jamie Malanowski, "Nerdfile,"

New Yorker, March 15, 1999; Samuel G. Freedman, *New York Times,* June 20, 1998; Richard Turner, "Of Books and Bar Codes," *Newsweek,* November 24, 1998; Joanne Lipman, *Wall Street Journal,* July 21, 1992; Paul Farhi, *Washington Post,* September 6, 1990; Patrick M. Reilly, *Wall Street Journal,* September 7, 1995; Eliza Truitt, "Industry's Best-Seller Lists," *Slate,* September 2, 1998. Karen Angel wrote the *Publishers Weekly* article on the public demand for books created by the Internet, "Independents Trace Title Shortages to Internet Booksellers," January 26, 1998. The QVC reference is based on Doreen Carvajal, *New York Times,* February 14, 1998.

In concluding, I should note that I have not paid attention to a distinction sometimes made between *reviewing* and *criticism.* Reviewing, some say, is a report about a book, while criticism considers the wider significance of a book. I prefer to think that criticism must report what is in the book, and that reviews must tell us if the book is any good. In the words of Orville Prescott, a longtime reviewer at the *New York Times,* "A reviewer must be blunt. A wretched book must not be let down gently. I believe in violence in reviewing; only with violence can you be of much use to your readers."

Notes to Chapter Six

In his classic on best sellers, *Golden Multitudes,* Frank Luther Mott wisely observed that "Every book published is more or less a gamble—less, of course, for the man of experience and good judgment, but never free from a large element of luck." Few, though, have tried to make sense of book luck, or even bothered to recognize it as the predominant phenomenon in publishing.

This is not surprising. Book luck is not a profitable line of inquiry. What is there for a scholar to say about successful writing if success comes down to a roll of the dice? Where is the pattern? As a result, professional observers of the literary scene treat book luck as an aberration: "Imagine! Author so-and-so really fell into some good/bad luck here. How strange!" But the book lover who dares not to make sense out of books soon realizes that book luck *is* the pattern. Our daily newspapers are full of stories about books that have had a lucky bounce. The real news is about books that succeed without a turn of good fortune.

Here are some news stories that provided the good-luck examples used in this chapter: On bon mots, Michael K. Frisby, *Wall Street Journal*, January 2, 1997; "Footnotes," *Chronicle of Higher Education*, July 10, 1991; Esther B. Fein, *New York Times*, May 17, 1993; Ken Ringle, *Washington Post*, September 27, 1990; Robert Frank, *Wall Street Journal*, February 18, 1999. On Ronald Reagan, the son of the president, Andy Meisler, *New York Times*, August 11, 1991. On Schulberg's *What Makes Sammy Run?* Ralph Blumenthal, *New York Times*, August 11, 1998. On Joanna Trollope, Joanne Kaufman, *Wall Street Journal*, April 10, 1997. On Victoria Gotti, Wendy Bounds, *Wall Street Journal*, April 22, 1997. A number of articles described the proliferation of Gulf War books: In the *Washington Post* were David Streitfeld, March 24, 1991, and April 14, 1991, and Paula Span, February 2, 1991. In the *Wall Street Journal*, Meg Cox, January 21, 1991, and Meg Cox and Kathleen A. Hughes, March 1, 1994. Calvin Sims wrote on *The Anatomist* in the *New York Times*, May 17, 1997. The Fred Hanna quotation appears in James F. Clarity's article, *New York Times*, February 10, 1991. The Bessie quotation is from Roger Cohen, *New York Times*, June 12, 1991. The Lincoln anecdote about poet William Knox is in Douglas L. Wilson's book, *Lincoln before Washington: New Perspective on the Illinois Years* (1997).

On death, I used these articles: The Gore Vidal quip about Capote is from George Plimpton's *Truman Capote* (1997). On Seth Morgan, Art Harris, *Washington Post*, February 12, 1991. On Anne Frank, Daniel Pearl, *Wall Street Journal*, January 28, 1997. On Jessie Lee Brown Foveaux, Clare Ansberry, *Wall Street Journal*, March 7, 1997, Bruce Knecht, *Wall Street Journal*, March 14, 1997, and Trip Gabriel, *New York Times*, March 24, 1997. On sequels to *Gone With the Wind*, see Martin Arnold, *New York Times*, November 5, 1998, and March 25, 1999. On books far beyond the grave, Richard Sandomir, *Los Angeles Times*, May 12, 1991, and Linton Weeks, *Washington Post*, August 6, 1999. David Streitfeld wrote on V. C. Andrews, *Washington Post*, May 7, 1993. The biographer of Victor Hugo quoted in the essay is Graham Robb; appropriately enough, the book is titled *Victor Hugo* (1997). Joan Didion wrote a thoughtful article on Hemingway's right not to publish in "Last Words," *New Yorker*, November 9, 1998; see also Ralph Blumenthal, *New York Times*, August 24, 1998. J. Gerald Kennedy, former chair of the English department at LSU, checked—and made useful corrections to—the list of posthumous books by Hemingway.

For a revealing article about the Beardstown Ladies, see Elizabeth Lesly Stevens, "He Cracked the Numbers Racket," *Brill's Content,* July/August 1998. James B. Twitchell sees life-after-death writing as marketing run amuck in his *Carnival Culture: The Trashing of Taste in America* (1992). This chapter does not begin to exhaust the list of elderly successes, for instance, the Delany sisters. Sarah and Elizabeth wrote (with help) *Having Our Say: The Delany Sisters' First 100 Years* (1993). By many accounts it is not a bad book, still in use in schools as a text for those who would understand the African-American experience. They published a later book, which also made the best-seller lists: *The Delany Sisters' Book of Everyday Wisdom* (1994).

The Graves quotation at the beginning of the chapter is from "Mostly It's Money That Makes a Writer Go, Go, Go," *Opinions and Perspectives from the New York Times Book Review* (1964), edited by Francis Brown. The quotation from the man who thought Napoleon should have shot a publisher is from Siegfried Unseld's *The Author and His Publisher,* already cited. Unseld, a German publisher, has written in-depth studies of the author-publisher relationship in the aforementioned book as well as in *Goethe and His Publishers* (1996). The publisher whom Napoleon shot was Johann Philipp Palm of Nuremberg. Strachey's quotation about Asquith is in Michael Holroyd, *Lytton Strachey: The New Biography* (1994).

The observation on slightly improved sales for *Leaves of Grass* is based on calls to booksellers made by my graduate assistant, Bonnie Bauman. The jump in sales of *OY VEY!* was reported in "Ticker," *Brill's Content,* December 1998/January 1999.

Background on prizes is found in Paul Levy, *Wall Street Journal,* October 30, 1998, and James Atlas, "The Booker Is More Than Just a Prize," *New Yorker,* October 13, 1997. Book awards deserve a chapter all to themselves. For one thing, we have good reason to wonder how accurate they are. For another, much about them is hilarious. Sir Michael Caine, chief executive of Booker P.L.C., an international food company, founded the Booker Prize. His obituary (Warren Hoge, *New York Times,* March 24, 1999) noted all the troubles he had administering the award: "Beryl Bainbridge once spent the entire ceremony lying on the floor because she said she was most comfortable there. Philip Larkin, a judge in 1977, threatened to throw himself out of a window if a particular book he favored was not short-listed, and a presenter once stilled the proceedings with anti-Semitic jokes." On another occasion, a winner denounced Booker's colonial history and threatened to give the prize to the Black Panthers. Meanwhile, people think up awards to embarrass authors. The *Literary Review*, edited by Auberon Waugh, came up with the Bad Sex Award for the most trite, stupid sex scenes.

Finally, let it be admitted that while there are some clear categories of book luck, some defy categorization and are best called dumb luck, a type of luck to which I alluded in the first paragraph of this essay. One example of luck dropping from nowhere makes the point. It is from *Who Does What & Why in Book Publishing* by veteran publisher Clarkson Potter. Jean Kerr, an author with whom Potter worked, agreed to sell her novel-in-progress to Doubleday, provided that it also publish a collection of the short essays she had written for magazines. She "thought it would just be nice to be able to give her friends something in hard covers that would last awhile," Clarkson recalled. The resulting book, *Please Don't Eat the Daisies*, was a best seller and sold to Hollywood.

Notes to Chapter Seven

"Information is scarce on why theft and mutilation occur and on how much they cost libraries," said Terri L. Pederson ("Theft and Mutilation of Library Materials," *College and Research Libraries*, March 1990). "From 1972 to 1987, less than fifteen articles and papers have been written on the subject."

As noted in the chapter, librarians dislike discussing the subject because they don't want to look bad and, besides, they do not want to encourage theft. Book authors spend considerable time thinking and writing about the stealing of words, as in plagiarism. But they, too, say little about the stealing of books. This lapse is best explained as self-interest. Writers don't want their words lifted and placed into someone else's book. That costs them money. Agitated, they write lamentations on the subject, occasionally producing an entire book. They do not become as exercised about having books stolen because, when a book is not returned to a library, librarians must buy a new edition. If a book is stolen from a bookstore, the store owes the publisher, who owes the author. Why ruin business?

Nevertheless, some worthwhile historical articles do exist and, roaming through various books on books, one occasionally finds an interesting clue about book theft. One of the most extensive articles I could find on the subject is Lawrence S. Thompson's "Notes on Bibliokleptomania," *Bulletin of the New York Public Library*. It was published in September 1944. I also used Manguel's *History of Reading*, especially the chapter "Stealing Books"; Lawrence W. Towner, "An End to Innocence," *American Libraries*, March 1988; and Alan J. Lincoln, *Crime in the Library: A Study of Patterns, Impact, and Security* (1984).

Of course, we do get stories on individuals, such as Blumberg, the Al Capone of book theft. Two examples of such stories are Miles Harvey, "Mr. Bland's Evil Plot to Control the World," *Outside*, June 1997, which is about a gent who cut valuable old maps out of books, and Christopher Reed, "Biblioklepts," *Harvard Magazine*, March–April 1997, which mentions the *Library Journal* survey. Many of the above authors have written versions of the Pope Innocent X story. The one I like best is in Grant Uden's chapter "Some Types of Bookmen," in *Strange Reading* (1900). David Maraniss wrote a long article about the Blumberg case in the *Washington Post*, April 1, 1990; see also the verdict reported in *Library Journal*, March 1, 1991. Nicholas Basbanes devotes a chapter to Blumberg and has other choice anecdotes on book theft in *A Gentle Madness: Bibliophiles, Bibliomanes, and the Eternal Passion for Books* (1995). The Online Computer Library Center volunteered to work with the FBI in returning the books Blumberg stole to their rightful owners. Afterward, the OCLC produced a videotape showing what that project involved. The public relations tape is called "The Omaha Project: A Rare Book Adventure."

The story about the Chinese pirating Stiglitz's economics textbook comes from a column by Thomas L. Friedman, *New York Times*, January 8, 1995. The *New York Times* ran useful articles about Russian thefts from the Germans, October 31, 1994, and New York book theft tastes September 28, 1986, and June 19, 1999. David Streitfeld wrote articles about losses from the Library of Congress, *Washington Post*, March 29, 1992, and October 21, 1992. Other anecdotes came from Charles Hymas and Cyril Dixon, *Sunday Times* (London), November 29, 1992; Press

Association Newsfile, *Los Angeles Times,* November 21, 1992; Roy Rivenburg, *Los Angeles Times,* October 11, 1992; Kristin N. Sullivan, *Fort Worth Star-Telegram,* August 29, 1996; Lloyd Ferriss, *Portland (Maine) Press Herald,* September 28, 1997; Alice Ann Love's Associated Press story in the *Chattanooga Times,* March 26, 1997; Sheila Toomey, *Anchorage Daily News,* April 11, 1998. Nero's interest in poetry is mentioned by Eleanor Clark, *Rome and a Villa* (1952). Background on Andrew Carroll is from Craig Wilson, *USA Today,* May 1, 1998.

When I wrote a similar, albeit shorter, version of this chapter for the *New York Times Book Review,* a number of people wrote to me. One, Vera Liebert of Rhinebeck, New York, related the Sean O'Faolain story. Thanks, too, to my friends Trudi Schafer and Louis Day for their nuggets.

The study on attitudes toward the Bible was published in the *New York Times,* October 28, 1996. The market for Bibles is described in *Publishers Weekly,* October 14, 1996.

Since we have so few books on stolen books and these endnotes need a little heft, I offer examples of books written about that other evil, plagiarism: Thomas Mallon, *Stolen Words: Forays into the Origins and Ravages of Plagiarism* (1989); Curtis D. Macdougall's chapter on "Literary Hoaxing" in *Hoaxes* (1958); William P. Alford, *To Steal a Book Is an Elegant Offense: Intellectual Property Law in Chinese Civilization* (1995) (this work also has some comments on the sort of book theft described in this chapter); and Neal Bowers, *Words for the Taking: The Hunt for a Plagiarist* (1997). Bowers's book is devoted to plagiarism of his poetry, but he includes an example of theft relevant to this chapter. Bowers wrote a poem, "Art Thief," that commemorated a sculpture stolen from his Iowa State University campus. The poem, cast in bronze, was displayed where the sculpture had been—until it, too, was stolen.

Notes to Chapter Eight

The worst part of writing this chapter was reading all the bad writing produced by presidents. Fortunately, we have very good writing on the evolution of our democracy and on our presidents.

Among the good books about our political system used in this chapter are: Theodore Draper, *A Struggle for Power: The American Revolution* (1996); Eric Hoffer, *The True Believer: Thoughts on the Nature of Mass*

Movements (1951); Alexis de Tocqueville, translated by Alan S. Kahan and edited by François Furet and Françoise Mélonio, *The Old Regime and the Revolution* (1998); and Leonard W. Levy, *Emergence of a Free Press* (1985). Pauline Maier, *American Scripture: Making the Declaration of Independence* (1997), revises our view of Jefferson's role in writing the Declaration of Independence.

Václav Havel is an excellent writer-politician; for an example of his thoughts on this subject see *The Art of the Impossible: Politics as Morality in Practice* (1997). Another good politician-writer is François Mitterrand; some of his ideas on writing come out in Franz-Olivier Giesbert, *Dying without God: François Mitterrand's Meditations on Living and Dying* (1998).

Useful discussions of public attitudes toward the First Amendment are found in Herbert McClosky and Alida Brill, *Dimensions of Tolerance: What Americans Believe about Civil Liberties* (1983), and Samuel A. Stouffer's classic study, *Communism, Conformity, and Civil Liberties* (1955). The study of attitudes about expression at work is found in David C. Korten, *When Corporations Rule the World* (1995), and Geoffrey Hull, "Free Speech in the Workplace: Public Desire and Emerging Law," a paper presented at an annual meeting of the Association of Education in Journalism and Mass Communication in the early 1990s. Business attitudes toward worker education are discussed in Bernard Avishai, "What Is Business's Social Compact?" *Harvard Business Review,* January/ February 1994. Alecia Swasy is the author of *Soap Opera: The Inside Story of Procter & Gamble* (1993).

Congressional and presidential disdain for free speech is depressing and well covered. One example is Floyd Abrams, "Clinton vs. the First Amendment," *New York Times Magazine,* March 30, 1997. Robert Bork's quotation is from his book *The Tempting of America: The Political Seduction of the Law* (1990). For details on Congress's slow payment to the printers of the Constitution, see Daniel Boorstin's "Printing and the Constitution," a chapter in his book of essays *The Republic of Letters* (1989), edited by John Y. Cole. Robert A. Rutland wrote a short monograph on what the delegates to the Constitutional Convention had read, "'Well Acquainted with Books': The Founding Framers of 1787" (1987).

For background on presidential writing I looked at Joseph Nathan Kane, *Facts about the Presidents: A Compilation of Biographic and Historical*

Data (1981, 4th edition). Various presidential biographies were helpful as well, among them: L. H. Butterfield's introduction to James Bishop Peabody, editor, *John Adams: A Biography in His Own Words* (1973); James Truslow Adams, *The Adams Family* (1930); Paul C. Nagel, *John Quincy Adams: A Public Life, A Private Life* (1997); Joseph J. Ellis, *American Sphinx: The Character of Thomas Jefferson* (1997); Fawn M. Brodie, *Thomas Jefferson, an Intimate History* (1974); Arthur S. Link, *Wilson: The Road to the White House* (1947); Herbert Parmet, *Jack: The Struggles of John F. Kennedy* (1980), along with a recent discovery of letters substantiating Professor David's role in writing *Profiles in Courage*, which was reported in *New York Times,* October 18, 1997. The book based on Adams's marginal notes is Zoltán Haraszti, *John Adams and The Prophets of Progress* (1952). Adams's statement about Washington's poor writing is quoted in Marcus Cunliffe's *George Washington, Man and Monument* ([1958] 1982). Benjamin Harrison told about his busy White House days in *This Country of Ours* (1897). James M. McPherson describes Grant's writing ability in "The Unheroic Hero," *New York Review of Books,* February 4, 1999. The history of FDR's inaugural speech is in Kathleen Hall Jamieson's *Eloquence in an Electronic Age: The Transformation of Political Speech Making* (1988). On Reagan's writing, see Garry Wills, "The Man Who Wasn't There," *New York Review of Books,* June 13, 1991, and Michael Korda, "Prompting the President," *New Yorker,* October 6, 1997. Larry Speakes tells how he put words in Reagan's mouth without the president knowing it in Larry Speakes, *Speaking Out: The Reagan Presidency from Inside the White House* (1988). For this book, Speakes hired someone to put words in his mouth, a professional writer named Robert Pack.

I used the following for Calvin Coolidge: John Earl Haynes, editor, *Calvin Coolidge and the Coolidge Era: Essays on the History of the 1920s* (1998); Howard Shaff and Audrey Karl Shaff, *Six Wars at a Time: The Life and Times of Gutzon Borglum, Sculptor of Mount Rushmore* (1985), Gilbert C. Fite, *Mount Rushmore* (1952), and Rex Alan Smith, *The Carving of Mount Rushmore* (1985). Calvin Coolidge talked about the difficulty of writing in *The Autobiography of Calvin Coolidge* (1929).

A good deal of writing exists about Lincoln's writing. I used David Herbert Donald, *Lincoln* (1995); Alfred Kazin's essay on Lincoln in *God and the American Writer* (1997); James M. McPherson, "Lincoln's Herndon," *New York Review of Books,* March 26, 1998; Gore Vidal, "Lincoln

Close Up," *New York Times Book Review,* August 15, 1991; Meg Cox, *Wall Street Journal,* November 26, 1990.

Stanley I. Kutler gives us Nixon's tapes on Watergate in *Abuse of Power: The New Nixon Tapes* (1997). Nixon's comments on writing being hard work are in Brian Lamb's *Booknotes,* mentioned earlier. The book contains interviews with other politician-writers as well.

William Greider, *Washington Post,* March 20, 1977, tells why Carter's instincts to work things out for himself, as good writers do, got in the way of presidential leadership. Similar negative comments on Carter can be found in Martin Schram, *Washington Post,* December 30, 1977; see also, Gabriel Schoenfeld, *Wall Street Journal,* December 13, 1996. On Bush as a writer of notes, Sarah Booth Conroy, *Washington Post,* February 5, 1989. Quayle's dumb statements are quoted nearly everywhere. He is a national sport. I made especially good use of an *Esquire* special about Quayle, August 1992. The critical review of Clinton's campaign book is by Richard Bernstein, *New York Times,* September 4, 1996. On Clinton's interest in solitaire, see Karen Ball, "It's in the Cards," *New Yorker,* March 31, 1997. Clinton's Lewinsky woes are described by Michael Isikoff in *Uncovering Clinton: A Reporter's Story* (1999); one typical story on Lewinsky's book is by Doreen Carvajal, *New York Times,* February 28, 1999. On Starr's report writing, David W. Chen and Neil A. Lewis, *New York Times,* September 12, 1998. On Gore as a writer, see Keith Schneider, *New York Times,* July 27, 1992.

John M. Barry tells the story of Speaker Wright's demise in *The Ambition and the Power* (1989), an inferior book that should have an index but doesn't. The book in which Spiro T. Agnew opened himself to prosecution is *Go Quietly . . . or Else: His Own Story of the Events Leading to His Resignation* (1980). An essay on Sinclair is found in Greg Mitchell, "When Writers Think They're Politicians," *New York Times Book Review,* November 1, 1992. A discussion of the historical use of political diaries is found in Michiko Kakutani, *New York Times,* October 1993.

On George Wallace's claim that words were put in his mouth, see Carl T. Rowan, *Washington Post,* September 6, 1991. As an interesting historical note, the guy who ghosted Wallace's infamous remarks, Asa Earl Carter, was a white supremacist from Alabama, who at one point commanded a one-hundred-member paramilitary unit called the Original Ku Klux Klan of the Confederacy. Carter, like Wallace, went from racist to warm and fuzzy. Under an assumed name, Forrest Carter, he wrote a book that purported to be the childhood memoir of an American Indian orphan, *The Education of Little Tree.*

The studies of presidential greatness go on and on. As noted in the chapter, the best known ranking has been done through a survey of great contemporary thinkers conducted by Arthur M. Schlesinger Jr., "The Ultimate Approval Rating," *New York Times Magazine,* December 15, 1996. A survey conducted by William J. Ridings Jr. and Stuart B. McIver, *Rating the Presidents: A Ranking of U.S. Leaders, from the Great and Honorable to the Dishonest and Incompetent* (1996), reaches more or less the same conclusions about who is good and who is bad; also like most other such surveys, the poll does not look at presidential writing ability. Some studies are keyed to a narrow range of issues of contemporary concern, such as randiness. As an example, Marvin Olasky, *The American Leadership Tradition: Moral Vision from Washington to Clinton* (1999), bases greatness on "religious beliefs and sexual morality," which is to say he is pretty annoyed with Clinton; Olasky argues that it is misguided to judge presidents based on "political rhetoric." Other studies of presidential greatness are Dean Keith Simonton's *Why Presidents Succeed: A Political Psychology of Leadership* (1987); Stewart J. H. McCann's "Alternative Formulas to Predict the Greatness of U.S. Presidents: Personological, Situational, and Zeitgeist Factors," *Journal of Personality and Social Psychology,* 1992, 62:3; James David Barber's *The Presidential Character: Predicting Performance in the White House* (1992); Thomas A. Bailey's *Presidential Greatness: The Image and the Man from George Washington to the Present* (1966); and Nathan Miller's *Star-Spangled Men: America's Ten Worst Presidents* (1998). Some works examining greatness suggest that vertigo is a determining factor. One of the dizziest such studies is *Cradles of Eminence* (1962), written by a husband and wife team. Victor and Mildred George Goertzel looked for trends in the youthful years of famous people who had books about them in the Montclair, New Jersey, Public Library. Along with their son, they subsequently wrote *Three Hundred Eminent Personalities* (1978), this time using the Menlo Park, California, Public Library. Apparently they had moved.

Miscellaneous comments in the chapter come from these additional sources: Mario Vargas Llosa is quoted in *U.S. News & World Report,*

November 5, 1990. The quotation about Baldwin is from John Campbell in John P. Mackintosh, editor, *British Prime Ministers in the Twentieth Century*, vol. 1, *Balfour to Chamberlain* (1977). John Keegan, *The Mask of Command* (1987), offers the insight on Alexander the Great's attitude toward his court historian. Robert Conquest's comment on Hitler as an artist is from "Terrorists," *New York Review of Books*, March 6, 1997. Theodore Roosevelt's spelling reform is discussed in H. W. Brands, *TR: The Last Romantic* (1997); Cullen Murphy wrote an amusing story about Clinton's Plain Language Initiative for *Slate*, posted September 9, 1998. Irving Lazar talks about selling Nixon's memoirs in *Swifty: My Life and Good Times* (1995). The comment on the Nixon library is from Stephen E. Ambrose, *Nixon: Ruin and Recovery, 1973–1990* (1991).

I conducted a number of interviews in researching this chapter. James McGregor Burns, Ray Price, Sam Vaughan, Tim Seldes, James David Barber, Mark Green, and Ken McCormick were especially helpful.

One is always tempted to look abroad for lessons and insights. And, as the chapter only begins to suggest, heads of state everywhere offer much to marvel at.

President of Belarus, Aleksander Lukashenko, who once ran a collective farm in the good old days of communism and gleefully douses the lights of newspapers that try to do their jobs, is far more enlightened about politicians such as himself writing. According to Article 86 of his Constitution, "The President may not hold other offices or receive any monetary remuneration other than his salary, apart from royalties for works of science, literature and art." Our Congress might learn something from this.

Mostly, though, other nations seem to be borrowing from us. The imperious Lee Kuan Yew, former prime minister of Singapore, came out with memoirs in 1999. *The Singapore Story: Memoirs of Lee Kuan Yew* has all the signs of an autobiography written by an American president. "I did most of my uninterrupted work on the PC at night after the day's work was done," he says in the book. "Several of the young men and women to whom I sent my drafts asked if the time stamp on my PC was wrong, because they were frequently stamped as 3 or 4 A.M. I assured them that it was correct." Lee wants us to know that he did the writing himself, yet, in making it clear that he is not letting writing get in the way of real work, he reveals that others did much of the work for him. His comments are reminiscent of Nixon's in the chapter, "Writing a book is very, very hard work. . . . And then I have good people that work with me."

With the end of communism, former Soviet-dominated countries have contracted some of our worst literary diseases. A former dissident I met in Vladivostok in the early 1990s told me that in the old days he had a secure job during the day, which let him spend his evenings translating quality literature. Now, Maxim said, people are watching television and reading less, so there was no market for his work. "I'm tired of waiting for things to get better," he said. The situation became so desperate in the Czech Republic that Václav Havel signed a petition appealing to western publishers for aid. Meanwhile, writing politicians have suffered like their American counterparts. In 1991, coauthors of a book lost their high government posts when it was learned that they had accepted an advance from a publishing house owned by a bank. Maybe this sort of thing will end if Lukashenko has his way and Belarus becomes part of Russia. More likely, though, Lukashenko will change and follow the American example.

As Dan Quayle and his family said in their 1989 Christmas card, "May our nation continue to be a beakon of hope to the world."

Notes to Chapter Nine

First, let it be said that of all the places I have conducted research, the Library of Congress is one of the most exhilarating. I have held interviews twice at the library, the first time in the early 1990s and again in 1998–1999. On both occasions, most (but, of course, not all) the staff stood out for its enthusiasm and sense of dedication. For this chapter, I have woven incidents and quotations from both sets of interviews so as not to muddy the narrative. I particularly appreciate the help of one Library of Congress staffer who agreed to review the entire chapter and made useful suggestions for improvement without suggesting changes any of my negative comments. She wants to remain anonymous, and I hasten to add for the benefit of senior management at the library, you will never guess who she is.

The Library of Congress's self-publishing efforts are prodigious. In 1997, for instance, it published more than forty books, calendars, CDs, and "other products" about itself. I have used some of this material: three books by James Y. Cole, *Jefferson's Legacy: A Brief History of the Library of Congress* (1993), *On These Walls: Inscriptions and Quotations in the Buildings of the Library of Congress* (1995), and *Copyright in the Library of Congress* (1995); Daniel J. Boorstin, edited by John Y. Cole, *The Republic of Letters* (1989); Barbara W. Tuchman, *The Book* (1980); Josephus Nelson and Judith Barley, *Full Circle: Ninety Years of Service in the Main Reading Room* (1991). Cole, who runs the library's Center for the Book, is the de facto historian of the Library of Congress. Most of what he writes is name-date-place history, but the books are useful as well as visually attractive. One of the most picturesque books about the Library of Congress was published by the University of New Mexico Press in association with the library's Center for the Book: *Library: The Drama Within* (1996), with photographs by Diane Asséo Griliches and text by Boorstin. The General Accounting Office report on the Library, *Financial Audit: First Audit of the Library of Congress Discloses Significant Problems*, was published in 1991.

I also used several histories of libraries. These included Frederick Lerner, *The Story of Libraries: From the Invention of Writing to the Computer Age* (1998); Elmer D. Johnson, *A History of Libraries in the Western World* (1965); Luciano Canfora, translated by Martin Ryle, *The Vanished Library: A Wonder of the Ancient World* (1990); Roger Chartier, *The Order of Books: Readers, Authors, and Libraries in Europe between the Fourteenth and Eighteenth Centuries* (1994); Abigail A. Van Slyck, *Free to All: Carnegie Libraries & American Culture, 1890–1920* (1995); David C. Mearns, *The Story up to Now: The Library of Congress, 1800–1946* (1972). Despite the seeming narrowness of its title, Anthony Smith's *Goodbye Gutenberg: The Newspaper Revolution of the 1980s* (1980) is valuable for its information about books and libraries. Likewise Alfred W. Crosby's *The Measure of Reality: Quantification and Western Society, 1250–1600* (1997) has a useful chapter on writing and organization of information. *Daedalus* devoted its Fall 1996 issue entirely to "Books, Bricks, & Bytes." Manguel's *History of Reading*, cited in earlier chapters, has a good chapter on library classification systems, "Ordainers of the Universe."

Association of Research Libraries' data are in *ARL Statistics 1996–1997* (1998). Robert L. Oakley, *Copyright and Preservation: A Serious Problem in Need of a Thoughtful Solution*, published by the Commission of Preservation and Access (1990), discusses book deterioration. The July

10, 1997, *Wall Street Journal* article about deacidification of books was by John J. Fialka. Two articles about digital preservation, by Katie Hafner and Irvin Molotsky, appeared in the *New York Times*, April 8, 1999.

An astonishing number of books are appearing about the future of books, many of them directed at whether words on a computer screen will conquer words on paper. I used Roger Chartier, *Forms and Meanings: Texts, Performances, and Audiences from Codex to Computer* (1995); Geoffrey Nunberg, editor, *The Future of the Book* (1996); Peter Ludlow, editor, *High Noon on the Electronic Frontier: Conceptual Issues in Cyberspace* (1996); Sven Birkerts, *Readings* (1999); Michael E. Hobart and Zachary S. Schiffman, *Information Ages: Literacy, Numeracy, and the Computer Revolution* (1998). Neil Gershenfeld made his comment about the value of traditional book technology in *When Things Start to Think* (1999). Robert Darnton wrote about electronic books in "The New Age of the Book," *New York Review of Books*, March 18, 1999.

Nicholas Baker wrote about the trauma of maintaining the San Francisco Public Library in "The Author vs. the Library," *New Yorker*, October 14, 1996. Joel Achenbach wrote about the overflow of words at the Library of Congress in the *Washington Post*, March 12, 1999. The quotation from the *Times Literary Supplement* is from "NB," August 28, 1998. The Barnes & Noble quotation is from Kara Swisher's article, *Wall Street Journal*, June 11, 1998. Jacob Weisberg wrote an article, "The Modern Library," in *Slate*, an electronic magazine delivered by the Internet; the posting date was October 24, 1998. Weisberg proudly notes that with technological advances we can take *Slate* to the bathroom with us. The book *Jefferson and Wine: Model of Moderation* is edited by R. de Treville Lawrence III and is published by the Vinifera Wine Growers Association (1989).

Alexander Stille wrote an article about the National Archives, "Overload," *New Yorker*, March 8, 1999. The National Archives have many of the same problems as the Library of Congress. In 1996, it concluded that it would take 120 years for a staff of the current size to transfer its backlog of nontextual material, such as videos and audiotapes, to stable formats. Some of the media to which it would be transferred will not last more than twenty years, estimates Charles Mayn, who heads the archives' media preservation laboratory. Mayn spends a good deal of his time trying to keep obsolete equipment running.

The scene set at the beginning of the chapter is based on—but does not re-create exactly—a Capitol Hill tour my graduate assistant Bonnie Bauman took. The faithful reader of this book will note that this chapter does not heavily rely on newspaper articles about the Library of Congress. In fact, the library is not well covered in the press. The problem is that news stories about libraries are usually boring. "Even the name library is boring," one newspaper book review editor once told me. The same can be said of librarians depicted in novels. Fictional librarians seem as one-dimensional as Bodley could have ever wished. One exception I can think of offhand is Kingsley Amis's *That Uncertain Feeling*. And remember what happens to the highly sexed Welsh librarian in the end. He takes a sales job with a small collier. But reporters who actually get inside the Library of Congress, and beyond the exhibits, discover a fascinating world.

Notes to Appendix A

P. T. Barnum's promotional exploits are chronicled in Irving Wallace, *The Fabulous Showman: The Life and Times of P. T. Barnum* (1959), as well as in Barnum's autobiography. The examples of book promotion used in this chapter come from some of the following sources: On hyping at the ABA convention, Nicholas A. Basbanes, "It's a Mad, Mad World," *Biblio*, November–December 1996. On book contests, Michael Ryan, "Agent Bill Adler's Best-Seller Is an Endless but Rewarding Do-It-Yourself Mystery," *Time*, October 17, 1983; Eric Pace, *New York Times*, September 2, 1994; David Brauner, *Jerusalem Post*, December 25, 1997. On the Baker-Mitgang back-scratching, Howard Kaplan's "Logrolling in Our Time," *Spy*, October 1990. King gives us the dope on Bachman in "Why I Was Bachman," an introduction to *The Bachman Books: Four Early Novels by Stephen King* (1986); also Mark Singer, "What Are You Afraid Of?" *New Yorker*, September 7, 1998. Another look at the marketing value of pseudo names is Donald E. Westlake, *Washington Post*, May 2, 1999. On the millennium book craze, Robert Dahlin, "Turning the Page on the 20th Century," *Publishers Weekly*, May 17, 1999. On Manchester's book, Jonathan Yardley, *Washington Post*, October 21, 1991. On Colette, Katy Emck, (London) *Times Literary Supplement*, May 1, 1998; Colette, heavily into marketing to go with her erotic Claudine novels, created Claudine perfume, ice cream, and cigarettes. The Abbé Migne is ably unmasked in R. Howard Bloch, *God's Plagiarist: Being an Account of the Fabulous Industry and Irregular Commerce of the Abbé Migne* (1995). For Alexander Pope, see Martin Seymour-Smith in Louis Kronenberger's already cited *Atlantic Brief Lives: A Biographical Companion to the Arts*, and George Paston, *Mr. Pope: His Life and Times* (1909). Joe Klein, our modern Pope, explains why he doesn't care about the money in "No, Really, I Am Anonymous," *New York Times Book Review*, May 19, 1996.

Notes to Appendix B

There is no need to repeat the names of the books on self-publishing by the Rosses and Jenkins. One book I did not mention in the appendix is Susan Page's *The Shortest Distance between You and a Published Book* (1997). Page's book seems neither better nor worse than the rest on this subject. It includes advice on forming groups of "writing buddy" relationships to help each other out and, of course, tells people to promote their own books. David Dempsey wrote about vanity presses in "How to Get Published, More or Less," *Harper's Magazine*, July 1955. There is no better book on Twain, including his terrible business (and publishing) sense, than Justin Kaplan's *Mr. Clemens and Mark Twain: A Biography* (1983).

Notes to Appendix C

As noted in the appendix, a number of writers have decried the state of book editing: John Brodie, "Brought to Book," *New Republic*, March 16, 1992; Martin Arnold, *New York Times*, November 12, 1998; Jonathan Yardley, *Washington Post*, August 6, 1990; Doreen Carvajal, *New York Times*, June 29, 1998; Steve Weinberg, "Why Books Err So Often," *Columbia Journalism Review*, July/August 1998; and John Simon, "Pathetic Fallacies," *New York Times Book Review*, November 22, 1998. Jacob Weisberg has been especially critical, for example, in "Rough Trade," *New Republic*, June 17, 1991, and in "The Courtly Contrarian," *New York Times Magazine*, March 15, 1998, which dissects Paul Johnson's carelessness with facts in his *History of the American People*. Weisberg received intense criticism for singling out editor Alice Mayhew in his *New*

Republic article. Many of her authors rose to her defense in letters to the magazine; the letters were published in the July 15–22 issue.

Nuggets in this appendix surfaced as a result of a list serve inquiry from Maureen Hewitt, assistant director and editor-in-chief of LSU Press. Those I used were provided by onetime Denver bookstore owner David Perkins, now at the University of Illinois Press; Debra Turner, at the University of Nebraska Press; and Bruce Barton, at the University of Chicago Press, who told the story of mixing *Knowledge* with *Ignorance*.

Charles Scribner Jr.'s comments about Maxwell Perkins are in "'I, Who Knew Nothing, Was in Charge,'" *New York Times Book Review*, December 9, 1990. John Updike's statement appeared in "Me and My Books," *New Yorker*, February 3, 1997. The story about Allen Ginsberg coming up with the title for *Naked Lunch* is in Barry Miles, *William Burroughs: El Hombre Invisible: A Portrait* (1993). Burroughs's rationalization for the title is in André Bernard's *Now All We Need Is a Title: Famous Book Titles and How They Got That Way* (1994). Penn and Teller's backfiring trick was reported in Esther B. Fein, *New York Times*, December 14, 1992. The anecdote about Thomas Harris is from Cathleen McQuigan's "Second Helping," *Newsweek*, June 7, 1999. The publishing turn-arounds for *Jane Eyre* and *Silas Marner* are from the Pool book, *Dickens' Fur Coat and Charlotte's Unanswered Letters*, cited earlier. The anecdote about Pope Sixtus was in Uden's *Strange Reading*, also cited earlier. The story about Timothy Dexter's book is from Irving Wallace, *The Square Pegs: Some Americans Who Dared to Be Different* (1954).

Two books that describe the publishing process are Leonard Shatzkin, *In Cold Type: Overcoming the Book Crisis* (1982), and Marshall Lee, *Bookmaking: The Illustrated Guide to Design/Production/Editing* (1979).

Index

In which the reader is shown how to find the interesting stuff in this book without having to read the whole thing.

—ᴂᴂ—

And in such indexes, although small pricks
To their subsequent volumes, there is seen
The baby figure of the giant mass
of things to come at large.
—WILLIAM SHAKESPEARE,
Troilus and Cressida

—ᴂᴂ—

A&E Biography, 69
About Books, Incorporated, 269–71
Academic journals, 45
Acknowledgment. *See* Dedications and
    acknowledgments
Acton, Lord, 141
Adams, James Truslow, 133
Adams, John, 198–99, 201, 202–03
Adams, John Quincy, 205
Addison, Joseph, 34
Adler, Bill, 263
Advances to authors, 65, 67, 71, 72, 73,
    120, 201, 217, 224, 227–28
Advertising. *See* Marketing
Age of Smoke and Mirrors, in presidents'
    writing, 202, 209–13
Agents. *See* Literary agents
Agnew, Spiro, 216–17, 227
Albert, Harold, 101
Albro, Tom, 242–43, 244, 246, 249
Alexander the Great, 221
Alexandrian Library, 179, 234, 247, 256
Alfred A. Knopf. *See* Knopf
Alger, Horatio, 28
Algonquin Books, 112
Algonquin Hotel, 4
*All You Need to Know About the Music
    Business* (Passman), xiii
Almanacs, 59, 60
Amazon.com, 74–75, 139–40, 151, 152,
    161–62, 262
Ambrose, Stephen, 140
American Baseball (Voigt), 136
American Book Award, 146*n*
American Book Prices Current, 183, 192
American Booksellers Association, 24, 46,
    48, 65, 111, 122, 261
American Express, 249
American Hotel & Motel Association, 183
American Library Association, 189
American Life (Reagan), 211–12
"American Names" (Benét), 4

American Nazi party, 200
American Philosophical Society, 60
American Poetry and Literacy, 190
American Psycho (Ellis), 168
American Scholar (Rovere), 93–94
Americans with Disabilities Act, 142–43
Amy Vanderbilt Complete Book of Etiquette,
    123
Anatomist (Andahazi), 166
Anatomy of the Mass, 276
And Ladies of the Club (Santmyer), 173
Andahazi, Federico, 166
Anderson, Richard, 238
Anderson, Sherwood, 28, 104
Andrews, V. C., 170
Angels Don't Die (Davis), 159–60
Anna Hastings (Drury), 103
Anonymous writings, 265
Any Given Day (Foveaux), 173
Apellicon of Teos, 179
Appalachian Spring, 235
Apple, R. W., 64
Appleton, Victor, 49–50
Arabella Stuart, Lady, 90–91
Arabesque, 69
Archer, Jeffrey, 123
Areopagitica (Milton), 20
Argentina, 166
Aristotle, 179, 221
ARL. *See* Association of Research
    Libraries (ARL)
Arnold, Matthew, 28, 53
Art of War (Machiavelli), 46
Ascent into Hell (Greeley), 33
Ascherson, Neal, 98
Asimov, Isaac, 48, 100, 169
Asphalt Nation (Holtz), 98
Asquith, Lord Herbert, 165–66, 209
Association of American University
    Presses, 165
Association of Research Libraries (ARL),
    239, 249, 255

139–40, 151–52, 161–62, 262; author's treatment of, 122–23; thefts from, 181–82, 183, 186; and computer technology, 255
Boorstin, Daniel, 149, 152, 255
Borders, 64, 111–12, 255
Borders Group, 255
Borges, Luis, 153
Borglum, Gutzon, 223
Bork, Robert, 215
Born to Rebel (Sulloway), 27
Boston Athenaeum, 236
Boston Globe, 139, 141
Boston Public Library, 236
Boswell, James, 38
Bouton, Bobbie, 101–02
Bouton, Jim, 101
Bowker, 269
Bradlee, Ben, 146*n*
Bradley, Bill, 74
Brady, Mathew, 248
Braindroppings (Carlin), 139
Brand-name writers, 65
Brazil, 48
Bridges of Madison County, 75, 140, 173
British Library, 252
British Museum, 55
Brodkey, Harold, 153
Brodsky, Joseph, 189
Brokaw, Tom, 72
Brontë, Anne, 28
Brontë, Charlotte, 28, 276
Brooke, Edward, 240
Brookner, Anita, 164
Brooks, Van Wyck, 262
Brown, Helen Gurley, 67–68
Brown, Larry, 28
Brown, Mark Malloch, 214
Brown University, 254–55
Bryce, James, 215
Bucaram, Abdala, 218
Buchanan, James, 205, 220
Bukowski, Charles, 186

Bulgaria, 198
Bulletproof *New Testament,* 11
Bunyan, John, 28
Burden, Carter, 8
Burden, Jerry, 184
Burgio, Kathryn L., 165
Burman, Sheldon O., 77
Burney, Fanny, 92
Burns, James McGregor, 225
Burns, Robert, 35
Burroughs, Edgar Rice, 28, 66–67
Burroughs, Joan, 279*n*
Burroughs, William, 28, 30, 186, 279, 279*n*
Buru Quartet (Toer), 43
Bush, Barbara, 212, 219*n*
Bush, George, 212, 216, 220, 228
Business Week, 150, 151
Byatt, A. S., 140
"By-pass" marketing, 270
Byron, Lord, 22, 30, 103, 129–30, 146

Cable television, 69
Calder, Robert, 94
Callendar, Newgate, 105
Cambodia, 198
Campaign books of presidential candidates, 218–20
Campbell, Laura, 248, 251, 253
Cancellation of contracts by publishers, 71–72, 167–68
Canterbury Tales (Chaucer), 18, 53
Capote, Truman, 168, 172
Cardinal Sins (Greeley), 33
Care Packages for the Home (Glanz), 79
Carey, Matthew, 262
Carl August, Duke, 34
Carlin, George, 139
Carlisle, Earl of, 130
Carlyle, Thomas, 6, 8, 152
Carnegie, Andrew, 247, 247*n*
Carr, John Dickson, 105
Carroll, Andrew, 190

About the Author

☺

John Maxwell Hamilton is the Hopkins P. Breazeale Professor at Louisiana State University and dean of LSU's Manship School of Mass Communication. He previously reported in the United States and abroad for a variety of publications, including the *Milwaukee Journal* and the *Christian Science Monitor*. In addition to journalism, Hamilton held a political appointment in the U.S. Agency for International Development during the Carter administration, and later served on the staffs of the House Foreign Affairs Subcommittee on Economic Policy & Trade and at the World Bank. He is a commentator on "Marketplace," broadcast nationally over public radio.